Drug control in a free society

9.75

9.75

Drug control in a free society

JAMES B. BAKALAR

LESTER GRINSPOON

Harvard Medical School

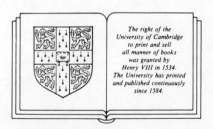

The right of the
University of Cambridge
to print and sell
all manner of books
was granted by
Henry VIII in 1534.
The University has printed
and published continuously
since 1584.

CAMBRIDGE UNIVERSITY PRESS

Cambridge
New York   New Rochelle
Melbourne   Sydney

Published by the Press Syndicate of the University of Cambridge
The Pitt Building, Trumpington Street, Cambridge CB2 1RP
32 East 57th Street, New York, NY 10022, USA
10 Stamford Road, Oakleigh, Melbourne 3166, Australia

First published 1984
First paperback edition 1988
Reprinted 1988

Printed in the United States of America

Library of Congress Cataloging in Publication Data

Bakalar, James, B., 1943–

Drug control in a free society.

Bibliography: p.

Includes index.

1. Narcotics, Control of. 2. Drug abuse.
3. Narcotic habit. I. Grinspoon, Lester, 1928–
II. Title. [DNLM: 1. Drug and Narcotic Control.
QV 33.1 B166d]
HV5801.B314   1985   363.4'5   84–11347
ISBN 0-521-26572-X hard covers
ISBN 0-521-35772-1 paperback

Contents

Preface

The problem of how a free society should deal with drug use and abuse remains unresolved despite years of bitter dispute and a century of efforts at government control. The modern world seems unable to form a consensus or even a consistent attitude about the subject.

We propose to review the peculiar medical, legal, and social status of drugs by examining the formal and informal controls used in modern industrial societies and comparing them with other methods that have been or might be used. From a historical and sociological point of view, the question is how ambiguous phenomena of drug use have been classified for social purposes; from a moral and practical point of view, the question is how to balance the requirements of health, safety, and social order against the need for individual freedom and diversity of experience when we regulate drugs. Drug research has produced historical narratives, pharmacological and clinical studies, theories about the nature of addiction and dependence, discussions of practical law enforcement problems, and polemics on drug policy that often combine impassioned certainty about what should be done with ignorance about what is the case. The clinical and pharmacological studies are useful but have a narrow range; the theories about addiction and dependence are inconclusive and rarely related to larger social issues; the debates on policy tend to be distorted by a lack of historical background and indulgence of passions and prejudices. The sociological and historical studies rarely relate what they say about drug use and drug controls to other tendencies in modern society. Lessons from the vast literature on alcohol and alcoholism are not applied to other drugs. And political theory usually receives too little attention in analyses of drug policy.

Some of the questions that arise are how problems in enforcing drug laws come out of confusion about justifying them; how medical ideas about addiction and dependence affect the politics of drug regulation; and how studies in the cultural symbolism of drug use can illuminate the issue of legislating morality. The subject must always be analyzed in social terms. When we ask what kind of drug regulation is reasonable or possible, we have to take account of the nature of modern societies. In discussing the medical aspects of drug control, we are talking about the way adaptation, normality, health, and sickness are defined in the modern world.

Most books on the control of drug abuse are concerned mainly with the effects of the drugs, who takes them, why, and how to stop it. A few books are opposed to present drug policies and their allegedly baneful consequences. In either case, the theoretical basis for legal controls on drug use is usually mentioned as a brief afterthought, if at all, and the history of drug control is often ignored or treated as an occasion for polemics. We prefer to work in a different way, one that may seem abstract and circuitous. That is partly because we are not trying to prevail in an argument or achieve some immediate practical effect. Advice and consolation of varying quality for drug users, parents, police, legislators, and doctors are copiously available, so we do not feel obliged to remind the reader of familiar facts (a useful job that has never been neglected) or contribute new, immediately practical wisdom (in this field even old practical wisdom is scarce, especially in proportion to the total number of words devoted to the subject). We certainly do not want to produce one more denunciation of either drugs or the drug control system. Instead, we would like to enable readers to draw back for a moment and consider the reasons for the modern social response to drug use.

It is important to be clear about what we mean by a drug. Some of the substances we will discuss have medical uses, but they are not ordinary medicines. What distinguishes them is the fact that they act on the central nervous system and are used to change thoughts, feelings, perceptions, or behavior. Among them are the opiates heroin and morphine, the stimulants amphetamine and cocaine, sedatives and tranquilizers like the barbiturates and diazepam (Valium), hallucinogens like lysergic acid diethylamide (LSD) and mescaline, alcohol, tobacco, marihuana, and phencyclidine (PCP). Because they affect the mind, they are often called "psychoactive." Some, especially alcohol and tobacco, are not usually regarded as drugs at all. Most of the others were at one time called "narcotics," a term now reserved for the opiates. Psychoactive drugs are sometimes called "recreational drugs," although they may be used for work, spiritual comfort, or therapy as well as for fun. They are also known as "drugs of abuse," a term that emphasizes a common social rather than pharmacological property: the fact that when people use them as they wish, the effects are considered dangerous enough to create a health hazard or a social problem.

We begin with some reflections on old problems of political liberty and their relevance to drug control. Then we discuss the ideas of addiction, dependence, and compulsive drug use, which are so important to both medical and legal definitions of drug abuse. We supplement political and medical theories by examining some aspects of the history and sociology of modern drug control. In Chapter 4, we offer a typology of the forms of drug control, with some judgments on their historical roots, theoretical bases, and comparative advantages and drawbacks. Finally, we consider alternative ways of looking at what is usually called the "drug problem."

Acknowledgments

We would like to express our gratitude to Alice Jelin and Dr. Robert Cserr for their moral support and the Medfield Foundation for its financial support. We would also like to thank Herminie Irving and Nancy Palmer for their help in typing and assembling the manuscript.

1 Questions of risk and liberty

In discussing drug control and freedom, it still makes sense to start with John Stuart Mill's essay *On Liberty* (1859), for all its flaws "the clearest, most candid, most persuasive and most moving exposition of the point of view of those who desire an open and tolerant society" (Berlin 1959, p. 50). Mill's basic principle is that the freedom of adults to live their own lives in their own way should be abridged only to protect others. No people who are "in the maturity of their faculties" and capable of "being guided to their own improvement by conviction or persuasion" (Mill 1859, chap. 1) should be forced to do anything just because it would be good for them, or forcibly prevented from doing anything just because it would be bad for them. Drug control was an important political issue at the time when *On Liberty* was published, and Mill had it very much in mind while writing the essay. In the name of the liberty of the Chinese opium smoker, he defended the opium trade between British India and China, which was under constant attack by reformers. He opposed laws requiring a doctor's prescription to buy certain drugs, including opiates. It goes without saying that he was against the alcohol prohibition laws passed in several U.S. states in the 1850s. In fact, he opposed most legal controls on alcohol, including penalties for drunkenness and taxes designed to keep consumption down (he did not object to taxation solely for revenue). Obviously he would have regarded almost all present drug laws as violations of his principle.

The libertarianism of Mill's essay, exemplified by his classic defense of freedom of speech, was regarded as radical in his own time. But his views on drug control, odd as they seem today, were largely in accord with established policies that reformers were only beginning to challenge. Today, Mill's views on free speech are considered prophetic, and his suspicion of paternalism is still attractive to many people. But only a few libertarian theorists like Thomas Szasz and Robert Nozick agree with him about drug control, and they are regarded as a radical fringe. Some study of history is ultimately needed to understand this change in attitude, but to see why there is any disagreement at all about the legitimacy and the basis of drug controls, we must first explore Mill's reasoning and the objections to it. The question is where and how Mill's principle can properly be applied, and what exceptions and qualifications have to be introduced to make it workable.

Mill was taught in the school of utilitarianism by his father James and by Jeremy Bentham, but *On Liberty* represents a partial break with the ideas of that school. Bentham had no objection to the exercise of paternalistic authority. He did not regard liberty as a good in itself, but only as a political instrument that was of value wherever it helped to achieve the overriding goal of the greatest happiness for the greatest number. He did not hesitate to recommend laws to prevent self-inflicted injury and punishment for what he called "self-regarding crimes." Mill does not abandon the principle of greatest happiness – he says he will "forgo any advantage which could be derived . . . from the idea of abstract right" (Mill 1849, chap. 1), but he insists that the principle itself demands that we treat certain liberties as inviolable. (It is doubtful whether any such case can be made on purely utilitarian grounds, but that is not the issue here.)

Mill thinks that three kinds of activity should be covered by the rule against paternalistic state coercion. Speech and opinion should be absolutely free; even harm to others should not be taken into account. "Combination," or joining with others to act in concert, should also be free as long as it harms no immediately identifiable innocent third parties. Finally, "tastes and pursuits," including the use of drugs and alcohol, should almost always be allowed free cultivation without government interference. Each person is the guardian of his or her own health and morals. The prohibition movement employs doctrines that "ascribe to all mankind a vested interest in each other's moral, intellectual, and even physical perfection, to be defined by each claimant according to his own standard." Of this idea he says that "there is no violation of liberty which it would not justify" (Mill 1859, chap. 4). Drug and alcohol laws, he believes, treat the people as though they were savages or children and punish all for the intemperance of a few.

Mill has to consider whether the issue of paternalism can be avoided. It might be said that no harmful act of any significance hurts only the actor; other people must be affected too. To justify a law this way is more attractive than telling protesting adults that something will be forced on them for their own good. In fact, indirect and long-term harm to others has always been the main justification given for suppressing individual drug use. The situations are familiar. Overdoses, accidents, and physical or mental illness caused by drugs may require the use of public medical resources; society may be damaged by crimes committed under the influence of drugs; drug users may neglect their families, who will require public support, or they may become unproductive and dependent on others because of chronic drug abuse.

Other devices can be used to avoid the question of paternalism. For example, to justify the helmet requirement for motorcycle riders, it has been proposed that we regard the cyclist who blithely refuses to put on a helmet as actually harming another person – the repentant cyclist after the accident. Presumably the same judgment could be made on the beginning drug user who gives no thought to the addict he or she may become some day. The problem is to stop the division into multiple personalities at some point before each of us is treated as a different person at each moment; without some persisting self, there can be no responsibility and no freedom.

Mill fears that indiscriminate state intervention in the name of protecting the public would reduce his antipaternalistic principle to a verbal scruple. So he insists that harm to others justifies state coercion only if it has actually occurred or is at least a definite risk. Indirect, remote, or merely possible harm is not enough. In one place he even suggests that the state should intervene only in cases of force, fraud, or treachery. Elsewhere he allows it more authority; for example, he says that drunkenness itself should not be punishable, but that a soldier should be punished for being drunk on duty. Still, he regards an activity as none of the state's business so long as it "neither violates any specific duty to the public, nor occasions perceptible hurt to any assignable individual" (Mill 1859, chap. 4). You may educate and persuade people not to misuse drugs (or not to use them at all), and you may punish them for actual harm to others produced by their use of drugs, but it is a clear violation of the antipaternalistic principle to prevent them by law from using drugs in the first place.

By setting narrow limits on the kinds of harm the law can take into account, Mill avoids such difficult issues as how much productivity society has a right to demand from an individual, or how great a probability of serious harm to others constitutes a reason for state intervention. He acknowledges that some health and safety standards may be necessary to protect consumers, but otherwise he is devoted to free trade; at any rate, he believes that no one should be restrained from selling drugs, alcohol, or any other commodity to a willing buyer as long as the transaction is not fraudulent. Anything can be misused or used in excess, but the state should interfere only when the misuse hurts an innocent third party.

Mill wants to limit the numbers and kinds of acts that are described as directly harming other people. By implication, his principle also requires limits on the numbers and kinds of acts that are described as involuntary or forced. An act that is not voluntary is, in a sense, not a true act, and therefore is not protected by the rule against paternalism. Prohibiting it only prevents an internal or external force from harming the apparent actor, who is unfree and not responsible. But Mill hardly considers this question, because he takes it for granted that adults are responsible for almost all of their acts. Even the most obvious ignorance or foolishness is no justification for treating an act as if it is involuntary. He does not discuss extreme psychological and social pressures (for example, what is now vaguely called "brainwashing"), but in any case it is questionable to describe that way the conditions that produce most drug and alcohol abuse. He does admit that people might need restraint to prevent them from exposing themselves to danger while "in some state of excitement or absorption incompatible with the full use of the reflecting faculty" (Mill 1859, chap. 5), but he understands this to be a special, rare, and temporary condition; today we tend to treat it as a persistent and recurrent one. For example, the legal theorist H. L. A. Hart, a successor in Mill's liberal tradition, criticizes him for using his principle to disallow restraints on self-inflicted injury caused by inadequate reflection, transitory impulses, weak will, and other subtle pressures (Hart 1963). But few actions are entirely free of all these defects, so taking them into account might in effect nullify the prohibition on paternalism. That is what drug laws, like consumer protection regulations, are designed to do.

Certainly we are much less inclined than Mill to treat drug use as the free, rational act of an autonomous person. It is usually considered a product of ignorance, impulsiveness, or, worst of all, addiction – conditions in which the drug user's freedom becomes a minor concern. For example, almost every heroin addict is introduced to the drug by friends who use it but are not addicted and never become addicted. But we do not want to believe that anyone takes this drug out of free will and with full knowledge: The user must be mentally disturbed, a child victim of evil adults, or, finally, a slave to addiction. So we have developed the myth of the pusher who lures innocent children with free samples. An addict who began to use heroin as a child can never have been free to choose whether or not to use it.

The easiest way to limit Mill's principle, then, is to accept it but at the same time to insist on taking into account many external causes and consequences that Mill himself would have considered politically and legally irrelevant. Acts that Mill would have regarded as free are treated as in some way socially or psychologically compelled; effects on other people that Mill would have considered too remote, indirect, secondary, or uncertain to require government intervention are treated as good reasons to pass preventive laws. Contemporary drug laws are readily justified in this way without appealing to paternalism in the strict sense.

Maybe it is true that the whole concept of paternalism is otiose in this case, because drug use is intrinsically less free than most other acts, or because the extent and severity of the drug problem give us good reasons to take into account consequences of an individual act that would otherwise be considered too remote or uncertain. We will eventually explore these questions. Meanwhile, let us assume what seems intuitively plausible to Mill – that some laws, including many drug laws, are truly paternalistic, directed mainly at self-injury.

These laws can still be defended, but only if Mill's two strong arguments against paternalism are rejected. The first one is that people in general are the best judges of their own interests. The opinion of others about what would benefit me is likely to be wrong when it conflicts with my own opinion; when authority tries to force me to do what is good for me, it is likely to interfere in the wrong place, at the wrong time, in the wrong way. Even when someone seems to be mistaken, it is best to educate and persuade rather than to use coercion, and resorting to force discredits those better means. Mill's second objection to paternalistic coercion is that it prevents people from making "experiments of living" (Mill 1859, chap. 3) that encourage the realization of individual potentialities, development of human faculties, variety of character, and richness of experience. By prejudging the value of the individual's desires and ends, paternalism imposes a conformity that limits human possibilities.

Almost no one rejects these arguments outright, but many people insist that the exceptions are much more numerous and, above all, more easily identified than Mill thinks. They believe that they can clearly define situations in which some external authority is able to judge a person's interests better than he or she can. They also claim to identify experiments in living that do not encourage individuality, diversity, and the fulfillment of human capacities. In some of these situations, education and persuasion alone are inadequate, because there is not enough time for them to work before serious harm occurs or simply not enough chance that they will ever work. Recreational drug use is usually put in that class.

Childhood is the most important situation in which we universally recognize some paternalistic discipline as necessary. Children are not assumed to be the best judges of their own interests, and restricting the experiments in living they are allowed to undertake is thought to promote rather than hinder their self-realization and the development of their individuality. The very word "paternalism" implies that the paradigm of coercing a person for his or her own good is the biologically natural authority of adults over children. That is why Mill insists that his principle applies only to people in the maturity of their faculties. Most of the reasons given for paternalistic coercion of adults are related to this model of childhood. They all assume that beneficiaries of paternal discipline are in some way incomplete – not, or not yet, fully developed human beings who must be granted the right to determine the course of their own lives. Even a writer who calls himself an anarchist can criticize "absolute tolerance" by comparing it to permissive child rearing (Wolff 1965). One common assumption is that whole societies and peoples can be historically immature, as a child is biologically immature; they require paternal government to realize their full historical potential. For this reason, Mill is willing to allow paternalism in the societies he calls "savage" and "barbarian"; in fact, one of his objections to alcohol control laws is that they treat the English laborer like a savage. Mill assumes a special status for nineteenth-century industrial society, but there is no need to follow him. Marxists, for example, insist that every class society is historically immature. We will cease to be barbarians only when humanity comes to its self-realization under communism. Until then, at least, Mill's worries about paternalism are beside the point.

But liberals generally refuse to treat every existing imperfection in individuals and societies as analogous to the biological immaturity that makes a parent's authority necessary. They require another principle to decide when individuals are so imperfect or incompetent that the state must protect them from themselves. One idea is that the state should be allowed to intervene whenever the situation is one in which a reasonable person would choose to be protected from the consequences of doing what he or she wants. The unreasonable person in the actual situation – ignorant, incompetent, foolish, impulsive, driven by forces beyond individual control – is placed under the authority of a hypothetical reasonable self whose agent is the state insofar as its laws are just and sensible. In effect, the coercive external authority is referred back to an individual taking prudent precautions for self-protection. And, as Mill insists, persons are usually the best judge of their own interests.

Gerald Dworkin has represented this situation in its simplest form by reference to the myth of Ulysses and the Sirens. Ulysses wants to hear the Sirens sing, but he fears being lured to death by drowning. So he has himself lashed to the mast of his ship and orders his men (who will be protected from the Sirens by wax in their ears) to ignore the anguished demands for release that he knows he will make when he hears the seductive and deadly song. When the sailors refuse to untie Ulysses, it could be said that they are exercising paternalistic authority over him; and yet, from another, more obvious point of view, it is they who are recognizing his authority. No moral or political problem arises here, and it is certain that when he comes to his senses Ulysses will approve of the sailors' actions (Dworkin 1971). The alcoholic writer Jack London is said to have proclaimed that he favored women's suffrage because the women would enact prohibition laws and save him from himself. This anecdote suggests a modern political version of the Ulysses story.

Unfortunately, in politics the command of the reasonable self is rarely so explicit, and a person who has not explicitly asked for the restraints is not nearly so certain to approve of them afterward. For that matter, in practice it is not easy to tell which self is the reasonable one. John Rawls touches on the problem with his theory of the original position in which individuals meet to frame a social contract behind a veil of ignorance. Each fictive person in this imaginary situation is conceived as fully devoted to rational self-interest but completely ignorant of his or her personal characteristics and social circumstances in any real world. Rawls believes that paternalistic coercion or restraint is appropriate whenever someone in the original position would judge it necessary to ensure against the possibility of undeveloped powers or self-destructive impulses. In a way, this person is the solicitous parent of the empirical self – a child with whom he or she is truly one flesh. No one could be a better judge of the interests of this imperfect real person or a better guide to that person's self-development and self-realization, so both of Mill's arguments against paternalism are eliminated. Judgment on what constitutes self-destructiveness or undeveloped powers is left first to the individual's rational, settled preferences. If we cannot say what these preferences are in a given situation, we must introduce a theory of "primary goods" – a notion of what is good for people in general (Rawls 1971, pp. 248 ff).

This takes us a long way from Ulysses' command and an even longer way from Mill's principle. Mill mistrusts paternalism because he believes that no conceptions of what is desirable for human beings are so fixed and certain that they need only be applied by a wise authority. But Rawls's abstract person in the original position, the creator of the social contract, is made out to be just that kind of authority on the good. The proper exercise of liberty in effect becomes identified with choosing rightly or rationally by a standard that has nothing to do with the individual's actual desires. The effect is a broad license for paternalistic restraint, ostensibly to promote genuine freedom.

Suppose that Ulysses forgets to order his men to ignore later commands given under the influence of the Sirens. Still, few would object if they denied his wishes for his own good. By refusing to untie him, they would be obeying the orders that an ideal Ulysses would have given, and the actual Ulysses will thank them for it later. Rawls might call this deference to his rational settled preferences, but he also might call it an application of the theory of primary goods. In this case, life is the primary good that would be chosen by the rational person in the original position. Even if the sailors do not know their captain's rational settled preferences – even if they imagine that later he might tell them that he would rather have died a blissful death – they should rely on the notion of primary goods and treat him as though they were obeying the command of a man in the original position.

A more practical example is legislation setting maximum hours and minimum wages for labor. In effect, the individual worker's freedom of contract, such as it is, is limited for the collective benefit of all workers. Workers actually fight for this ostensible limitation on their individual freedom, and they certainly do not regard it as paternalistic. Nor does Mill; he insists that such laws actually grant rather than deny power to the people affected by them. But this is ostensibly a case of paternalism, since the law is being used to protect workers against temptation. A worker who votes for a law or signs a union contract setting maximum hours and minimum wages is in somewhat the same position as Ulysses commanding that certain wishes he might later express should be denied. But these laws and contracts are also enforced against (or in favor of) workers who have not agreed to them and may even object to them. Ulysses neglecting to give his command was not in the same situation. There the sailors could assume an oversight, because refusing to untie him served not only his own rational preferences but also a primary good recognized by everyone. Mill would certainly have judged Ulysses to be in a state "incompatible with the use of the reflecting faculty," but even here some extreme libertarian might defend letting him go. In most cases it is less clear what the person under restraint would prefer if he or she were reasonable, and in many cases it is not obvious to everyone that a primary good is being served. For workers to believe that wage and hour limitations do them more harm than good is not obviously irrational, although it may be wrong. So a few individualist libertarians would allow maximum hour and minimum wage restraints to be applied not to workers in general but only to those who have actually contracted for them.

The larger issue here is which self-injurious actions are compatible with rationality and therefore with freedom. If free acts, however wrong or mistaken, are in some sense products of a fully developed rational capacity, it is hard to see how Mill can dispense with some conception of human nature or the meaning of human life that gives content to the idea of rationality. He actually alludes to this in the epigraph of his essay, where he quotes Wilhelm von Humboldt as saying that the aim of government is human development in its richest diversity. Mill objects to paternalism partly because it assumes the existence of primary goods or rational preferences so obvious that they can be imposed on people against their will. But to speak of rich human development implies some conception of fulfillment appropriate to human beings and therefore some idea of rationality as a rule directing action toward such a fulfillment. By that standard some acts must be irrational and, if there is no freedom without rationality, possibly unfree. And maybe such acts should be prevented by paternalistic coercion.

Mill himself hardly considers the matter further after making exceptions for children (and "savages") and for acts performed in a state of "excitement or absorption." But promoting the highest development of human powers could easily require much more work by government. The tension is inherent in Mill's conception of the individual; he is uncertain which of our characteristics demand that freedom should be defended against paternalistic coercion. He is concerned about developing and exercising the capacity to conceive our own ends, shape the meaning and course of our own lives, and maintain our own conceptions of happiness, so he emphasizes the value of the individuality and diversity that result from such choices. But it is easy to think of acts (including some kinds of drug abuse) that are free by Mill's definition, yet actually seem to destroy the capacity to shape our lives and therefore reduce individuality and diversity. The shaping of my life should be guided by what is significant for me, but I am not always the best judge of that. And even when I do know what is really important for me, I may be the victim of other desires that prevent me from attaining it – desires I wish I did not have. Alcohol and drug dependence are the paradigms. A life dominated by impulse, drift, or restricting habits is not free. Mill himself actually writes in *Logic* that "none but a person of confirmed virtue is completely free" (Himmelfarb 1974, p. 108). This conception of freedom is obviously not the same as the political one of *On Liberty*.

The trouble is that to justify paternalism by distinguishing meaningfully free acts from those produced by impulse, drift, and compulsive habit would be to smuggle in the idea of obvious primary goods and universal rational preferences that he has already rejected by denying that there is any fixed human nature capable of serving as a political standard. From another point of view, the distinction implies that a more or less balanced, fully developed character is required for politically protected free action.

But once we introduce that criterion, it is hard to know where to stop short of identifying free acts with rational and virtuous acts as defined by a standard independent of the individual's will. And Mill fears the political implications of doing that.

The requirement of wholeness, integrity, consistency, and ultimately rationality as conditions for freedom can be extended beyond the individual. No one is self-sufficient; no one is even himself or herself outside of a context created by other people in families and societies. Mill's distinction between harm to oneself and harm to others becomes unimportant in this perspective. Any injury done anywhere affects both individual interests and the common good at once, and the freedom of a whole person is also the good of a whole society. These ideas are worked out most clearly in the theory of positive liberty. Mill's contemporary, T. H. Green, used the term as a contrast to negative liberty, permission to do what you want, which is central to Mill's conception of political freedom. The distinction has been analyzed by Isaiah Berlin (Berlin 1969). Advocates of positive liberty insist that a free individual must be a whole person, and no genuinely whole person can exist outside of a free society, that is, one which allows the full development and self-realization of each person. As long as social arrangements are imperfect, all individuals are unrealized, incomplete, and to that extent, at least, like children. In the terminology of Hegelian idealism, the empirical will, which exercises the dubious freedom Mill defends, is distinct from the real or essential will, which is in total harmony with reason and can have full effect only within a society that is also totally reasonable. In Marxist terminology, people in a class society are alienated, estranged from their true natures. They are in a socially transitional stage; alienation will end only when the human species comes to full maturity under communism. In either view, freedom is best conceived not as the exercise of an imperfect individual's will but as the product of a good life in a reasonable society. What Mill regards as paternalism may be one of the ways to attain that freedom.

The idea of positive liberty goes back in Western thought at least to the remark of Socrates that no one willingly errs. Montesquieu characterized this concept succinctly in his statement that liberty consists of being able to do what you ought to want to do. In this tradition, persons who consider themselves free may be slaves to impulses that destroy the capacity for meaningful, rational choice. All action opposed to the common good is unfree in the deepest sense, and it may be necessary to coerce people for an end they are too depraved or foolish to recognize – as Rousseau put it, to force them to be free. Green (1895) defines natural rights as the powers individuals need to attain the ends human society is meant to realize. He believes that many restraints called paternalistic by Mill, such as laws restricting the use of alcohol and drugs, actually create new rights by preventing behavior that interferes with the possibility of free action contributing to the public good. Benevolent restraint nullifies a hidden coercion that destroys human powers and therefore violates natural rights.

The central question about all paternalistic authority is who will guard the guardians, or, to put it more abstractly, how the authority is to be appointed and what justifies its rule. Where the beneficiary is a child, as we saw, the answer is easy: The authority is appointed by nature and its justification is maturity. A problem arises only where adults are involved. Marxists often vest authority in those social classes or groups that are historically mature and therefore understand the present potentialities of humanity. Rawls believes that just laws, including paternalistic restraints, derive their authority from the refined rationality of the person in the original position; we need only imagine ourselves to be divining the thoughts and wishes of that person, which are those of an ideal parent who is also, somehow, ourself. Superior hereditary capacity and a vision of the idea of the good give the guardians of Plato's Republic the right to rule.

But there are always doubts about what group is historically mature, what the person in the original position would think, who has been granted a vision of the good. And as long as this is so, paternalistic authority may be under suspicion as a disguise for tyranny and a danger rather than an aid to the development of human capacities. Kant writes of the need to liberate humanity from its self-imposed tutelage and says that paternalism is the greatest despotism imaginable. Von Humboldt says that the incapacity for freedom can arise only from a want of the moral and intellectual power supplied by freedom itself (Chomsky 1973, p. 398). Many advocates of positive liberty also see the problem. Green admits that some kinds of external restraint reduce "the capacity for spontaneous action regulated by a conception of a common good" (Green 1895, para. 209) and thus retard the development of freedom; these are the restraints he is inclined to regard as paternalistic. In fact, he believes that very few acts are so necessary or so dangerous to the public that we must enforce or prevent them with threats of punishment. He admits, in effect, that negative liberty is necessary to develop the capacity for positive liberty – a point not far from Mill's justification of his antipaternalistic principle as a way to develop human powers.

Some compromise is necessary. Everyone wants to put limits on the state. The term "paternalism" is suspect even to Green and others who approve of laws that Mill would certainly have called paternalistic. Rawls would say that we must be left to make our own decisions about some things, either because the rational person of the original position would have no opinion about them or because he would believe that we should be free to choose. The Marxist has to consider whether some kinds of benevolent restraint are incompatible with the historical level of social forces and therefore unacceptable to their beneficiaries. Green admits that not every power whose exercise would ideally be desirable can be claimed as a right in a given society at a given time; the claim must also be acceptable to the public. Even supposing it desirable that no one should ever drink alcohol, the state would have no right (as well as no capacity) to enforce a prohibition law if the populace was not willing to tolerate it.

The idea of positive liberty in its purest form actually tends toward anarchy rather than any sort of state control. It suggests a vision of a world in which my freedom is always fully compatible with yours, total self-mastery is joined with complete absence of overt coercion, and impulse coincides with deepest reflection in a perfect harmony of will and reason. At some ideal point humanity reaches adulthood, its compulsory education ends, and there is no more need for coercive law or a state. Marxists say that the state will wither away when the condition for the free development of each is the free development of all. Green's political theory has similar implications: "For a positive and detailed criterion of just punishment, we must wait till a system of rights has been established in which the claims of all men . . . are perfectly harmonized. . . . And this is perhaps equivalent to saying that no complete criterion of just punishment can be arrived at till punishment is no longer necessary; for the state of things supposed could scarcely be realized without bringing with it an extinction of the tendencies which state-punishment is needed to suppress" (Green 1895, para. 189). On the assumption described (and rejected) by Isaiah Berlin, that the rational ends of our true natures must coincide (Berlin 1969, p. 154), there is no right to negative liberty in existing societies, but no need for any coercive state once our true natures have been realized. Mill, in contrast, does not believe that even the highest and most harmonious development of human powers could ever become so perfect that both coercion and formally prescribed liberties would be unnecessary.

Theorists of positive liberty seem to be justifying a strong state authority under some conditions and an ideal anarchy under others. But in either case they treat the distinction between harm to self and harm to others as unclear and difficult to apply in practice. The result is the same as if they avoided the issue of paternalism entirely by finding, in every act the state proposes to restrain, causes beyond the actor's control or consequences affecting other people. So long as no one even has a self outside of a social context, any harm that a person does must have social as well as personal causes and effects. Theories of positive liberty therefore have the same effect as insistence on external causes and consequences.

Whether they speak of positive liberty or external harm, the critics of Mill's principle are making an important point. In modern societies many laws, including some of which almost everyone approves, can be regarded as violating Mill's principle on Mill's interpretation of it. As Green points out, the principle is much too broad even to fit our commonsense notions of what is paternalistic. The laws that govern building inspection, practicing medicine without a license, minimum wages, consent as a defense in assault charges, the dispensing of prescription drugs, seat belts in cars, gambling, obscenity, prostitution, swimming in public pools without life-guards, laetrile, food additives, dueling, suicide, and selling oneself into slavery have little in common. They cover very different areas of social life, they were established in very different circumstances, and they are enforced in very different ways. Some deal with what we ordinarily call consensual crimes, and others do not; some would be regarded as paternalistic by most people, and others would not. It is true that all of these laws involve or might involve violations, modifications, or qualifications of Mill's principle, but that does not tell us much about them, and it gives little guidance to legislators or the public. Knowing how to regulate minimum wages, dueling, or the use of swimming pools hardly helps in handling the problem of recreational drug use. Analogies that may be interesting to political theorists seem to have little practical use. It is not surprising that most people prefer to avoid Mill's formulation of the issues. Certainly legislators rarely consider it on his terms; they are no more disinclined to enforce, punish, or prevent self-regarding acts than Bentham was.

Yet, as we saw, even among writers who reject most of Mill's applications of his principle and most of the theory behind it, a feeling persists that there is something worth preserving, some inner core of negative liberty that should be inviolable. Unfortunately, it is hard to define that inner core in a principled way that is neither so broad and abstract that it takes in almost everything we do, nor so limited and concrete that it amounts to nothing more than a list of policy recommendations for specific situations. For example, Ronald Dworkin proposes a distinction between the "force" of Mill's principle, which he says is great, and its "range," which he considers quite limited. Liberty as "independence" is what Mill endorses, not liberty as "licence" (Dworkin 1970, pp. 261ff.). But unless this distinction is the same as the one between positive and negative liberty, it is merely rhetorical. Dworkin seems to be using it to justify ad hoc whatever policies he considers desirable. The "force" of the argument against state interference with sexual acts between consenting adults is said to be enormously powerful because sex comes within the proper "range" of the principle; but outside that range, in the territory of drug use or consumer protection, the principle may have no force at all. This is a statement of preference, not an argument, and it is not Mill's preference – he defends the sale of potentially deleterious commodities.

To resolve the issue, we need to know not only whether laws on drugs, sex, or any other subject can be justified on some grounds, paternalistic or nonpaternalistic, but also why paternalistic or preventive legislation is socially distributed the way it is. Why, in societies where so many actions dangerous to the actor and to others are permitted and sometimes encouraged, do we impose such strong restrictions on drug use? Why are these laws often controversial, and always difficult and expensive to enforce?

Utilitarian calculation might seem capable of proving that a certain system of control does more good than harm when applied to drug use but would do more harm than good in some other area of social life. But when an issue is at all complicated, the utilitarian calculus simply does not supply the necessary distinctions; comparing different kinds of benefit and harm on a single scale is too difficult. It is important to mention, incidentally, that in actual policy discussions about drugs, we rarely concede that there are any benefits to be had from using them. As the Canadian Commission of Inquiry into the Non-Medical Use of Drugs said in its 1973 report, there is "no clearly established framework" for assessing the good effects of drugs (*Final Report* 1973, p. 50). Legislators show no interest in whether or when recreational drug use does any good, and little interest in comparing the harm done by drugs to other kinds of harm. So in practice, the only utilitarian issue is whether the reduction in harm caused by the drugs is worth the cost of enforcing a drug law. And even that issue is rarely given much serious attention.

Analogies do help to explain the controls on recreational drug use, but not just anything that seems paternalistic will do. The present system of drug regulation can be analyzed using three analogies: rules relating to dangerous sports and hobbies; consumer protection laws, including public health and the control of medical practices and technologies; and the regulation of public morality or public order. Twentieth-century governments have been forced to recognize, implicitly or explicitly, the power of these analogies, which in their encounter have produced the history of modern drug laws and the form taken by our modern drug problem.

In practice, the analogies are used in combination to justify severe social disapproval and legal restraints that we would probably not tolerate for equivalent dangers (if it were possible to speak of them) produced by acts other than drug use, while at the same time supplying apparently inconsistent exceptions for two especially dangerous drugs, alcohol and tobacco. The current drug control arrangements and their justifying analogies have the weight of twentieth-century history behind them, and they are similar everywhere in the world. They are the accepted and perhaps inevitable response, in our time, to a need for classification and control of a complicated and ambiguous social situation. Whether we want to protest against this system, modify it, or defend it, we need to become more aware of just what we are doing and describe it more candidly.

Consider a typical article on the dangers of what is colloquially known as "getting high." The alarming interest in this dangerous behavior is pointed out, its social roots are examined, the epidemiology of the habit is analyzed, and the motives of the young people who take the trips are discussed. Some are depressed, others bored; some want escape, adventure, or a way of testing themselves in the search for identity. A few have personality disorders, and others suffer from feelings of inadequacy. The roles of parents, peers, and social conditions are considered. The author notes the euphoria often produced by the experience and describes the process of going up to a peak and coming down. The sometimes remarkably complex and expensive paraphernalia used and the proliferation of shops displaying and selling it without interference from the law are mentioned and deplored. The abnormal mental and physical states produced by the habit are analyzed, and the danger of serious accidents, even death, is emphasized. The question of psychological dependence is discussed. The article ends with a call for more effective law enforcement and a re-examination of the moral and spiritual condition of the society that has produced the epidemic.

It sounds unremarkable; the ideas and vocabulary are familiar to the point of boredom. But a few years ago, when a satirical piece with this theme was published, its title was "Alpinism: The Social, Scientific and Treatment Aspects of Getting High and Its Prohibition" (Phallow 1978). The point, of course, is that much of the descriptive language used in writing about drugs applies to mountain climbing as well; only the customary denunciations, anxious soul searching, and earnest recommendations sound absurd when transferred. For mountain climbing you can also substitute the still more dangerous sport of flying small planes (Lindsey 1980) or even, say, high school football, which produces several dozen cases a year of permanent quadriplegia (Torg et al. 1975). It would be silly to suggest that drug use is just like these other pursuits and should be subject to similar rules, but the analogy is not entirely irrelevant. As the satire implies, we tend to ignore similarities between drug use and other voluntary activities that may injure the participant. Obviously we do not want to find ourselves comparing the effects of marihuana on high school students with the effects of football.

Mill supplies the justification for not prohibiting dangerous sports; it preserves liberty by protecting individual tastes and pursuits from paternalistic coercion. The same reasons can be given for not prohibiting potentially unhealthy eating habits. But official policy rejects the notion that a drug trip might resemble an airplane trip or a drug habit might resemble a habit of eating candy. One possible reason is that drug use is not considered a free act in the same sense as eating candy or flying small planes; another is that, unlike these other activities, drug use has little or no value that justifies the risk. In practice, the two ideas reinforce each other, because of the connection between freedom and rationality. If we decide that something has no value and its pursuit is therefore irrational, we look for ways to show that people who want it are not making a truly free choice.

Mountain climbing is dangerous, but its pleasures are virtuous ones; it provides an opportunity for physical exercise, adventure, achievement, and the enjoyment of natural beauty. In making public policy, the illness caused by enjoyable but unhealthy eating habits or the accidents suffered by careless mountain climbers and motorcycle riders are balanced against the satisfaction of human needs and desires that these activities are assumed to provide. But drug use for anything but the treatment of disease is not regarded as satisfying a legitimate need or desire. There is some underground lore about the alleged beneficial effects of illicit drugs, and there is also a more respectable lore about the virtues of alcohol. But they tend to be nervously jocular or embarrassed, and have little effect on public policy. Permitting drug use is often defended in the name of individual freedom, but rarely on the ground that there is any good in it.

As Mill apparently fails to understand, in this case circumstances can make talk of individual liberty trivial or even hypocritical. In a complex industrial society, where far more needs to be known than any single person can learn, there are some things about which the average person is simply incapable of making an informed and rational choice. To use the jargon of neoliberal economics, the cost of information processing is too high. In less scientistic language, everyone is in a sense limited and underdeveloped for this purpose, and therefore needs the kind of protection Mill mistrusted as paternalistic (we may also call it, more aggressively, "consumers' rights"). Outlawing marihuana smoking is not like outlawing motorcycle riding, a taste or pursuit to which people have a right, however dangerous it may be to themselves and others. Instead it is seen as something like outlawing the sale and use of a motorcycle with a defective part. People might be willing to buy that motorcycle, but only out of ignorance, carelessness, or impulsive folly. Since it has practically no value, society does not have to respect the freedom (if it can be called that) of those who choose to do it. Another example is the regulation ensuring that electric chainsaws cannot be sold without shields to protect the user. Someone might want to buy a chainsaw without a guard, because it is cheaper or less clumsy to handle, but we do not respect that wish. Using a chainsaw without a shield may not be more dangerous than alpine climbing, but we also assume that it has little value. These analogies could be carried further. Drugs with no accepted medical uses are treated like defective motorcycles; they are pleasure vehicles that have a deadly flaw. Only in this case, the flaw is such an integral part of the design that the vehicle itself must be banned. Drugs with medical uses are more like the chainsaw – acceptable as a tool for certain purposes, but only with safeguards that cannot be left to the individual user to supply.

Certainly drugs are potentially dangerous instruments that can be ignorantly misused and sometimes produce serious ill effects. But it is hard to believe that the risk of, say, marihuana smoking is so obviously great, the benefits so obviously negligible, and the consumer's ignorance so substantial that the drug has to be treated as something from which all consumers must be protected. Consumer protection laws imply that sometimes we cannot rely on the commonsense rule that greater dangers are also much more obvious and therefore more likely to be avoided. People are not scientific calculators of risk, and they tend to underestimate the probability of unlikely events. With a product like the chainsaw, the danger might seem too remote and contingent to outweigh the immediate inconvenience of a safety device if there were no special regulation. But presumably the more you think about it, the more you are likely to demand a chainsaw with a shield. The situation is different with drugs. Studies show that the *less* people know about the effects of recreational drugs, the more dangerous they consider the drugs to be (Glaser and Snow 1969; Swisher 1971); this has even been used as an argument against drug education in schools. If people who know more about the facts are wrong in their attitudes, which is quite possible, the mistake is obviously not caused by the kind of ignorance or preoccupation usually said to justify consumer protection laws.

Another peculiarity of drug laws as a form of consumer protection can be illustrated by comparing them with pollution control laws. Here we have to balance two goods, industrial productivity and a clean environment. We try to estimate how much loss of productivity we can tolerate for the sake of a given degree of improvement in air or water quality. If we followed the same policy in regulating drugs, we would try to estimate how much loss in the benefits of recreational drug use we should tolerate for the sake of a given reduction in their ill effects. But in fact the issue does not even arise, since benefits from recreational drug use are not conceded to exist for policymaking purposes.

An even more interesting analogy is the laws on seatbelts in cars. It took a long political struggle to get them installed, and now most people will not use them. But it is still very doubtful, in this country, that buckling of seatbelts will be made compulsory. Most legislators who regard driving without a seatbelt as a right would reject as absurd the notion of a right to smoke marihuana. And yet the argument against individual freedom of choice seems at first glance much better in the seatbelt case. The risk of driving without a seatbelt is overwhelmingly greater than any benefit, a fact not nearly so obvious in the case of marihuana; and driving without a seatbelt is not an active taste or pursuit like marihuana smoking, so it is more likely to be done automatically, without conscious choice or genuine thought – the kind of situation in which people need protection most and the threat to their freedom is least.

Driving without a seatbelt resembles drug use because it may cause accidental harm. Looking at television is sometimes said to resemble drug use in another way: It is said to be an "addictive," psychologically pernicious, and socially debilitating practice, especially dangerous to children, which can seriously damage the quality of life. But we have no laws defining a permissible amount of television viewing, just as we have no laws requiring the use of seatbelts. It is true that these matters are not left to individual choice everywhere. In many countries drivers are fined for not wearing seatbelts; in some places television viewing is restricted by law. What is interesting is that drug use, except for alcohol, is left to individual choice nowhere. Drug laws are not typical protective laws, but a special set of regulations for a very special case.

Another anomaly makes this situation clearer. If it ever became necessary for the government to use vast amounts of money and personnel to curb an organized illicit traffic in chainsaws without shields, or most other commodities forbidden by consumer protection laws, the law would probably be repealed. If people wanted the commodities so much, we might conclude that they have a legitimate interest and value strong enough to outweigh any argument for prohibition. In other words, we would handle the problem as we handle mountain climbing, hang-gliding, or motorcycle racing: We would treat it as a matter of preferred tastes and activities (however questionable) rather than consumer error. But it is considered normal and necessary for the police to devote a large part of their resources to combatting the drug traffic, and the size of the problem is not regarded as a reason to change our way of dealing with it. Besides, every activity connected with any of the banned drugs is a crime, including simple possession. Possessing some of these drugs is still a felony in many states, and the sale of a few grams is often subject to the same punishment as rape, armed robbery, and second-degree murder. Obviously more powerful feelings are at work here than those that produce the average consumer safety law.

If the comparison with seatbelts or chainsaws sounds strained, that is because psychoactive drug control is usually regarded as something more than an ordinary health and safety measure. The regulations for drugs of pleasure, drugs of abuse, or "controlled substances" are not the same as the controls on other drugs. The two systems have different historical origins (regulation of so-called narcotics started much earlier) and remain different today, despite some convergence. The controls on pleasure- and performance-enhancing drugs not only protect consumers but also contain what is believed to be a threat to the social fabric and the moral order. This is the third analogy popularly used in thinking about drugs: They belong to the group of problems that includes prostitution, pornography, and gambling. Iran since the revolution of 1979 supplies another example, more interesting because more alien. A police campaign has been instituted there against alcohol, drugs, and Western popular music, which are all regarded as parts of a single social problem. The music has to be outlawed because it is "addictive," causes disorderly conduct and sexual excess, and ultimately produces undesirable moral and social changes. In other words, the Iranians think of music the way we think of drugs (and a few other vices). We do not believe that governments have a right to issue decrees on the forms and uses of music, and most of us do not regard musical listening habits as a moral issue. What makes us so sure that legal restraints on music are not just as sensible, or just as pointless, as legal restraints on drug use?

The defense of public morality can be used as a justification for ignoring Mill's principle in two familiar ways: Either the victims of gambling, drug, and sexual habits are not free, or their behavior by its very nature harms others. But the legislation of morality has been much more disputed in modern liberal societies than consumer protection laws, usually because of doubts about the notion of morality involved and the assumed connection between the disapproved behavior and various social ills. A public debate on the subject took place in England in the early 1960s, when the jurist Lord Devlin defended laws against homosexual acts. He argued that when a society decides whether to make an act a criminal offense, it must consider the effect on the common morality as well as harm done to a victim. A society, he said, is a community of ideas, and acts offensive to deep common convictions disintegrate the bonds that enable people to live with one another. For example, the principle barring consent or forgiveness as a defense to an assault charge ensures that even if the victim acquiesces in violence, society will enforce its own idea of what is intolerable among human beings living together in a community. When the man on the street, or, as English lawyers say, "the man on the Clapham omnibus," feels strong enough intolerance and disgust, the law must ratify his feelings for the sake of social cohesion (Devlin 1965).

Several writers challenged Devlin's argument. The legal theorist H. L. A. Hart argued that feelings of intolerance and disgust do not constitute a moral conviction (Hart 1963), and Ronald Dworkin later expanded this argument into a distinction between "sociological" and "discriminatory" senses of the word "morality." In the first sense, morality includes anything that any sufficiently large social group considers to be part of its system of ethical beliefs. In the second sense, a conviction is not moral unless the person who holds it is able to give reasons for it – reasons not contaminated by prejudice (for example, racism), personal emotion, false factual beliefs, or rationalization, and not dependent solely on the beliefs of other people; for example, "Everyone knows that homosexuality is a sin" is not a discriminating moral statement. A certain degree of sincerity, consistency, and lack of arbitrariness is also necessary; to say that the wrongness of homosexuality is self-evident, like the wrongness of cruelty, would be to fail this test. Dworkin says that Devlin wants the law to ratify morality in the sociological sense, although in fact it should be concerned only with morality in the discriminatory sense. A consensus of prejudices and passions that presents itself as morality deserves no legal respect, and by ignoring it, a legislator or judge vindicates the true implicit morality of the community (Dworkin 1971, pp. 248–55).

Hart adds that Devlin assumes a degree of social solidarity not common anywhere at any time and especially unlikely in modern society. He identifies Devlin's idea with what the nineteenth-century judge Leslie

Stephen called the "denunciatory" function of punishment. But without the backing of an overwhelming moral majority, denunciation by official punishment becomes merely an idiosyncratic and excessive expression of anger and disgust. We have no single universally accepted code of sexual conduct, only a number of mutually tolerant sexual moralities.

Hart also points out that in his defense of legal moralism, Devlin effectively defines a community as a set of shared moral assumptions, and therefore allows no way to distinguish between a breakdown in the social order and the emergence of a new moral consensus. He implies that any unpunished act defying the moral consensus in any area of social life is a potential threat not just to a particular custom but to the whole life of the community. On this assumption the fabric of society is woven so that a break anywhere causes it to unravel everywhere. Moral change becomes either impossible or catastrophic. Devlin responds that not every deviation from the accepted code is dangerous enough to be made a crime, but he gives no rule for deciding which ones are – or, rather, no rule except the lawmaker's estimate of the intensity of popular feeling, the intolerance and disgust felt by the man on the Clapham omnibus (Devlin 1971). Although Mill does not discuss legal moralism explicitly, he anticipates this response when he criticizes those who "consider as an injury to themselves any conduct which they have a distaste for" (Mill 1859, chap. 4). So Mill, Hart, and Dworkin all agree that Devlin tries to introduce legal coercion where it is not desirable, but only Mill would regard drug laws as illegitimate coercion of that kind.

Devlin's argument derives some of its plausibility from being an extension of a special case: the need to preserve public order and decency against offensive public behavior. Laws against the open display of obscene material, sexual acts in public places, or public intoxication might be justified because the affront to the sensibilities of the majority is immediate, direct, and unavoidable. In this case it may make some sense to regard producing disgust or annoyance as a form of injury. The laws defended by Devlin treat private behavior as though it were a public nuisance, a stink in the public nostrils. Devlin's legal moralism implies that if the very thought of someone looking at pornography or performing strange sex acts or smoking marihuana offends people enough, it should be outlawed just as if they were being unwillingly confronted with it on the street – having the smoke blown into their faces, so to speak. This is an old idea. Brothels used to be called "disorderly houses," a term that assimilated breach of the moral order to breach of the public peace. But the modern tendency has been to insist more and more on the difference. For example, in New England in the seventeenth century, courts interpreted common law doctrines on drunkenness to make intoxication in private a crime, but later reinterpretations established that the law's concern was not sin but breach of the peace. Devlin's implicit blend of moral disorder with offensive public behavior represents a reaction against that historical trend.

Another way in which legal moralism can be injected into criminal law is the notion of alarm and fear as types of harm that must be taken into account in calculating the utilitarian balance. Bentham feels no reverence for tradition, and he certainly does not credit popular feelings of intolerance and disgust with special moral weight. But for him, bad feelings, especially if they are strong enough to be described as "alarm," are bad things; and to the extent that any behavior produces general alarm, it works against the greatest good of the greatest number. This is only one consideration among many in deciding what to treat as an offense or crime, but it could be important. General alarm is related to the concrete fear provoked by a robbery or assault in somewhat the same way that the offensiveness of private drug use and unusual sexual behavior is related to the offensiveness of public intoxication or obscene gestures in public. If marihuana use, for whatever reason, provokes this kind of public alarm, it may have to be treated like robbery and assault in order to preserve social tranquility. The point is that here a private act has public consequences. Whether or not the public's intolerance is rational is a secondary question.

Most American cities and states now have laws against the sale of drug paraphernalia – special pipes and cigarette papers for smoking marihuana, mirrors engraved with the word "cocaine," and so on. Ostensibly these laws are meant to make drugs less attractive by getting rid of accessories that have a glamorizing effect. It is as if we tried to prevent alcohol abuse by banning fancy wine glasses, bottled mixers, or swizzle sticks with drinking jokes printed on them. This sort of law has practically no effect on drug use. Its real purpose is to eliminate an affront to propriety and decency. Closing down a shop that sells paraphernalia is a way to remove an offensive sight from the streets and put an annoying thought out of people's minds; it is like insisting that pornographic bookstores be inconspicuous. This is a clear case in which a law justified as a way of reducing drug use is actually a way of reducing the anxiety caused by excessive public consciousness of drug use.

Two interesting examples of what seem to be pure legal moralism are criminal laws against desecrating the flag and mutilating a corpse. These acts, Mill would have said, neither harm any assignable individual nor violate a specific duty to the public; nor do they injure the person who performs them; but they are very offensive. In one recent model penal code (Schwartz 1971), flag desecration is a crime only if done in public, but mutilation of a corpse is a crime under any circumstances; public outrage, in this rare case, is assumed to be carried over to private activity. Today it would be hard to get general agreement on outlawing any private behavior that outraged sensibilities less than mutilating a corpse. Many people may regard flag desecration, even in private, as a symbolic threat to communal order, but that does not justify making it a crime. In this view, it also makes no sense to treat private homosexual behavior as a crime, even if many people think that homosexuality is a danger to the community. Drug use might be treated the same way, as the Alaska Supreme Court suggested when it ruled that smoking marihuana in the home was protected by the right of privacy proclaimed in the state constitution, but other courts have not followed it.

One underlying reason for our uneasiness about legal moralism is that we lack any traditional, fully accredited source of authority. We have little sense of social solidarity, and existing customs are under constant attack. At one time the worst crimes included sacrilege, heresy, witchcraft – acts that could bring down the wrath of a deity who would destroy the community. In a more abstract form, the idea of natural law justified the punishment of acts that injured an objective public good based on an inherent human nature. Modern liberal societies no longer endorse the idea of a universal moral order backed by either a god's commandments or a natural law prescribing the proper ends of humanity. T. H. Green agreed that it was wrong to punish conduct that violated no one's immediate rights, just because it was thought likely to weaken belief in some divine authority or bring on the wrath of unseen powers. Mill himself, of course, rejected the theory of natural law as well as all divine authority, since he did not believe in a fixed human nature and fixed goods that everyone had to recognize.

But the presumed outrage of the man on the Clapham omnibus, unsupported by any broad principle, is a poor substitute for the anger of a god or an accepted conception of public virtue based on a view of humanity's natural ends. The U.S. Supreme Court declared contemporary community standards to be the basis for judging whether a legal definition of obscenity is constitutional, in effect endorsing something like Devlin's view for this purpose; but its decision satisfied no one, because people cannot agree even on what these standards are, much less on why they should have the authority of law. Devlin's deference to the alleged indignation of the common man merely exchanges a set of serious ideas that are no longer tenable for a set of unconsidered attitudes that never were tenable. The conviction that some acts are destructive to the common moral order becomes dubious when we no longer believe in an avenging deity who has the power to destroy the community; the conviction that some basic human standard is being violated becomes questionable without the support of assumptions about human nature that would justify it. In these circumstances we have to fear that, as Dworkin suggests, a consensus (not even universal) of prejudices and passions – what Mill calls "the tyranny of prevailing opinion and feeling" (1859, chap. 1) – will fill the gap, disguising itself as a moral imperative.

So, the current Iranian idea of a moral order remains much more comprehensive than any available to Western liberal secular societies. Most of us are inclined to say that in its campaigns against rock music (and homosexuality), the Iranian government is legislating not morality but taste. Where to draw the line is the problem; in liberal societies, more and more things once considered moral issues become matters of taste, or, as Mill would say, tastes and pursuits. We have become reluctant to justify laws by what look to us like confused generalizations about the social fabric or the moral order. We are committed to being at least a little more precise about what we want to protect – public health, public tranquility, aesthetic values, productivity, the welfare of children, and so on. Thus, we free ourselves from the difficulties of legal moralism while retaining its main advantage in avoiding the consequences of Mill's principle: the way it extends the notion of long-term effects or secondary harm. If nothing less than the health of the community or the fate of its children is at stake every time someone performs an apparently innocuous sex act or casually uses a drug, we need no subtle arguments about whether people should be allowed to injure themselves.

Unfortunately, there remains the problem of adjusting legal means to social ends when the harm contemplated is so vague and all encompassing. In discussing issues such as a decline in productivity or public tranquility, it is almost impossible to distinguish causes from symptoms. Is the behavior that worries us the source of any social miseries associated with it, or is it just a by-product of them or an ineffectual attempt to cope with them? We are often uncertain how to justify laws for such purposes; unlike most consumer protection laws, they apparently lack a clear, limited purpose and a well-defined effect.

But drugs are much easier to legislate against than music or sex. The greatest authoritarian philosopher, Plato, thought music and sex required government regulation; the ruling Iranian clerics and other successors in the authoritarian tradition tend to agree. Liberal theory, and now also liberal society, have put this in doubt. But all of us except a few libertarian eccentrics think that drug use requires government restraint. A police campaign against popular music looks absurd to most of us, and a government attack on homosexual behavior looks sinister to some of us, but the point of view from which a war on drugs looks absurd or sinister is hard to achieve today.

The familiar explanation is that drugs are not like sex and music; they are poisons that can produce deadly habits as well as accidents and crimes, a threat to life and health. No one could say that objections to drug use are merely a matter of taste. Cause and effect seem clear enough here, and talk about poisoning or pollution is more than a metaphor; the consumer protection analogy is available to fall back on. But then all the questions that made it necessary to consider the issue of legal moralism arise again. Why are drug laws so severe compared to other consumer safety laws, and why are they so much harder to enforce? Why do we make an exception for alcohol? Why do Iranians (and even some Americans) blame drugs and rock music for some of the same evils? Why do well-informed people often see less danger in drugs than ill-informed ones? What sort of consumer protection is this? In fact, drugs are regarded as both a dangerous commodity and part of a disapproved way of life, so they are subjected to two kinds of moral and legal censure. But the rules appropriate for these two situations are not the same. The problem is circumvented by using a very broad conception of public health.

Selling or using a drug once may seem harmless, but that is an illusion if it is the start of an epidemic. Some acts may be a surrender to impulses that have no natural bounds and would spread enormously, overpowering and disintegrating us, if they were not confined by law. Since this is not like the ordinary case in which consumers merely need protection from their own carelessness and the rapacity of others, it is hardly a surprise to find studies showing that people who know something about the actual dangers of illicit drugs are often more rather than less willing to use them. For anyone who regards drug use as a plague, that only makes the threat worse and fierce resistance more necessary. The failure of education and information is evidence that drugs disturb the brain, robbing us of reason, and create addictive habits, robbing us of freedom. It might even be better to keep people in ignorance about them, just as we preserve them from contact with plague germs. Popular indignation can then be regarded as a sound basis for public policy even if it is apparently ignorant, for it acknowledges a basic vulnerability.

In its 1980 campaign platform, the Republican party called the U.S. drug problem a "murderous epidemic." Many social problems are described from time to time as "epidemic," and this is a legitimate use of the word, but it still refers primarily to physical disease. It is significant that drug use evokes the image more often and more powerfully than any other social problem. Traditionally, a plague was the vengeance of the gods on a community whose leaders had transgressed the moral law: the plagues of Egypt in the Old Testament or the plague of Thebes in Sophocles' *Oedipus*. Epidemic physical disease can no longer be regarded as merely a sign of moral disorder, because we know its causes, but drug abuse is another matter. By calling it an epidemic, we suggest a public health campaign that is also a moral crusade.

If drug abuse is a communicable disease, and drugs are a menace like the typhoid bacillus or the smallpox virus, the reasons for intervention become overwhelming. The imagery of disease has tremendous social potency. It eliminates most moral and political doubts, since disease has nothing to do with free action. Preventing an epidemic of typhoid presents no moral problems, so why should the prevention of a drug abuse epidemic? The infectious disease carrier, the Typhoid Mary, has to be quarantined, so why shouldn't heroin addicts be locked up? If the persuasion and imitation by which drug use spreads are regarded as a form of infection, the drug as a disease agent, and the drug user as a carrier, freedom and individual desires obviously deserve no consideration. We grant no one freedom to be infected with typhoid. The thought that everyone might perform homosexual acts or read pornography may be troubling, but on this analogy the prospect that everyone might constantly use drugs for pleasure is worse and also more likely – as though half of the population contracted a horrible disease. Worries like Mill's dissolve, because we no longer have to think of the problem as one created by people doing things to themselves that others consider bad for them; instead we can picture an external agent, the drug, invading the individual and social body and spreading irresistibly. Preventing disease has been regarded as a government responsibility for at least a hundred years; that is the meaning of public health medicine. The international system for control of pleasure drugs developed along with the first international institutions devoted to preventing the spread of infectious disease, and today the World Health Organization (WHO) serves both functions.

Since so many people are so obviously threatened by any outbreak of contagious drug abuse, Mill's claim of freedom to do what affects only oneself cannot be raised. And in this situation we have to act even on remote and indirect possibilities of harm, as we do when we quarantine and vaccinate. Thus public health, like legal moralism, provides a way of emphasizing external causes (the germ, the drug) and consequences (the transmission of illness to others). And if paternalism is acceptable at all, preventing disease is one of the best possible reasons for it. Rawls's rational person, for instance, would certainly want to be protected against anything likely to cause illness; health is a candidate for the status of primary good. Even the idea of natural law is still socially effective in matters of health, because all people have similar ends here merely by virtue of their biological humanity.

Above all, the language of disease tends to foreclose the issue of whether there is any benefit in using drugs for pleasure (after all, some diseases produce an unhealthy euphoria in the early stages). Therefore it eliminates all acknowledgment of any important resemblance between drug use and other tastes, pursuits, and indulgences. We know that it would be absurd to speak of a murderous epidemic of mountain climbing. If we can solemnly refer to a murderous epidemic of drug use, we do not have to consider whether marihuana or LSD, for example, actually causes as many deaths as mountain climbing. It also becomes harder to think of marihuana use as something like an eating habit – an indulgence that may be healthy or unhealthy, good, bad, or morally indifferent, depending on the persons, amounts, and circumstances involved, and that is normally subject only to informal social pressures (or Mill's education and persuasion). A community threatened by infectious disease must simply take the necessary measures to stop it.

The vocabulary of public health medicine also permits a smooth transition from physical health to psychological and moral health and finally to social health: The "murderous epidemic" is crime and illness at once, without careful distinction. In this way, consumer safety becomes mixed with morality, and the two different kinds of justification reinforce each other. Mill rejected alcohol and other drug control laws on the ground that they gave the majority a legally enforceable interest in every citizen's moral, intellectual, and physical perfection, to be defined as the majority saw fit. A plausible reply is that curbing mass drunkenness is not a form of officious meddling aimed at remaking some people in the image of others; it is a matter of elementary public health as well as social order. Like the idea of order, the idea of health is ambiguous; it has social and moral as well as biological elements. The World Health Organization once defined it as not just freedom from disease but total well-being, physical, mental, and social. By this definition, anything desirable is healthful and vice versa. In effect, it allows positive liberty to be introduced as an aim of government in the guise of public health, sweeping away most barriers against paternalism. This way of thinking about health recognizes its etymological and actual kinship to wholeness; to be cured is to be reintegrated, restored to oneself, and returned to society. But it also allows public health to develop connotations that belong to political philosophy as much as to physiological medicine. At the turn of the century, the German physician and statesman Rudolf Virchow wrote, "Medicine is a social science, and politics is nothing but medicine writ large." This open-ended conception of health has left its sources in biology far behind. It is characteristic of what is sometimes called the "therapeutic state" – a twentieth-century development that undoubtedly would have disturbed Mill.

Besides, disease is the realm of medical expertise; WHO has even officially identified "drug abuse" with nonmedical use. The British Committee on Obscenity and Film Censorship (Williams 1981) pointed out that banning pornography had become hard to justify, not only because the actual effects of pornography are unclear, but also because we do not know who should judge whether those effects are good, bad, or indifferent; there are no experts on moral health, as there are on medical matters such as drug addiction. The committee's faith in medical expertise on drugs is probably too firm; it remains doubtful to what extent drug use really is a medical rather than a moral or cultural problem. But what matters is the effect of a medical definition; it obviates the problem of guarding the guardians, appointing and justifying an authority. In the twentieth century, medicine has finally become a science, so medical control seems to be based on objective standards supplied by the most reliable intellectual authority we have. Medical regulations are our most stringent consumer protection laws. A free market in this service is considered an invitation to fraud, so practicing medicine without a license is forbidden. The ordinary citizen has no more claim to judge the proper uses of drugs than the theories of biology. Mill did not approve of the taste for opium, but he objected to laws making it impossible to indulge the taste without a doctor's prescription. Today, taking opiates is no more considered a matter of taste than using an x-ray machine. To do it without supervision is simply a dangerous misuse of an instrument valuable only for certain purposes understood by the medical profession. And the rules against taking risks in medicine are much stricter than the rules against taking risks in the pursuit of pleasure or ambition. If the sport of boxing came under medical control, it would be banned immediately.

H. L. A. Hart criticizes Mill for assuming implicitly that most people are "rational middle-aged men with settled preferences" (Hart 1963, p. 33) – in other words, that they resemble Mill himself. Hart thinks that Mill's antipaternalistic rule would enhance the freedom and welfare only of a minority, perhaps an elite. Medical control is an interesting variation on this idea. It would be convenient if we could find a way to refuse drugs directly to only those people who would use them impulsively or unwisely, and make them available to others, but that is administratively impossible. Instead, control of drugs is turned over to an elite of presumably rational and mostly middle-aged men and women who are assumed to know how other people should use them. But their authority is not derived from being generally sensible and well-balanced; it comes first from professional knowledge and only secondarily from personal character and wisdom.

The history of ordinary medical drug regulation shows that even this authority becomes more and more restricted as the presumed objectivity and certainty of medical knowledge increase. The first federal drug law, the Pure Food and Drug Act of 1906, was hardly a consumer protection law by modern standards of drug regulation. Its main purpose was to guarantee fair value by prohibiting "false and misleading" labels. Mill would not have disapproved, since he agreed that people need protection against fraud. In a 1910 Supreme Court case, Justice Oliver Wendell Holmes pronounced that the phrase "false and misleading" could apply only to claims about the contents of the package, not to claims about its usefulness. On that issue, he said, opinions are far apart and consumers should be allowed to judge for themselves.

In 1910 there were very few effective drugs and very little solid evidence on which ones were useful or harmful in which situations. Today disagreements about these matters are less common, and there are scientific procedures – especially double-blind clinical trials – designed to resolve any differences. Lay persons now have little more to say about whether most drugs work than about whether opium use is a matter of taste. The Food, Drug and Cosmetics Act of 1938 was the first federal law requiring sellers of medicines to provide directions for use and proof of safety. These provisions were soon interpreted by administrative regulation to require doctors' prescriptions for many drugs; the assumption was that laymen could never properly follow directions for using those drugs on their own. In effect, the law established a distinction between prescription and nonprescription drugs for the first time. More elaborate restrictions introduced in the 1950s and 1960s gradually took decisions on which drugs could be prescribed away from doctors and transferred them increasingly to the government. Not even ordinary doctors, much less lay persons, would be allowed to choose, even when they were fully informed. The whole development could be described from one point of view as a vast extension and transformation of the principle allowing laws to prevent fraud – an extension to the point where any doubts about paternalism are dissolved. It would have been impossible without the conviction that appropriate experts can determine with scientific confidence which drugs work and which do not.

Medical terminology and medical metaphors seem natural in dealing with psychoactive drugs. Most ordinary therapeutic drugs are dangerous enough to cause illness as well as cure it. (Drugs taken for pleasure are sometimes said to produce a special kind of illness – addiction or dependence.) Most pleasure drugs also have regulated therapeutic uses. So it is plausible to apply the same strict rules. We do not have to worry about whether marihuana smoking is more dangerous than boxing or flying a small plane; medicine is not in the same conceptual realm as voluntary tastes and pursuits.

But medicalization can never be the whole answer for pleasure drugs. The regulation of these drugs has a separate historical origin and remains distinct today. Prohibition of so-called narcotics began long before the government required prescriptions for ordinary therapeutic drugs. Consumers have not had the right to choose opiates or cocaine since 1914 or marihuana since 1937. The government was telling doctors that using opiates to maintain an addict was not a legitimate medical practice long before it started to substitute its judgment for the doctor's about any other kind of drug therapy. And the usual forms of medical control have, of course, always been inadequate for the drugs now designated as controlled substances. Even when they have therapeutic uses, prescriptions are recorded and limited by law, and doctors may be called on to justify their use to the federal government.

The language of medicine was introduced in the first place to make the special severity of drug controls plausible where justifications based on public morality or even simple consumer protection might have been inadequate. But since the usual forms of medical control are obviously too mild, we continually turn back to the other justifications to supplement the medical one. The circle is never made explicit, since the transitions are blurred by the ambiguity of a term like "public health"; this special public health problem includes psychological, social, and moral health. So the use of drugs for pleasure is believed to present three kinds of threat to human welfare. It is an offense to morality, or at least a danger to public tranquility, productivity, and so on; in some ways, it is also like an epidemic disease; and in some ways, it resembles the ignorant use of a dangerous instrument like a chainsaw. Social attitudes and legal regulations conform to each of these three analogies in different ways, and each one reinforces the others at weak points to supply reasons for stricter controls. For example, viewed as a way to enforce a consumer protection measure (or promote public health), spraying marihuana with the dangerous weed killer Paraquat would be absurd. But viewed as a severe deterrent to immoral behavior, it makes excellent sense. We officially reject the idea that drug use might be a risky taste or pursuit that nevertheless sometimes has value for some people, like climbing mountains or eating rich food. Marihuana smoking can be seriously described as an epidemic, but to call mountain climbing "getting high" is only a joke.

This way of using analogies is possible only because drugs are assumed to do little or no good. Since the pleasure they provide is seen as trivial (if not bad in itself), freedom to use them is trivial, too. Where drugs are concerned, we all have to be treated like children, unable to judge our interests well and in need of guidance from coercive rules. Making our own choices about drugs is not thought to develop richness, diversity, or unity in human experience – on the contrary. A utopia in which no one wants to do anything so dangerous as climbing mountains is absurd, but a society in which no one wants to use drugs for pleasure is still regarded as a plausible ideal – the drug-free society.

One way to avoid this conclusion is to redefine the value of drug use so that it looks almost as good as mountain climbing. In the late 1960s and early 1970s, there was much talk of consciousness expansion. Today we sometimes hear about a natural desire to alter consciousness that appears even in children and that could be said to justify the use of drugs (Weil 1972), just as a natural desire for adventure or competitive achievement justifies mountain climbing. There would be no need to seek pathological causes. In practice, altering consciousness to diversify experience (in the abrupt way that drugs do it) is not generally recognized as a natural desire with a value of its own. But in one interesting exceptional case, U.S. law has recognized the use of a drug for other than medical reasons as an activity with intrinsic value.

Members of the Native American Church, an Indian group, are allowed to take peyote in their religious rituals. Here federal courts have found a fundamental right of the individual that overrides a state interest in suppressing nonmedical drug use: the guarantee of religious freedom in the First Amendment to the Constitution. In other words, drug use has to be more than a pleasurable taste or pursuit before the law will allow it. To refute the presumption that nonmedical drug use is negligent, ignorant, and generally worthless, there must be overwhelming evidence that the drug users know what they are doing, consider it important in their lives, and believe seriously in its intrinsic value. But even that is not enough. The courts have made it clear that they will not accept merely individual religious beliefs (much less consciousness expansion) as a justification for drug use, and they have said that they will scrutinize very skeptically the claims of any new organized churches. The drug must be not only religiously important to its user but also an essential part of a traditional rite with a communal significance. So far, the exception made for the Native American Church is unique. It is as though mountain climbing were regarded as generally so dangerous and useless that climbers would be fined and jailed unless they could prove they were making a pilgrimage to a holy site on the peak certified by an established church.

The peyote eaters have been allowed to escape from the standard system of categories. Their drug use is not for pleasure, it is not exactly medicine, and it is not illness or impulse or error. The religious context makes this an obvious case for Mill's view that people should be free to shape their lives, guided by what is significant for them. But there is also a special social context. Peyote eaters are thought to deserve respect because they demand something different from the abstract liberal individualist freedom to do what they want if it injures only themselves. The idea of liberty involved is inseparable from the maintenance of a community and a common way of life. We are implicitly endorsing a kind of positive liberty in the guise of religious freedom.

The Native American Church is one small exception. Alcohol is a different kind of exception. We know that it is not absurd to treat drug use as a matter of taste, because that is the way we have always regarded alcohol. It is not just that alcohol is legal and most other pleasure drugs are illegal; our whole public discourse about alcohol, even that of pro-hibitionists, is different from the way we talk and think about other drugs. No one pretends that alcohol prohibition can be treated as a consumer safety measure. For example, during the campaign for Prohibition, it was understood that a ban on alcohol would require a constitutional amendment, unlike other drug laws and consumer laws in general. To begin outlawing opiates and cocaine, all we needed was a law based on the taxing power granted to Congress in the Constitution (the Harrison Act of 1914 was formulated as a revenue measure, because most police powers were thought to be reserved to the states by the Tenth Amendment). But possession of alcohol was never a crime even under the Volstead Act, and since repeal we have relied almost entirely on education and appeals to self-restraint instead of paternalistic coercion in dealing with alcohol problems – a limitation unimaginable in the case of any other drug. Alcohol has never been under medical control either, except briefly during Prohibition. We do use disease analogies in talking about alcohol abuse, but the emphasis is on the susceptible individual and not the irresistible infectious agent. Few people, except those in Moslem countries, dream of an alcohol-free utopia, and even fewer want to impose it by law. Alcohol escapes the net of analogies used to control other drugs.

The most common argument used to justify the inconsistency is that alcohol prohibition, unlike other drug prohibitions, just does not work. It is true that even in a completely free market, alcohol might be the most popular drug; that makes banning it harder. But prohibition may well reduce the consumption of alcohol and the harm done by drinking; we do know that American alcohol use declined in the 1920s, and the incidence of diseases such as cirrhosis of the liver dropped sharply (Burnham 1968–9). Prohibition is also said to cause more harm than it prevents, but if that is true, it is equally true of other drug laws. Alcohol prohibition in the 1920s and marihuana prohibition today may have produced the same nasty side effects: costs of arrest and punishment, growing disrespect for the law, organized criminal violence, police corruption and oppression, poisonous adulteration, and misrepresentation. The parallels are ridiculously precise, including the tendency (in the past, if not more recently) for research to be monopolized by prohibitionists and the appointment of national commissions (the Wickersham and Shafer commissions) that investigated the problem and came to self-contradictory but cautious and therefore politically acceptable conclusions. In fact, allowing for differences in the size of the original problem, alcohol prohibition probably worked just about as well (or badly) as present drug prohibition laws work. Repeal came not because prohibition was totally ineffective, but because we decided – although we seldom express it this way – that we wanted the pleasure of convenient, legal alcohol more than we feared an increase in drunkenness and alcoholism. It is still unthinkable to make the same kind of balancing judgment about any other drug, even to come to a different conclusion.

We concede that alcohol is a very dangerous substance and creates a vast health problem, while recognizing that it can also be a harmless indulgence. But apparently the strain of tolerating the ambiguity is too great, because we are unable to do the same for any other drug, even when there is little evidence that the drug could ever be as dangerous as alcohol. In public discussions, drugs are a dangerous commodity, a public health problem, and a moral menace that requires the full force of the law. That is the official view. But unofficially it is different; in polls a large part of the population says that drug use should be a matter of individual choice (Glaser and Snow 1969). What may seem to be hypocrisy here is largely confusion and doubt. Drug use is a difficult social policy issue because it is so complicated and ambiguous. It is a hard test for modern ideas about freedom and modern ways of differentiating classes of behavior. Many analogies seem applicable to it, and we easily fall into inconsistencies when thinking about it. Before considering historical and other explanations, it is important to examine one more topic that is closely connected with the theoretical issues discussed here: addiction or dependence.

2   The meanings of addiction and dependence

The most important justification for strict legal and social controls on drugs is dependency or addiction. This is the kind of drug use that produces the most serious effects on health, productivity, and family life. Even more important, it provides the best reason for saying that the drug user is not free, and that anyone exposed to the drug may lose personal freedom. Respecting a person's freedom may not require respecting his or her desires if those desires are addictive or may produce a dependency. Besides, addiction and dependence are what make us think of drug abusers as sick and drug use as primarily a medical problem rather than a mere taste or pursuit. Dependency makes the drug user resemble a child or a patient, who can justifiably be deprived of autonomy.

But human lives are inconceivable without habitual actions; virtues and vices are habits; our personalities, and the very continuity of our selves, are partly constituted from habits, in the sense of learned dispositions to certain ways of responding and behaving. There is no sharp line between acts determined by choice and those determined by habit. And any self-destructive or immoral habit can be pictured as a kind of enslavement, in accordance with the view that only positive liberty is true liberty:

. . . each of these petty beings [habits] held secretly a Chain in her Hand . . . though they were always willing to join with *Appetite*, yet when *Education* kept them apart from her, they would very punctually obey Command. . . .

Though they grew slowly in the Road of *Education*, it might however be perceived that they grew; but if they once deviated at the Call of *Appetite*, their Stature soon became gigantic, and their Strength was such, that *Education* pointed out to her Tribe many that were led in Chains by them, whom she could never more rescue from their Slavery . . . but with little effect, for all her Pupils appeared confident of their own Superiority to the strongest *Habit*, and some seemed in secret to regret that they were hindered from following the Triumph of *Appetite*. . . .

Others were enticed by *Intemperance*. . . . I observed that the *Habits* which hovered about them soon grew to an enormous Size. . . . Habit had so absolute a Power, that even *Conscience*, if *Religion* had employed her in their Favour, would not have been able to force an Entrance. (Johnson 1950, pp. 150, 157)

"Intemperance," in this eighteenth-century text, means what we call "alcoholism." The term "intemperance" was used mainly to refer to habitual drunkenness even before the term "addiction" came to mean chiefly opiate abuse. Obviously people have always been conscious of the unusual strength and devastating effect of some drug habits. But it is only recently that we have come to think of those habits as somehow different in principle from others.

It is not easy even to decide whether the issue is an empirical one or merely an argument about words. The philosopher W. B. Gallie has introduced the idea of "essentially contested concepts." The criteria for applying these concepts are multiple and involve moral and social evaluations, and the relative importance of the various criteria is recognized by users of the concept to be unsettled. The life of the concept is debate. Like such political ideas as democracy and tyranny, addiction or dependence qualifies as "essentially contested" in this sense. That values are involved is obvious; we do not usually call any habit an addiction or dependency (except as a joke) unless we mean to say that it is harmful. It is probably not so clear that the criteria for application are unsettled, since the prevalence of medical terminology in the field may make it appear, falsely, that drug dependence is as clearly defined as cancer, smallpox, or even schizophrenia. But in fact, today as in the past, even medical authorities have not been able to agree on what drug dependence is. In one recent collection of essays on the subject, twelve psychological theories, eight biological theories, twelve sociological theories, and fifteen mixed theories are offered, all with at least some claim to respectability (Lettieri et al. 1980).

An addiction once meant almost any strong habitual inclination, as in this line from Shakespeare's *Othello*: "Each man to what sport and revel his addiction leads him." It was common to talk of an addiction to gardening or theater going without deliberate humor or any sense of incongruity. But to many people today, addiction means simply a mysterious and utterly debasing enslavement to certain dread chemicals. Other meanings are felt to be secondary, metaphorical or jocular. This change has come about partly because the concept of addiction has been medicalized (with few corresponding advances in the discovery of either causes or solutions). And yet, ironically, the medical profession is now beginning to abandon the term; it is no longer applied, as it once was, to almost any habitual drug use that incurs social disapproval.

One medical definition of addiction that still has some currency is the following: a condition induced in certain higher mammals by chronic administration of central nervous system depressants like alcohol, barbiturates, and opiates, in which a gradual adaptation of the nervous system to the drug causes a latent hyperexcitability that becomes manifest when the drug is withdrawn and produces physiological symptoms that are interpreted as a physical need for the drug. This definition implies no moral or political attitude, and it does not intimate anything implausibly horrible and debasing (the much-publicized heroin withdrawal reaction at its most intense is no worse than a bad case of flu, and exaggerating it only serves the interest of the addict's self-dramatization). Emphasis on the withdrawal reaction, which is physically identifiable, at least keeps medicine out of the business of judging which drugs are detrimental to society or trying to solve the problem of free will by distinguishing between compulsion and desire. But there are some problems even with this definition. Other drugs – stimulants, caffeine, and nicotine – produce various physical withdrawal reactions in many people, and withdrawal from a person – the breakup of a love affair, for example – sometimes produces similar symptoms. But the main problem is that physical withdrawal reactions are simply not one of the most important causes or (with the exception of some high-level barbiturate addictions) one of the most serious consequences of drug abuse. If they were, it would be more plausible to define it as a purely medical problem.

Pharmacological tolerance is another symptom that often accompanies addiction. It is usually described as an adaptation of the nervous system to the effects of a given amount of a drug that makes it necessary to keep taking more to get the same effect. Tolerance is most conspicuous in amphetamine abusers, alcoholics, and heroin addicts, but most drugs will produce it if they are taken often enough for a long enough time. Again there is a question of whether this reaction is something specifically induced by drugs; all routine pleasures tend to pall and may have to be revived by an injection of more of the same. The call for madder music and stronger wine does not distinguish between the wine and the music. Tolerance to drugs also varies a great deal with the individual and the particular effect; for example, some amphetamine abusers take twenty times the amount an ordinary person could tolerate, but the drug can be given for years to a person suffering from narcolepsy without any need to raise the dose.

Little is known about what, if anything, distinguishes drug withdrawal reactions and drug tolerance from other forms of compensatory response and adaptation. One theory is that withdrawal reactions occur because a drug has taken over the work of a chemical normally made by the body itself and has caused the mechanism that produces it to atrophy, like an unused muscle. Another theory is that in supplying chemical stimulation to nerve cells, drugs produce physical changes that increase the nerve cells' demand for stimulation, creating a need that normal body processes can no longer serve. But analogous theories might be needed to account for the symptoms of habituation to things other than drugs; body chemistry has to change in either case. Nor do we have evidence that the induction of drug tolerance and withdrawal reactions is in general so much simpler, more reliable, and more mechanical than other forms of habituation – so much more independent of what we usually call free will and choice – that it deserves to be treated quite differently for moral and political purposes.

As the term "addiction" has come to be used in medicine less often and with a more restricted meaning, "dependence" has taken its place in many official formulations. In 1969 WHO's Expert Committee on Drug Dependence defined it as follows: "A state, psychic and sometimes also physical, resulting from the interaction between a living organism and a drug, characterized by behavioral and other responses that always include a compulsion to take the drug on a continuous or periodic basis in order to experience its psychic effects, and sometimes to avoid the discomfort of its absence. Tolerance may or may not be present" (World Health Organization 1969, p. 61). The apparent neutrality of "dependence" seems attractive as a way of avoiding premature theoretical commitments, and the word is used by so many people for so many purposes that it is unlikely to suffer the fate of that captive of the drug-abuse vocabulary, "addiction." But many are still dissatisfied. Some authorities, who might be called humanists, think that it suggests a kind of enslavement and falsely implies that people who use drugs are not choosing to do so. They point out that in the vague WHO sense, drug dependence is no different from dependence on television, a religious ritual, a parent, or even trousers. A life centered on drug use may be unreasonable and self-destructive, but so are many other devotions and commitments. Explanatory terms like "compulsion," "craving," and "overpowering need" apply just as well to love of chocolate cake or, for that matter, to love of another human being.

Some writers who take this attitude consider themselves defenders of pleasure against a life-denying puritan morality; others see themselves as defenders of individual liberty against state power and medical technocracy. Thomas Szasz, for example, insists that a person is neither more nor less responsible for misuse of psychoactive drugs than for any other bad habit or vice. For him the idea that some chemicals have a mysterious power controllable only by coercive authority removes the main actor from "the drama of temptation and restraint" and makes it a meaningless exercise (Szasz 1974).

The trouble with "compulsion," "craving," and other such expressions is that they suggest a simple state of mind that produces a simple, uniform pattern of behavior. But the behavior of drug abusers follows no such pattern; it is impossible to define when an established routine becomes a compulsion or a strong desire a craving. Alcoholics, for example, when asked why they relapse, usually blame it not on craving but on anger, frustration, and social pressures. "Loss of control" has become less popular as a way to describe what happens when alcoholics drink, because some of them can take one drink and stop if the time, place, and social setting are right (Paredes et al. 1973), and to say that alcoholics lose control only when they drink abusively would be tautological. Heroin addicts tend to lose their craving when they are in prison or some other place where they cannot expect to find the drug; they often feel it again when they return to their old environment (Meyer and Mirin 1981). Not only do even the most severe addicts and alcoholics exercise some control but, contrary to myth, the great majority of opiate users are not addicts at all (Jacobson and Zinberg 1975).

Alfred Lindesmith developed a theory of opiate addiction that defined craving as the feeling that arises when an addict interprets abstinence symptoms (withdrawal reaction) and attributes them to the drug (Lindesmith 1947). But it turns out that addicts tend to take more than they need to relieve the physical symptoms of abstinence, and most of them come to desire opiates with an intensity that can be called a craving before they are physically addicted; in fact, it is this desire that causes addiction, rather than the reverse. Craving for stimulants even more obviously develops without physical addiction. Craving can be defined in a commonsense way as a desire that is abnormally strong or hard to change, or that produces an abnormally intense reaction when it is not fulfilled. But drugs are not the only object of that kind of desire. The authorities we have called humanists therefore tend to regard it as obvious but irrelevant that people are likely to want to go on doing something that gives intense pleasure. As Szasz puts it, to talk about a euphoriant without the potential to produce craving, dependence, or addiction in some sense is as absurd as talking about a flammable substance that does not ignite. The humanists seek other reasons for the persistence or intensity of the desire, and for moral approval or condemnation of it, in personal history, environment, and culture.

On the other side are researchers who are trying to develop a scientific model of drug dependence; often they are behavioristic psychologists who want to measure the dependence in experimental animals with the help of their favorite conceptual apparatus of reinforcement schedules and operant conditioning. From the point of view of these scientists, the trouble with WHO's language is not its social implications, or some insult to human dignity, but its vagueness, which permits too many debaters' points in opposition. They would like to clean up and shave down this shaggy definition for laboratory purposes. For them, a drug produces dependence if it is taken repeatedly by animals in cages. Differences between animals and people, between one animal and another, or between one person and another are secondary. References to desires, cravings, compulsions, and other "mentalistic" phenomena are not allowed. Moral judgment, implicit or explicit, is forbidden as unscientific. Here we are beyond freedom and dignity, and everything must be cashed in quantitative, observational currency.

Since behaviorism has no use for the idea of free action, it tends in its own way to deny any special features to drug dependence. Drug habits are said to be produced, like other habits, by repeated stimulus and response. Objects differ only in their reinforcing power for a given organism in a given situation. Here is a typical behavioristic definition of drug dependence by M. H. Seevers: "Repeated use of psychoactive drugs leading to a conditioned pattern of drug-seeking behavior. A characteristic predictable and reproducible syndrome is associated with each drug" (Seevers 1972, p. 17). Experiments with laboratory animals do reveal distinctive patterns. Rats and monkeys will not repeatedly inject the psychedelic drug mescaline or the antipsychotic drug chlorpromazine, and these drugs do not produce what is called drug dependence in human beings. They will inject morphine, cocaine, amphetamines, barbiturates, alcohol, and caffeine. The pattern for opiates like morphine and codeine is a gradual increase to a dose that is then held constant, while the interval between injections varies. When the injection machinery is disconnected from the drug supply, the animal keeps trying to get more at a low rate for a long time – up to months. The pattern for cocaine and amphetamines is a cycle in which rapid injection of large amounts is followed by exhausted abstinence. When the machinery is disconnected, the animal keeps pressing for the stimulant at a very high rate, but only for a few hours before it gives up (Thompson and Pickens 1970). Significantly, human opiate and stimulant abusers may behave more or less the same way in analogous situations (Griffiths et al. 1980).

There are authorities who regard behavioristic explanations as not scientific enough; they object to definitions "based on social and behavioral criteria, not on any characteristic biologic, biochemical, or neurophysiological aspects of [drug] use" (Fink 1972, p. 384). They are impatiently awaiting a concept of drug dependence soundly based on physical tissue responses. So far even physical withdrawal reactions have not been fully explained in terms of tissue response. But psychoactive drugs do closely resemble the chemical neurotransmitters that are manufactured by the body to pass messages between nerve cells, and this suggests another explanation of drug dependence. A psychoactive or euphoriant drug is what biologists call a "supernormal stimulus." A herringcatcher will hatch a gull's egg in preference to its own, because it has an innate brooding mechanism that draws it toward the biggest egg in sight. Drugs apparently stimulate brain cells as gull eggs stimulate the herringcatcher, with a similar potentially maladaptive effect. They could be regarded as a neurophysiological shortcut that evades the environmental adaptations usually needed to obtain pleasure. Drug dependence has been called an "artifical drive," with the same kind of power as primary biological drives such as hunger and sex – not necessarily uncontrollable or unmodifiable, but something more than an ordinary habit (Bejerot 1972).

To the humanists, "conditioned pattern," "predictable syndrome," and "artificial drive" have the look of fighting words, weapons in a war between the two cultures. The main procedural objection is that the conditions of behaviorist experiments are too different from any encountered by animals in the wild or people in society. The animals are caged and under restraint; they have few sources of satisfaction except drugs. The conditioned pattern may be a laboratory artifact, and the animals might act quite differently in a situation that offered a variety of dangers and opportunities. Even in laboratories, the reinforcing properties of drugs vary from one animal to another. And most free-running animals in a more or less natural environment apparently do not use drugs in an intensive and compulsive way even when they are made available without limit (Alexander et al. 1978).

One of the most interesting animal experiments offers a particularly strong challenge to the idea of a simple, uniform pattern of stimulus and response attached to certain reinforcing chemical substances. Rats and other animals were kept at 80 percent of normal body weight and forced to press a lever for food, which was not delivered immediately but after a fixed or variable period of time. When the interval between deliveries of food pellets was very short or very long, they drank water normally. But when the interval was intermediate, they drank vast quantities of water in a compulsive, ritualized way. The thinner the animals were, the more of this compulsive behavior they exhibited. Putting them on a liquid diet or delivering water directly to their stomachs through a tube made no difference. After a while, the animals would even work to get the excess water. The result was similar when cocaine, avoidance of an electric shock, or water was substituted for food as the original intermittent reinforcer. The type of compulsive behavior varied, depending on the opportunity. A pigeon would attack another pigeon under restraint. When alcohol was available, rats would become chronically intoxicated, although they normally show only a mild interest in alcohol.

The experimenters interpret this excessive behavior as comparable to displacement activity. Limited quantities of an important commodity are being delivered at rather long intervals; the animal is tempted to escape from the situation prematurely, and delays action by a compulsive ritual. Since everyone is subject to frustration by nature and society, we are all on "a set of complex intermittent schedules" of reinforcement, which may produce "adjunctive behavior" unconnected with the immediate source of the frustration. Opportunities in the environment determine whether this behavior will take the form of irrational violence, drug abuse, or other excesses. The pattern is associated with a situation rather than a substance (Falk 1981).

In any of these cases, distinguishing between the laws of nature and the laws of culture is not easy. All drugs act physically on the brain, but the brain's perceptions of reward and punishment, pleasure and pain, depend largely on what we think, and that depends largely on our culture and the company we keep. At some point, the brain structure common to all mammals, or even all human beings, has to give way to personal histories and social conditions. Even laboratory animals, so long as they are pressing levers to inject drugs in an artificial environment free of competing interests, dangers, and exigencies, are in a sense culturally determined to crave drugs or to be psychologically disturbed. The limitations of ideas about psychoactive drugs based on animal experiments are amusingly illustrated by the fact that these animals show no interest in tetrahydrocannabinol, the active ingredient of marihuana, although international treaties classify it as a dangerous "narcotic" with dependence-producing powers that have to be coercively controlled. The neurophysiological effect of a drug's chemical action is usually necessary to produce the habitual inclination to use it, but this is not enough to sustain a coherent concept of drug dependence. In the real world, drug abuse has everything to do with psychological and social problems.

Looking at individual psychological problems, we come upon the notion of the addictive or dependence-prone personality. This label has been used, confusingly, both to complement and to contradict the notion of a dependence-producing drug. It is said that only an individual with an inadequate personality is inclined to take a bad drug (especially opiates) or that a deficient person will make bad use of any drug. There may be personalities, as well as drugs, associated with drug dependence; some people, for a variety of reasons, seem to need a drug's influence to gain respite from their troubles or surcease from pain. But it is not true that *only* and *all* people who have some special characteristics identifiable in advance will use or misuse drugs. For example, in studies of alcoholics, it appears that some are antisocial personalities (Robins et al. 1962); some tend to be depressed (Palola et al. 1962); some are concerned with power (Williams 1976) and others with dependency (Barry 1976). As for heroin addicts, no single variable of personality or circumstances predicts who will become addicted (Kandel 1978).

In other words, dependence proneness is not a useful diagnostic category (accordingly, the American Psychiatric Association no longer classifies drug dependence as a personality disorder). We cannot tell who will take to the habitual use of which drug. It is too hard to arrange control groups or compensate for the effects of differential availability. In any case, to impute a psychological deficiency to the drug user is circular reasoning if the only symptom of this tendency to drug dependence is precisely the habitual use of an illicit drug. Szasz points out that it is absurd for Ernest Jones to regard Freud's giving up cocaine as evidence that he was not an addictive personality, while ignoring his far more serious dependence on nicotine in the form of cigars. And William Burroughs commented:

In Persia where opium is sold without control in opium shops 70% of the population is addicted [this is a vast exaggeration]. So should we psychoanalyze several million Persians to find out what deep conflicts and anxieties have driven them to the use of opium? I think not. (Burroughs, 1956, p. 127)

Social policy can validate judgments about the personal weakness of drug users. Given existing laws and attitudes, it might be true that people who want to use heroin in the United States ought to have their heads examined, but the question is whether they should be called weak rather than daring to the point of foolhardiness. The serious argument here is that whatever the weaknesses and inadequacies of drug users, the idea of a private transaction between an aberrant personality and an overwhelming chemical compound is a myth. If, like most heroin addicts, a drug user is not permitted to lead a normal life, his or her inadequacies will appear magnified. The social conditions in which a drug is available determine the kind of person who will use it and the view that will be taken of his or her personality. As one sociologist has pointed out, if many opiate addicts were middle class in the 1890s and very few were in the 1920s, it was not the personalities of middle-class people that had changed but the social meaning and function of addiction (Duster 1970, p. 156).

There is another way in which the diagnosis of drug use as a symptom of personal inadequacy can be misleading. Learning to use a socially acceptable drug like alcohol is part of growing up; it is one of the symbols and rituals of adulthood. Marihuana, on the other hand, was until recently identified with youthful rebellion, that is, with immaturity. The rituals of marihuana use therefore had a different value, and one of the worries of parents whose children used the drug was that they were not growing up in the socially approved way. From this uneasiness, it was a short step to the judgment that anyone who used this "wrong" drug, following a slightly different ritual and passing into a slightly different social world, was emotionally immature, weak, unable to face problems – even "fleeing reality." Users of an unfamiliar drug are likely to be seen as menacing if they are far enough away, inadequate if they are too close to home. So a psychological judgment is made on a social situation.

The word "compulsion" in the WHO definition of drug dependence suggests both a pharmacological mechanism and a drive coming from somewhere in what Freud called our "inner alien territory." But in practice these cannot be separated from social situations. Carl N. Edwards describes a patient who became "addicted" to a placebo pill; he demanded dose increases and developed craving and abstinence symptoms (Edwards 1974). This extreme case illustrates in parody the importance of the social context, because here only the institutionalized relationship between doctor and patient produced and sustained the dependence. Even in the more ordinary case, social rules and customs may define the consequences of using a drug; the old word "addiction" too often meant little more than "the consequences of opiate use," many of them produced by laws making it necessary to commit crimes to pay for the drugs. If someone needed a barbiturate or whiskey to fall asleep every night, this habit was not called addiction mainly because it was not as expensive as injecting weak solutions of heroin (many so-called addicts do not use enough of the drug to produce a physical withdrawal reaction) or as likely to lead to prison, and therefore did not disrupt the drug user's life or society's routines so much. If medical terminology is used mainly to impose a moral judgment on a social situation (especially one created by the law), it is in danger of becoming meaningless.

It is hard to overstate how much social conditions influence the symptoms of drug dependence. In one study a group of alcoholics was placed in a hospital ward and each alcoholic, one at a time, was allowed to drink as much as he wanted for two days once every two weeks. The drinking was supposed to be done alone and in an assigned area. The result was that the alcoholics drank only where they were allowed to drink and stopped when told to stop without complaint. They even said that they did not enjoy the drinking very much. The supposed chemical tyranny of alcohol was easily suspended when it became dissociated from familiar bars and drinking buddies (Paredes et al. 1973).

Thomas Szasz is the most extreme advocate of the view that drug addiction or dependence is a social rather than a physical or psychological fact. He writes: "Addictive drugs stand in the same sort of relation to ordinary or nonaddictive drugs as holy water stands in relation to ordinary or nonholy water" (Szasz 1974, p. xvii). An addictive drug, in other words, is not a particular kind of chemical but something that has been labeled as such by an accepted ritual. Szasz even argues that addiction to a drug is in principle no different from a foreigner's "addiction" to speaking English with an accent, another habit that is hard to break. And he refers to abstention from drugs (or dieting instead of overeating) as another form of addiction. We should not allow these polemical exaggerations to put us off, even if Szasz does mean them literally. It is not necessary to adopt his radical individualism and the associated classical liberal view of the functions of the state and the medical profession (he would impose no restrictions at all on drug use and sale) to recognize that concepts like drug dependence may encourage people to avoid taking responsibility for the consequences of their habits by treating them as external forces rather than as part of the self. It also makes us more inclined to use an external countervailing force, and to apply it to the drug itself and the drug users rather than to other sources of misery and mischief in the environment. We avoid difficult decisions about whether the use of a particular drug in a particular way is a good or bad habit, and we do not permit the users to decide either, since, being dependent or addicted, they are by definition unable to make reasonable choices.

Drug dependence, then, involves pharmacology, individual psychology, and social background in varying proportions. This is more than a commonplace, because it shows that emphasis on the drug itself is often wrong. In its latest diagnostic manual, the American Psychiatric Association reserves the term "drug dependence" for what we have called addiction: tolerance or a physical withdrawal reaction. Other problems involving drugs are classified as organic mental disorders (acute drug intoxication, drug-induced psychosis, etc.) or substance use disorders (most habitual misuse of drugs). Thus psychiatrists now avoid the use of "dependence" in a way that implicitly judges any habitual or persistent drug use as abusive or excessive by its very nature.

But even if drug dependence is not a very coherent concept for analytical purposes, anyone who has tried to give up smoking cigarettes will testify that something is going on that requires that description. Attachments to drugs are too often felt to be unusually intense and yet somehow separate from the center where plans are made – the executive ego. Consider the following example of incipient alcoholism: A retired woman, aged sixty-four, living by herself, has begun to take sherry when alone and is now drinking two bottles a day. She has made a rule that she will not drink before 10 AM, but she feels shaky in the morning and sometimes finds it "difficult to hold out." She comments, "It's all so silly, I can't believe it's me" (Royal College 1979, p. 41). And drugs are often personified, as though they were agents with a will of their own: Amphetamines are "the Man" to a truck driver or football player who uses them at work; cocaine is "Lady" to someone having a romance with it; alcoholic drinks are "John Barleycorn" or "Demon Rum." The drug habit is felt to be something outside the self, or a fragment of the self that has become detached but is still on peculiarly intimate terms with it.

However the emphasis is distributed among biological, personal, and social causes, the common theme is imbalance, fragmentation, loss of wholeness, lack of internal direction. Things fall apart, the center cannot do its job of regulation. A part of the person somehow takes control, and the habit somehow both is and is not oneself in action: the paradox of habit. Members of Alcoholics Anonymous are taught that alcohol is an external power enslaving them, yet at the same time that being an alcoholic is their identity. Alcoholics who experience a conversion and give up drinking are not just dropping a bad habit; they are undergoing self-surrender, self-renewal, self-transformation. The American Psychiatric Association, as we saw, has narrowed the application of "dependency," but its broader definition of substance abuse still includes "inability to reduce or stop use," which implies feeling one's own impulse as an alien power.

The main effect of compulsive drug abuse is to make behavior simpler and more rigid; the adaptive repertoire is narrowed, and experience becomes less rich and diverse.* (The extreme case is that of a caged laboratory animal injecting drugs.) But for some people, this is a kind of solution. A heroin addict may be trying to reduce all the problems of life to a single one, so that it will no longer be necessary to make fundamental choices or be subject to ordinary emotional vicissitudes. A life is given structure by repetitive acts that produce an artificial stability. Addicts can be devoted as much to hustling – the daily routine of getting the next fix

---

* "The junk [heroin] merchant does not sell his product to the consumer, he sells the consumer to the product. He does not improve and simplify his merchandise, he degrades and simplifies the consumer" (William Burroughs).

– as they are to the drug itself. It becomes a way of life. So the chemical action of the drug is real, but its overwhelming power is a projection of a quality that belongs to the drug abuser. The same loss of adaptability can be found in any monomania – pathological gambling, "mainlining Jesus" in a religious cult, even all-consuming devotion to a beloved person or a game like chess. Avoiding addiction or dependence means maintaining balance by caring about more than one thing (or person). So addiction or dependence is a matter of degree; the ideal of autonomy can only be approached, never absolutely realized (see Peele and Brodsky 1975).

This is another way of stating the political dilemma that both positive and negative liberty seem to be fictions. If reasonableness is produced by a certain wholeness of character, a balanced relationship among desires, the victim of a dependency is incapable of reasonableness. If freedom is impossible without rationality, this person cannot be free. But total rationality, absolute freedom, are unattainable. John Rawls's perfectly rational person in the original position, lacking in any defining or limiting habits or qualities, is avowedly a fiction of negative liberty. The corresponding fiction of positive liberty is the wholly integrated person in a society combining the greatest possible easy self-possession and self-control in each person with nearly frictionless cooperation among individuals. Any limiting habit seems incompatible with both kinds of freedom, but we all have patterns of behavior that limit us.

Mill said that anyone who could potentially be guided to improvement by conviction or persuasion should be free of paternalistic coercion. But this may be impossible for alcoholics or heroin addicts, even though their reason is sound. Samuel Taylor Coleridge described alcoholics and opium addicts (including himself) as suffering from "idiocy and lunacy of the will" – a strange notion, since idiocy and lunacy normally prevent the formation of a genuine will. A remarkable feature of drug abuse is that it calls out such extreme comparisons merely by intensifying the paradox of habit. Yet Coleridge's phrase remains a metaphor; the reasons for denying the retarded and insane certain rights and excusing them from responsibility cannot apply where reason is intact and the victims are apparently suffering only from their own deliberate acts.

The problem is particularly difficult when criminal responsibility has to be determined, and in the hardest kind of case, the criminal act concerns drugs only – possession, use, sale, or intoxication. In *Robinson v. California* (1962), the Supreme Court considered a state law that made "using or being addicted to the use of" narcotics a crime. In an opinion delivered by Justice Potter Stewart, the majority declared that imprisonment for addiction would be cruel and unusual punishment under the Eighth

Amendment, because addiction is a status rather than an act; it is more like syphilis or insanity than criminal behavior. Justice John Marshall Harlan, in a concurring opinion, said that he would have allowed the imprisonment of Robinson, even though he was an addict, if the state had introduced evidence that he had actually taken narcotics in California, but the use of addiction as a way to circumvent restrictions on evidence was objectionable. In dissent, Justice Byron White said that Robinson was not being punished for a status but for habitual use of narcotics, a series of acts. The *Robinson* case seemed to establish addictive compulsion as a potential bar to conviction for drug possession or even being under the influence of drugs. But the case has been interpreted very narrowly, along the lines of Harlan's concurring opinion. If the state can show proof of narcotics use (which is almost always necessary for proof of addiction in any case), anyone can be convicted, addict or not.

In *Powell v. Texas* (1968), the Court decided that it was not cruel and unusual punishment to jail an alcoholic for public intoxication. Justice Thurgood Marshall, speaking for four members of the majority in a five-to-four decision, criticized the idea that alcoholism implies compulsion or loss of control. He called the *Robinson* case irrelevant, because being drunk in a public place was clearly an act rather than a status; the only question was whether the act should be regarded as freely chosen, and the *Robinson* decision did not imply that the drunkenness of an alcoholic or the narcotics use of an addict is involuntary. Justice Abraham Fortas, speaking for four dissenters, said that this alcoholic's public drunkenness was the symptom of a condition over which he had no control and therefore no responsibility. White agreed with the dissenters that people should not be subject to criminal penalties for acts not under their control, but he concurred with the majority because he thought that Powell's public drunkenness, as opposed to his alcohol abuse, was voluntary.

What could not be achieved by constitutional interpretation is now being partially achieved by legislation; more than half of the states have passed some version of the Uniform Alcoholism and Alcoholism Intoxication Treatment Act, which takes the handling of public drunkenness out of the criminal law system and transfers it to public health authorities (with uncertain results so far). But the *Robinson* decision is as far as the courts have been willing to go on their own. In *U.S. v. Moore* (1973), the Supreme Court rejected an addict's claim that he could not be convicted of possessing heroin; it said that even if his possession of heroin was a symptom of the disease of addiction (which the court did not concede), it could be regarded for criminal law purposes as voluntary. Where the charge is more serious – selling drugs, robbery, assault – a pattern of addiction or alcoholism has never been an excuse for denying responsibility (although actual intoxication may affect specific intent and therefore reduce the seriousness of the crime).

An insane person can plausibly be said to lack the *mens* of *mens rea* (guilty mind) – the coherent mind that in legal terms makes responsibility possible (Fingarette and Hasse 1972). Yet the insanity defense is much criticized and rarely successful. It is hardly surprising, then, that no court has dared to propose an addiction defense. Incapacity allowing exculpation has never been interpreted to include mere difficulty in not desiring something, or any mere habit, however powerful and well entrenched. Whatever loss of self-control or internal compulsion may be involved in drug dependence, we do not consider it an excuse for criminal acts. Coleridge's metaphor of "lunacy of the will" has never been carried that far.

The Court's decision in the *Robinson* case proved to be less important than a dictum in which it expressed approval of involuntary civil commitment instead of criminal penalties for addicts. Here the issue is the opposite of exculpation. May drug abusers be confined against their will, under the rubric of treatment or civil commitment, for a longer time than they could legally be forced to spend in prison, or in circumstances where they could not legally be imprisoned at all? By 1962 most states already had civil commitment provisions for alcoholics and narcotics addicts, but these were not often used. Civil commitment in the United States was mainly restricted to narcotics offenders in the federal hospitals at Lexington, Kentucky, and Forth Worth, Texas. In the 1960s, New York and California established civil commitment programs for addicts convicted of drug possession or sale, but they were of dubious effectiveness. Given a choice between prison and "treatment," addicts tended to choose whichever alternative meant a shorter term of confinement.

The constitutional basis for civil commitment of addicts has been litigated very little. In civil commitment hearings, courts have generally not required the procedural safeguards of the criminal law – the privilege against self-incrimination, right to confront witnesses, right to counsel, proof beyond a reasonable doubt, and so on. The District of Columbia Circuit Court suggested in 1971 that if there was no genuine treatment, civil commitment might be a cruel and unusual punishment in violation of the Eighth Amendment. The court was not clear about what would constitute genuine treatment, although it implied that more than an honest effort would probably be necessary. Despite this suggestion, civil commitment for addicts will probably never be rejected on substantive constitutional grounds (Dershowitz 1973). So courts have never analyzed the theoretical questions about civil confinement in cases involving addiction as opposed to insanity. In general, there are two requirements – incapacity or incompetency and danger to self or others. Is drug dependence the kind of incapacity that justifies preventive confinement? What likelihood and degree of danger should be required? Should the standards be different when persons other than the drug user are endangered?

The ambiguities of determining incapacity for free choice in drug users are familiar by now. At times a desire seems so irrational, wrong, or unwanted, and dominates a life so much, that we are prepared to treat it as a sign of incapacity and try to give effect to what the person who feels it would want if he or she were whole. On the other hand, giving in to an unwanted, irrational, or inappropriate desire is succumbing to temptation, and our literary paradigm of succumbing to temptation, Adam and Eve in the Garden of Eden, is also a paradigm of the exercise of free will. If we do determine that someone has become incapable of deciding freely whether or not to use drugs, Mill's principle is apparently no longer necessary. If free action is impossible, the right to do to yourself as you please has no meaning, and coercion is permissible to prevent harm to someone who is already unfree. Therefore the usual formula in involuntary civil commitment for insanity is "dangerous to themselves or others" without distinction. And in cases involving addiction, courts have never specifically required that the confinement be for the addict's own good. (An odd contradiction might arise if courts were more explicit, since it could be said that one of the main benefits of civil commitment for addicts, who are thereby in effect judged not to be responsible for their drug use, is that it might prevent them from being repeatedly jailed for drug possession – that is, held criminally responsible for the same drug use by the same legal system.)

It is interesting to contrast this situation to one in which courts have been unwilling to impose even a much milder deprivation of liberty, despite a much greater and more immediate danger to both self and others. People are allowed to refuse blood transfusions for religious reasons even when they are likely to die and children are dependent on their support. The basis is the guarantee of religious freedom in the Constitution; but behind that, as in the case of the Native American Church and its peyote use, lies an assumption that the refusal, however eccentric or even irrational it seems to most of us, is free, wholehearted, a desire of the undivided person, and therefore worthy of respect.

Existing law makes little formal use of the distinction between harm to self and harm to others. But even in a legal system that in theory does take harm to others more seriously, harm to self might be a better reason for involuntary preventive confinement simply because it is easier to predict (Brock 1980). Dangerousness in the mentally ill, for example, is notoriously hard to judge, but the chronic suffering produced by an illness like schizophrenia and the relief afforded by the available palliatives are fairly well understood. The important word here is "illness." The course of schizophrenia is more or less predictable because it is a disease. Courts rely on the same interpretation of narcotics abuse when they allow involuntary confinement; it makes the harm to the drug user seem predictable and the idea of a treatment or cure plausible. But are they?

This brings us back to medicine. We saw how effective the medical or disease model has been in justifying limitations on access to drugs, and we discussed some medical conceptions of addiction and dependence. Drug abuse and drug dependence are used as diagnostic classifications by psychiatrists because they are now regarded as being, in some sense, illnesses. Whatever we may think about the metaphysics of free will, surely an act that is a symptom or defining feature of a disease must have a special moral and political status. The question of illness and the question of freedom and responsibility are intimately related.

Alcoholism has been analyzed more than any other form of drug abuse, since it is the most widespread and most severe. By now there is general official agreement that it should be called a disease, yet many people remain stubbornly reluctant to accept that view, and many who do accept it are unsure of just what makes alcoholism a disease or what kind of disease it is. In detail, the picture is utter confusion, and it begins to look as though the convenient label "disease" disguises an almost total lack of reliable knowledge or plausible explanations.

One problem is that "in the first place, it is difficult to sustain *any* categorical statements about alcoholism" (Fingarette 1970, p. 801). The Royal College of Psychiatrists defines it as a craving, a "narrowed drinking repertoire," drinking that dominates a person's life, and relapse after abstinence (Royal College 1979, p. 42). Mark Keller, writing in 1960 as editor-in-chief of the *Quarterly Journal of Studies on Alcohol*, refers to "implicative" (suspicion-provoking) or marked and repetitive drinking that produces bad social, economic, or health consequences for the drinker (Keller 1960). The same author, writing in 1972, emphasizes the inability to choose consistently when to drink and when to stop (Keller 1972). Another authority, Morris E. Chafetz, calls alcoholism a behavioral disorder manifested by a preoccupation with alcohol to the detriment of health, by loss of control, and by self-destructive behavior (Chafetz 1979). Some advocates of what is called the "distribution-of-consumption" theory of alcohol control prefer to emphasize the amount of alcohol consumed, which they say correlates very well with health problems (DeLint 1976).

The diagnostic manual of the American Psychiatric Association shows an interesting change. In its first edition, alcoholism and drug dependence were classified as personality disorders and used in a diagnosis only as a last resort, if the drinking or drugs could not be regarded as secondary or symptomatic (American Psychiatric Association 1953). The third edition of the manual classifies alcohol abuse (the term "alcoholism" is not used) and other drug problems as substance use disorders, a special category. They are identified by a pathological pattern of use (this is a substitute for "psychological dependence" in older formulas), impairment in social or occupational functioning, and a duration of at least one month. Many indications of pathology and impairment are suggested, but none of them is set off as definitive or even more important than the others. The evidence for a pathological pattern of alcohol use includes such things as intoxication throughout the day, inability to stop or cut down, binge drinking, blackouts, repeated temporary abstinence, and attempts to restrict drinking to certain times of the day. Impairment is indicated by violence while intoxicated, absence from work, legal difficulties, and arguments with family or friends. Alcohol dependence is defined as alcohol abuse with either tolerance or a withdrawal reaction. Personality disorder, especially antisocial personality, is mentioned as a predisposing condition (American Psychiatric Association 1980).

So, this disease has a peculiarly diverse set of symptoms. Everything from the quantity of alcohol drunk to deviation from the accepted drinking practices of a social group has been used to define it. One respected authority lists more than a hundred definitions and hypotheses (Jellinek 1960). Such popular tests as craving, loss of control, tolerance, and withdrawal reactions are inadequate – either empirically wrong, too vague, or tautological (Maisto and Schefft 1977). Tests based on drinking at certain times of the day or in certain amounts include too many people or exclude some whose drinking is obviously abusive. It has even been contended that the skid row or Bowery dweller, long the typical representative of alcoholism in the public mind, is often not a "true alcoholic" at all (Straus and McCarthy 1951). There is no alcoholic personality, no definite progressive course (Trice and Wahl 1962), and, of course, no generally accepted treatment; even for selected groups of alcoholics, there is no clear evidence that any one kind of treatment is better than any other (Armor et al. 1976). The goal of treatment too is unclear; certain (angrily disputed) studies suggest that abstinence is not the only answer (or "cure") for all people defined as alcoholic (Pattison 1976). Wildly contradictory judgments about the aims and effectiveness of treatment are a natural result of confusion and vagueness in the definition of what is being treated.

In fact, alcoholics appear to have nothing in common which differentiates them from the rest of us, except that at some time in their lives they are regarded by others or regard themselves as persistent users of alcohol in a way that is harmful to themselves, their families, or society. In despair, some authorities have taken to using the plural "alcoholisms," suggesting that it is not one disease but many. The trouble is that there is no established way of classifying these alcoholisms and identifying causes and treatments. Many authorities are coming to think of alcohol abuse as simply one common effect of a great variety of biological characteristics, personal problems, social conditions, and situations in life. That is certainly what the studies of abusive behavior by frustrated experimental animals suggest.

Most of the basic ideas on this subject are old ones, systematized and elaborated but not much improved in the twentieth century. There has alway been doubt about the proper moral description of excessive drinking. The idea of classifying it as a disease, introduced in the eighteenth century but not ratified by the American Medical Association until 1958, did not arise from any new scientific knowledge; we know little more in that sense than we knew two centuries or twenty centuries ago. The disease concept of alcoholism at first "appears and disappears like a will-of-the-wisp, leaving no lasting impression" (Howland and Howland 1978, p. 40). Before the eighteenth century, habitual drunkenness was regarded as a moral weakness and a cause of disease, especially liver failure and insanity, but not as an illness. Jonathan Edwards used the example of the drunkard to illustrate his view that desire and will are one; the drunkard chooses his ruin, Edwards said. He gave no credence to the idea that the alcoholic is enslaved. But other Puritan divines did call habitual drunkenness a kind of madness or "an incurable habit," which at least hints at illness. Thomas Trotter, in his "Essay on Drunkenness," published in 1804, called it a "disease of the mind" and said that mere preaching against it was useless. Benjamin Rush, in *An Inquiry into the Effects of Ardent Spirits* (1811), described the physical effects of alcohol abuse and called it a "derangement of the will." But he also treated it as a moral weakness; this mixture is still very common (Levine 1978). By the 1850s the disease concept was well established, not among doctors but among some temperance reformers who believed that alcohol was the cause and abstinence for everyone the cure. By the 1890s alcoholism, along with morphine and cocaine addiction, had been added to some lists of mental illnesses.

But the churches still had the strongest influence in defining alcohol problems, and their view was essentially a moral one. Doctors were poorly organized and had little voice. The great change came after the failure of Prohibition, as the medical profession began to assert itself more aggressively. A new development of the disease concept, propagated by Alcoholics Anonymous and by the Yale Center of Alcohol Studies, emphasized individual susceptibility as opposed to the malignancy of alcohol itself. Since then the disease concept has become even more firmly established, although we now emphasize addiction or dependence less than abuse, which sounds suspiciously like bad behavior rather than illness.

Popular attitudes duplicate the confusion among the authorities. In one household survey (Linsky 1972), the main causes given for alcoholism were personality disorder, biological susceptibility, moral weakness, and, more rarely, social drinking and alcohol itself. The treatments most approved were medical attention, psychiatric care, willpower, religion, legal controls, education, change of spouse or job, and family pressure, in that order. In another survey, 58 percent described alcoholics as "sick," 37 percent described them as "weak," and the rest did not know how to label them (Boyd 1970). People have accepted the idea that alcoholism is a disease, and they are willing to turn alcoholics over to experts (although there are no established treatments except for the physical symptoms), but many of them also retain vestiges of the old moralistic conception. (Alcoholics too often regard their behavior as shameful; maybe that is why one of the symptoms alcoholism workers are taught to notice is denial.) It has been suggested that a theory of alcoholism should cover all societies and all levels of drinking, should be compatible with theories about other deviant behavior (pathological gambling, for example), and should be testable and useful in practice (Sargent 1976). No such theory is likely to appear. Maybe alcoholism, like creativity, is not susceptible to explanation by a testable theory, because it is a name for too many different things in different circumstances.

Let us examine what it means to say that alcoholism (and, by implication, other forms of drug abuse) is a disease. This is not simply a dispute about words, because the decision to classify something as an illness has many social consequences: It affects attitudes toward the alcohol abuser, the types of control considered appropriate, criminal responsibility during intoxication, and insurance payments. If alcohol abuse were considered to be not illness but "succumbing to temptation," as Thomas Szasz describes it (and as most people would have judged it before the nineteenth century), or a way of life, as others have claimed, we would have to think about these matters in a different way. E. M. Jellinek, one of the best-known American authorities, originally insisted that alcoholism implied loss of control, because he feared that too broad a definition – say, one based entirely on excessive use – would undermine the ethical basis of social sanctions against habitual drunkenness by identifying it as a symptom of illness. Later he decided that some types or stages of alcoholism were diseases and others were not; it was a disease only if the drinker had lost control or was unable to abstain (Robinson 1972). Apparently he, at least, thought it essential to make some clear distinction between misbehavior and illness. (The issue is further complicated by the need to avoid confusing alcoholism with the diseases it causes, such as cirrhosis of the liver and Korsakoff's syndrome, or with the effects of tolerance and withdrawal, which resemble a disease in the obvious physical sense.)

By itself, the fact that drug abuse has a social component or consists largely of repeated actions is no reason to deny the possibility of classifying it as an illness. A disease is, among other things, an abnormality that prevents adequate social participation or functioning, and cure always implies some kind of social reintegration. And of course, people can be responsible for their own illness, whether it is heart disease or drug abuse. Some destructive behavior seems so much more serious than a mere problem of living or a bad habit that it earns the description "behavioral disorder." The American Psychiatric Association, for example, includes pathological gambling and kleptomania as well as substance use disorders among its diagnostic categories. Even what we regard as physical illness varies with time and place; it has been said that in the lower Mississippi Valley in the early nineteenth century, malaria was so common that it was seen not as a sickness, an abnormality, but as one of the inevitable burdens of life. Illness may not be simply what doctors say it is, but the definition of disease also depends partly on the state of medicine, and for that reason, too, is subject to historical change. The gluttons Dante placed in hell as sinners would now probably be regarded as suffering from the behavioral disorder of overeating or the disease of alcoholism. Sometimes we even classify criminal behavior as a symptom of disease by branding it the product of sociopathy or an antisocial personality, although we have not reached the point of denying that criminals are responsible for their crimes.

The categories involved can be called, colloquially, "sick" (including "crazy"), "bad," and "weak." Despite the efforts of R. D. Laing, Szasz, and other antipsychiatrists, most people believe they can distinguish between madness and problems of living. And no matter how often we are told that criminals are antisocial personalities and therefore in some sense sick or crazy, we are likely to go on thinking of them as blameworthy. But the status of drug abusers and addicts has always been much more ambiguous. Twentieth-century institutions have tried to resolve the issue by classifying them officially as sick, but alcoholics are still often regarded, despite the apparent contradiction, as sinners against themselves (weak) and against others (bad) because of the same actions that are supposed to be symptoms of disease. A complication is presented by the fact that using alcohol, even in excess, is also a normal, quite respectable social activity. Some politicians have recently claimed alcoholism as an excuse (moral, if not legal) for taking bribes or visiting male prostitutes. They are trying to use the modern disease concept to excuse their actions while in effect avoiding the stigma of serious abnormality that is the usual price of denying moral responsibility. This kind of manipulation is presumably what Jellinek feared when he refused to describe merely excessive or abusive alcohol use as a disease. Admittedly, it could not be attempted with any other drug. No congressman in trouble would dare to introduce heroin, cocaine, or marihuana as an excuse, because using those drugs is almost as scandalous as extortion or homosexuality. And even in this case it did not succeed; the ambiguity that the politicians were trying to take advantage of worked against them in the end because it made for commonsense limitations in the public mind. But common sense can change, and the limits remain unclear.

In law the influence of the disease concept has been important, although indirect and usually inexplicit. One of the underlying questions in the *Robinson* and *Powell* cases was whether the defendant's criminal act was a symptom of disease, and whether, if so, that made him not responsible. The decisions did not formally depend on this issue, but they provided a rich source of metaphors and comparisons. The majority opinion in the *Robinson* case compared punishing the addicted defendant to jailing a leper for his disease. Harlan, in dissent, responded to this analogy by pointing out that courts had allowed the confinement, even in prison, of typhoid and venereal disease carriers. Justice Tom Clark, in dissent, justified Robinson's conviction on the ground that the penalty was criminal only in appearance but civil in intent, since the purpose was to arrest the disease of narcotic addiction in its early stages. In his opinion in the *Powell* case, Marshall explicitly criticized the disease concept of alcoholism, and the dissenter Fortas in effect defended it, saying that Powell's public drunkenness was symptomatic of a condition he could not avoid – implicitly a disease.

Deciding that alcoholism or addiction is a disease does not settle the issue of whether Robinson's or Powell's acts were voluntary, since people must often be held responsible for acts they would not have performed if they had not been alcoholics or addicts. Justice White made this distinction in the *Powell* case: Powell's alcoholism may have been involuntary; his public drunkenness was not. But when the act is regarded as merely a symptom, it seems harsh to ascribe responsibility to the actor. And since alcohol and drug abuse are defined as misuse of certain substances, almost any harmful action of the alcoholic or drug abuser might potentially be regarded as a symptom. The close association between alcoholism, drug abuse, and antisocial personality, sometimes regarded in the medical and sociological literature as an empirical correlation, is partly a matter of definition; as the term "substance abuse" suggests, this disease not only causes but often actually consists in part of antisocial acts (Grinspoon and Bakalar 1978).

In criminal law the disease concept is a minor issue, since courts have rarely been prepared to deny the criminal responsibility of alcohol and drug abusers. A defense of addiction used against a charge of robbing a drugstore would get the same short shrift as a defense of pathological gambling in an embezzlement case; the criminal courts must draw a line somewhere if they are to have any function at all. But in civil commitment cases, disease becomes a much more important issue. Addiction or alcoholism can be seen as a serious incapacity, rather than merely bad or self-destructive behavior, because it is pictured as a disturbance of adaptive functioning, biological and social at once. It is treated by detoxification, a medical procedure that allows the alcoholic or addict to recover from the physical symptoms of withdrawal with the least possible danger and discomfort. Methadone maintenance for heroin addicts also seems to be a form of drug therapy. This creates a certain aura of medical expertise that makes it more plausible to regard civil commitment as treatment for illness and therefore obviously for the addict's good. Unfortunately, detoxification provides only temporary symptomatic relief; and substituting one opiate for another, as we do in methadone programs, is not treatment for a disease (much less a cure) but a way to reduce the inconvenience of addiction for the addict and society. Evaluations of drug treatment programs show that once detoxification or methadone maintenance has ended, we have no clear idea of what to do (Ogburn 1978).

Some evidence supports the embarrassing suggestion that untreated heroin addicts are more likely to stop using the drug than those who are treated (Waldorf and Biernacki 1982). But maybe the addicts who are treated are simply the more severe cases, so that even after treatment they are not as well as the ones with a milder illness. To judge whether that is so, we first have to decide what constitutes a severe case of addiction. Many addicts, maybe most of them, have made a mess of their lives. They are socially isolated, neglect their health, and have no job or family; they pass the time committing burglaries, selling drugs on the street, waiting for a connection, and nodding off. Eventually, if they survive long enough, they are likely to end up in prison, civil confinement, a detoxification clinic, or a methadone maintenance program. Addicts who do not lead that kind of life often have enough fortitude and social support either to sustain the addiction on their own or to give it up on their own, untreated.

But this does not tell us what defines a severe case of addiction. In the purely medical sense, it means very little. Certainly it does not depend on the total dose. There is no evidence that the people who succeed in breaking the habit on their own are the ones who are least heavily addicted in a physiological sense. On the contrary, many of the soldiers who became addicted in Vietnam but immediately stopped taking heroin on their return to the United States had been using a drug that was purer and stronger than anything available to street addicts here. It is convenient to conclude that the least severely addicted persons are precisely those whose lives are not so wasteful and chaotic that they end up in the treatment system. But such reasoning is circular; under this definition, treatment can never be proved to have failed. Lacking an independent criterion of severity, we have to say that the evidence against the effectiveness of treatment is strong.

But if there is no effective treatment, civilly committed addicts may be in confinement solely because of some possible future misuse of drugs. This possibility properly makes many people uneasy, especially since addicts are usually referred to civil commitment after an arrest for drug possession.

This combination of medical diagnosis with moral or legal judgment may come perilously close to punishing people for drug use more or less as criminals, while denying them the procedural rights of criminal law and allowing sentences of indeterminate length on the ground that they are sick and should be confined for their own good until they get well. To civil libertarians, civil commitment of opiate addicts sometimes looks like a pilot program for that dubious utopia, the therapeutic state. There is no question that this disease-crime model of drug abuse allows great scope to the state by introducing disease concepts into criminal proceedings and identifying the presence of a disease in willed and often unregretted acts. As Nils Bejerot writes, "the addict generally does not suffer from his disease, he enjoys it . . . . the patients . . . must be . . . kept free from drugs for a long period, with or against their will" (Bejerot 1970, p. xvii). It becomes part of the definition of this illness that the patients may have no right to decide whether they want treatment for it. The only familiar similar situation is insanity; we are reminded again of "lunacy of the will." The treatment need not even be for the drug user's own good if drug abuse is regarded as an epidemic; then Mill's principle becomes irrelevant, as we saw in Chapter 1. Harlan's analogy in the *Robinson* case between civil commitment of addicts and quarantine of typhoid carriers shows the effect of this idea. In thinking of drug abuse as an infectious disease, we assimilate the voluntary process of persuasion and example by which it spreads to the involuntary transmission of infection.

This allows us to regard drug users as somehow both helpless victims and free persons who must be blamed for their actions. U.S. public policy on opiates especially has tended to follow this pattern. After the Harrison Act outlawed all use of opiates except for legitimate medical purposes, the government questioned whether maintenance of an addict on narcotics was a legitimate medical purpose. By the early 1920s, a doctor could write of "the shallow pretense that drug addiction is a disease" (Prentice 1921, p. 1553), and the medical profession was abandoning addicts. That was consistent; the law punished addicts as willful criminals, and doctors should so regard them.

Today, opinion has shifted again, and addiction (now called "opiate dependence") is fully recognized as a disease, but addicts are still subject to arrest, and, except for those in methadone programs, are not allowed treatment for their most obvious physical symptoms, the withdrawal reaction. We deny medical treatment for these symptoms and then treat the acts that produced the symptoms as themselves evidence of illness, without renouncing our moral disapproval or removing criminal penalties. The institutional restraints on coercion built into procedures for dealing with criminals and the quite different ones built into procedures for dealing with sick people can both be evaded in this way. A curious example is observed by Isidore Chein:

That the basic concern of compulsory therapy plans is suppressive rather than therapeutic and that ideologies of suppression and of therapy do not easily mix is most evident in the qualifications that are generally introduced as to which addicts are to be eligible for compulsory therapy as an alternative to jail sentences. . . . Thus, there is generally a limit set on the number of times a patient may avail himself of the therapeutic alternative, and a self-committed addict who seeks discharge before his time is up renders himself ineligible forever. It is as if one were to declare that an easily cured patient is sick, but a hard-to-cure patient is a scoundrel. (Chein et al. 1964, p. 333)

The most important restraint on our treatment of sick people is the requirement that the patient feel ill and want to be cured; the most important restraint on our treatment of criminals is the requirement that they have committed some harmful act. If the condition of addiction to certain drugs or the habit of using them is an illness and a crime, both restraints may come to seem unnecessary. Since drug use is a disease, there is no need for evidence of a harmful act or safeguards for individual rights; since drug use is a series of criminal acts, there is no need for consent to treatment.

The case of *In Re de la O*, decided by the Supreme Court of California in 1963, involved a man who was convicted of a narcotics misdemeanor and then given an indeterminate sentence of up to five years of civil confinement for addiction. The court rejected his contention that this penalty was criminal and therefore barred by the *Robinson* decision. He argued that he had been sentenced under the penal code, placed in the custody of the Department of Corrections, confined against his wish with visitation and mail restrictions, and subjected to the authority of a criminal parole board. The state pointed out that addicts who commit themselves voluntarily are subject to the same rules. The court said that despite the unfortunate use of criminal law terminology this place of confinement was not a prison; the petitioner was there for quarantine and treatment.

As medicine advances and society becomes more complex and rationalized, more and more things come to be regarded as disease, and once a condition or form of behavior is classified as a disease, we rarely look at it again in any other way. We move toward the therapeutic state that identifies health with positive liberty (thus the epithet "sick society"). Whether you approve of this tendency or disapprove of it depends on your views about freedom and about the institutional arrangements that define health and sickness. In any case, it alters the balance among the biological, personal, and social components that enter any conception of illness. The biological anchor for the disease of drug abuse is a chemical with definite effects on the body and brain. But even the change in emphasis from addiction or dependence to abuse is a movement away from biology. And now we have come to the point where one writer calls alcoholism a matter of "social learning" (Larkin 1979) and another, thinking about heroin use in the United States, says that "the natural history of drug addiction is like that of a society: it must be rewritten every few years" (Vaillant 1970, p. 497). It is hardly surprising that alcohol and drug abuse are the only common diagnoses associated with antisocial personality. Most heroin addicts, for example, are juvenile delinquents or petty criminals before they ever use heroin, and addicts who do not have this kind of history are the most easily "cured" (Bess et al. 1972). In the English clinic system for opiate addiction, the addicts are described not as patients but as clients – a designation they prefer (Judson 1975) – and the aim of the program is not mainly to make the addicts stop using the drug (as in the U.S. methadone maintenance system) but to find work for them and help them develop other interests. If those aims are accomplished, they tend to give up opiates.

The question is whether we should go on calling something a disease when its social component is so important that it can be said to lack a natural history in the ordinary medical sense and may at times be hardly separable from general antisocial behavior. From the personal rather than the social point of view, we can ask whether there is any other disease for which the best-known cure is a kind of religious conversion or meetings in which the sufferers confess their misdeeds and exhort one another to change their ways. The biological anchor seems to be lost.

Maybe art can help here. Drugs and alcohol are moving agents in a play many people believe to be the greatest ever written by an American – Eugene O'Neill's autobiographical *Long Day's Journey into Night* (O'Neill 1956). It is set in a summer house in Connecticut where the four Tyrones (O'Neills) are gathered together in the summer of 1910. The action takes up one day from morning until late at night, and it consists mainly of two revelations that are not really different – about illness and about the family itself. Mrs. Tyrone is a morphine addict; her actor husband James and two (adult) sons are heavy drinkers – alcoholics by most definitions. Early in the play, Mary Tyrone learns that her younger son, Edmund (Eugene), has tuberculosis, and the men come to realize with shame and despair that she has started taking morphine again. Her addiction is presented, at the start, as a disease like tuberculosis; the sons accuse their stingy father of causing it by hiring a cheap, incompetent doctor who gave her too much morphine during childbirth. The husband in turn scolds her: "I've been a god-damned fool to believe in you." But he also admits that "it was a curse put on you without your knowing or willing it." She complains of the local doctor, "When you're in agony and half insane, he sits and holds your hand and delivers sermons about will power." She says, "I've never understood anything about it except that one day long ago I found I could no longer call my soul my own." According to Edmund, she has said that she hopes she will take an accidental overdose some day.

But things turn out to be more complicated. She tries to convince herself that she is taking the morphine for her rheumatism. At one point she says, "I've become such a liar . . . , especially to myself," and she calls herself a "lying dope fiend." She asks Edmund not to believe that she used his illness as an excuse to take morphine again. And there are other suggestions that the addiction is purposeful. It enables her to achieve "a peculiar detachment in her voice and manner." James says, "Every day from now on there'll be the same drifting away from us." Under the drug's influence, she becomes "a ghost haunting the past," and Edmund says that she takes it "to get beyond our reach." Her memories go back to the happy days at a convent school, before her marriage, when she thought about becoming a nun. Edmund tells his father, "You've never given her anything that would help her to want to stay off it" – despite all the money he has spent on cures. Maybe it is a question of wanting, then, and the addiction is "a curse put on her without her knowing or willing it," just like the other misfortunes of her marriage – no more and no less. This is true to what we know of medical addiction; most people who are given morphine by doctors, even if they suffer a physical withdrawal reaction, do not go on craving and seeking the drug afterward.

Alcohol, too, is at times a sickness for the Tyrones. Edmund says of a poet with whom he feels an affinity, "Poor Dowson. Booze and consumption got him," implying that they are the same kind of thing. It transpires that Mary's father, too, died of drink and tuberculosis, and hereditary susceptibility is suggested. But more often the men's alcoholism is presented as a continuing problem of character and situation rather than something traceable to an outside cause such as a tuberculosis bacillus or a doctor's needle. When James criticizes Mary for her addiction, she accuses him of bringing up the older son, Jamie, to be an alcoholic by giving him whiskey to quiet him as a baby – implying an analogy with the morphine used on her when she gave birth. But this is presented only as a dubious suggestion prompted by anger and malice. In general, the characters are much less concerned about who or what to blame for the drinking, which is thought of more as something the men do than as something that has happened to them. And beyond the alcohol and morphine there are other, vaguer addictions – James's penny pinching and his habit of compulsively accumulating real estate, which his sons regard as a degenerate form of their peasant ancestors' attachment to the land.

Drink and drugs move the plot, too, because whiskey and morphine allow the Tyrones to think and say things they would otherwise not think and say; all the revelations and self-revelations are booze and drugs talking. Drug and alcohol problems illustrate remarkably how hard it can be to distinguish the press of circumstance from the unfolding of character. It is hard to draw a line between what these people have done and what has been done to them. As the action ends, late at night, with Mary Tyrone in a narcotic trance and her husband and older son stuporous from whiskey, we feel that it is inadequate to describe the morphine addiction and alcoholism as clinically identifiable illnesses; instead they represent what the Tyrones have made of their life together, and the definition of a "cure" would be to become different people leading a different kind of life.

Not all drug dependence includes the personality in this way. Nicotine dependence involves a much more limited set of symptoms, and is more easily interpreted as a specific disorder in an otherwise psychologically and biologically normal person. Maybe drug dependencies form a continuum on this scale. But in general, the trouble with calling drug abuse an illness is that the standard of health is so hard to identify once the biological level at which all human beings have a great deal in common is left behind. The danger is exemplified by the practice of imprisoning political dissidents in psychiatric hospitals for "reformist delusions." This makes sense if the norm of mental health includes agreement with existing social and political arrangements. And so it should if existing arrangements are fundamentally correct and health is defined socially. That is the ultimate dream of positive liberty. But such confidence about what is socially healthy seems monstrous; a society is not an organism.

To identify something as a disease is to set it off from other social and personal problems. Schizophrenia is not an exaggerated form of eccentricity or maladjustment; it is a very special condition. But it has never been shown that an alcoholic is a special kind of person with a special susceptibility, who drinks for reasons different from the ordinary social drinker's, in a different way, and with different effects. Distinguishing between alcoholics and social drinkers is not easy, and people slip back and forth between these categories (Miller 1979). In one study comparing people who described themselves as alcoholics with another group of heavy drinkers who did not describe themselves that way, the researchers found that the self-identified alcoholics were more likely to have been to meetings of Alcoholics Anonymous (AA) and more likely to believe in the need for abstinence, but were otherwise very similar to the control group. They had more alcohol problems, but the difference was one of degree (Skinner et al. 1980). Similar patterns exist in other forms of drug abuse – even heroin dependence (Vaillant 1970). That is only another way of saying that the social component in the definition of drug abuse is great.

Defenders of the disease concept have little to say about two problems that exacerbate each other and confound the treatment of drug and alcohol abusers: their unwillingness to assume the role of patient (sometimes called denial) and the medical community's reluctance to confer it. Here is what often happens:

. . .drug and alcohol abusers receive medical care of lower quality than that accorded to other patient populations . . . diagnosis is often delayed or missed, patients may be excluded from the health care system, referrals may be ineffectively made, if at all. . . .

Some of these deleterious effects for patients can be attributed to negative attitudes on the part of physicians and other health care staff. Institutional characteristics also contribute to the problem. . . . There are insufficient illness-categories for patients with alcohol, amphetamine, or other drug problems. These patients are often disruptive or diagnostically confusing. . . .

These patients are then assigned to a "management" category. . . . The shorter the time on the ward and the less staff time required, the more successful the case. (Chappel et al. 1979, pp. 253–4)

But ignorance, impatience, and hostility on the part of medical staff do not account for everything. In fact, these institutional and personal obstacles develop partly because health professionals realize, consciously or not, that they are being asked to solve a problem that is largely nonmedical in the context of their training. For similar reasons, health insurance programs often cover alcohol and drug abuse inadequately. We hesitate before taking on, in the name of curing illness, what may turn out to be an indefinitely protracted task of getting unhappy and troublesome people to live better or behave better. Alcoholism researchers also complain that supervisors in industry are reluctant to accept the diagnosis of alcoholism in employees. But this reluctance may be caused by understandable confusion. Diagnosis suggests a common, easily recognizable abnormal or diseased pattern of drinking, and it is often hard to extract any such pattern from the varying ways in which people use and abuse alcohol at different times in their lives.

The complaints of people who are called on to treat alcoholics can be quite touching:

. . . if we insist on total abstinence as the criterion, program results are not impressive. If we are more modest and reasonable, as we are with depression and diabetes, for example, then respectable improvement rates are not uncommon. Alcoholism may then be seen as a treatable illness rather than a revolving-door phenomenon, staff morale improves, patients become less fatalistic, better arguments can be made for funding purposes, and staff may be more easily attracted to the field. (Gottheil 1982)

Unfortunately, it is not just a historical accident that the idea of alcoholism as a treatable disease has been associated with the idea of abstinence as a treatment. No one doubts that depression and diabetes will continue to be regarded as illnesses no matter how imperfect the treatment. But alcohol abuse is so unstable as a disease entity that sometimes only the goal of abstinence seems to preserve its coherence. Without that goal, the disease theory of alcoholism might turn out to be a will-of-the-wisp after all.

The disease concept requires careful criticism because this, if anything, is the received view. But it would not have become so widely accepted if there had not been much to be said for it. Civil commitment of addicts convicted of possessing heroin is rarely as oppressive in practice as it seems in libertarian principle. Whether a term of civil confinement works as treatment or not, it rarely lasts longer than the alternative prison sentence, and addicts often prefer it. The rise of methadone maintenance has meant much less deprivation of liberty for addicts diverted from the criminal courts. The legal system is too conservative to draw out all the possible implications of the disease–crime model. And this model is, after all, very attractive; even police officers who are professionally trained to handle addicts as criminals do not object to their being assigned to methadone maintenance programs instead of prison after conviction (McDonald 1973). The model has become popular precisely because of the way it blurs the distinction between treatment and social control (or improvement); this vagueness may be inherent in any plausible conception of drug abuse.

In a book called *Models of Madness, Models of Medicine* (1974), Miriam Siegler and Humphry Osmond make a good case for regarding alcoholism and drug abuse as medical problems. They discuss various ways of looking at madness (in the sense of chronic psychosis) and conclude – as almost all psychiatrists would agree – that it is best regarded as a true disease (or diseases) and not, for example, as a problem of living or an inchoate romantic rebellion against an oppressive society. Heroin dependence and alcoholism are a much more difficult issue. Siegler and Osmond describe medical, psychosocial, and a number of what they call "moral" models. Admitting that all of these models have some validity and are used by most people at one time or another, they discuss the flaws in each one and conclude that the best one for most purposes is a mixture of medical and "restorative moral" models. The virtue of this approach is that they abandon the attempt to determine what drug abuse and alcoholism are in some unattainably objective, scientific sense. Instead, they concentrate on what kind of authority is best for dealing with drug abuse and what the drug abuser's responsibilities should be. Thus, they are more concerned with defining a medical or quasimedical model than a disease concept. They emphasize discontinuity rather than continuity between alcoholism and social drinking, because the passage from being a problem or nuisance drinker to being a patient is rarely gradual. Alcoholism is treated as a metabolic defect compounded by social and psychological problems. The "moral etiology" of this disease is irrelevant because it is of no use in treatment. Blaming society or the alcoholic's family leaves the alcoholic with no responsibilities and nothing to do. Reproaching the alcoholic for moral weakness is notoriously futile. In this medical–moral model, the alcoholic is not a bad person but can be a bad *patient* – one who does not fulfill the duty of seriously trying to get well. This way of conceiving the problem, they believe, is above all best for the alcoholic's morale and thus for the chances of improvement.

Siegler and Osmond are in effect clarifying, systematizing, and extending the views of AA. They believe that the successes of AA come from its definition of alcoholism as much as its treatment methods. AA regards alcoholism as both an illness (which can be arrested by abstinence) and a spiritual problem. It must be conceived as an illness because illness is ego alien: The formula is not "I am doing bad things with alcohol" but "Alcohol has gained power over me." Alcoholics are unfortunate, not evil, but their vulnerability is special, so they do not have to denounce liquor and all of their drinking friends. They do have the duties of making restitution to the people they have harmed and following the rules that will enable them to get well. And the decision to get well requires a spiritual crisis and renewal. Like the disease–crime model for treatment of heroin addicts, which it formally resembles, this model of alcoholism is somewhat incoherent logically; its incoherence reflects the medically and morally ambiguous nature of alcoholism. It also contradicts some of the evidence by making a sharp distinction between alcoholic and ordinary social drinking and by insisting rigidly on abstinence. But the model is humane and seems to work for many alcoholics.

Siegler and Osmond's approach to the analysis of medical authority is related to their views on alcoholism and addiction. They classify it into three types: scientific (biomedical), public health, and Aesculapian. The authority of scientific medicine is "sapiential," based on knowledge and expertise about physiology. The authority of public health medicine is supposed to have a scientific basis, but it is primarily moral and political, dependent on a social consensus. Aesculapian authority is the individual doctor's relation to the patient – sapiential, moral, and charismatic at once. Scientific medicine, unfortunately, has so far contributed little to the understanding of drug and alcohol abuse. Public health medicine is the realm of drug education and laws controlling drug use and sales. It is the Aesculapian relationship between individual drug abusers and medical professionals who care for them that Siegler and Osmond most want to identify and defend. To them it is the heart of the medical model as applied to drug abuse and alcoholism; the mixed source of its authority is most appropriate for a problem that evades categories.

For social reasons, Siegler and Osmond want to circumscribe medical authority carefully. They are somewhat wary of public health medicine's habit of using the language of health and illness for quasipolitical situations, and they insist on a discontinuity between drug use that is illness and drug use that is not. Their approach is most compatible with a political emphasis on negative as opposed to positive liberty. The most common justification for drug and alcohol prohibition, after all, is an intervention of public health medicine in the name of something very much like positive liberty. But the Aesculapian idea is not needed in all situations; for example, the disease concept of drug and alcohol abuse should not be used in judging criminal responsibility.

As Siegler and Osmond recognize, different conceptions of disease and different models of medicine are needed for different purposes. Doctors and other medical professionals have many roles, and there are many kinds of medical knowledge. The proportions of expertise, charisma, and moral authority in medicine vary with the situation, the illness, and the relationship between doctor and patient. Especially when dealing with drug abuse and alcoholism, we are always at the border between free will and compulsion, between illness and other forms of suffering. Szasz to the contrary, conceptual precision and logical fanaticism are wrong here. We are not able (and may never be able) to classify such situations into exclusive categories using a positivistic conception of disease and a simple, rigid notion of freedom. The "sick" label has its dangers, but especially in contrast to the "bad" label, it has the virtue of not narrowing the range of solutions too much. To use the label rigidly therefore is to repudiate its purpose.

Reflection on the nature of chronic drug problems has become much more sophisticated; for example, the latest formulations of the American Psychiatric Association on substance abuse are a great improvement over earlier ones. But what we have come to realize is mainly how much we do not know. References to dependence and addiction are no longer so promiscuous because the inadequacies of these terms are better understood. For lack of an alternative, the disease concept is widely used, but not without recognition that it is precarious and has some questionable social implications. We have probably gone about as far as we can in analyzing concepts and bringing commonsense knowledge to bear on them. Further developments in the field may depend on an unpredictable scientific breakthrough. Meanwhile, history and sociology illuminate some areas not reached by either political theory or medical knowledge.

3   The historical direction of drug policy

Political ideas and even medical categories are bound up with institutions that have histories. In *On Liberty*, Mill took little account of this fact, except for a few comments about savagery as a historical childhood and his warning against the tendency toward a tyranny of popular feeling in advanced democracies. But in other writings, even he paid more attention to history. Against the rationalistic radicalism of his first master, Bentham, who called tradition "the authority of inexperience," he eventually learned to balance the conservatism of Coleridge, who suggested that before denouncing an established institution or practice as irrational, we should ask, "What is the meaning of it?" The meaning of a practice, in the sense of its place in the life of a society, is inseparable from its development. Drug use may be one of those issues on which a page of history (or sociology) is worth more than a volume of logic.

Looked at as a series of incidents, the history of social and legal responses to drug use, especially in the last century and in the United States, sometimes seems melancholy and haphazard. It is easy to find inadequate pharmacology, inconsistent ad hoc responses based on poor information, indulgence of passions and prejudices, including racism, in response to drug scares, institutional self-aggrandizement by narcotics police, and a fair amount of hypocrisy and corruption. This has often been emphasized by people who are convinced that the drug control system is wrong and who want to find particular circumstances, institutions, or individuals to blame. But beneath the surface, there is a single trend and an established pattern not confined to the United States. The drug laws of all modern nations (except in the case of alcohol) are similar, despite some variations in severity. International treaties and supranational control institutions further guarantee unanimity and uniformity. In some corners, the system still contains fossil structures such as the classification of "narcotics" including three very different drugs (marihuana, opiates, and cocaine), but in general it has become more intellectually orderly.*

---

* The American Psychiatric Association's new diagnostic classification of drug abuse problems is an example of this kind of conceptual clarification; another (though still inadequate) is the Comprehensive Drug Abuse Prevention and Control Act, the major federal drug law passed in 1970.

In its broad outlines, it is not a product of accident, error, fanaticism, or corruption.

Twentieth-century society has moved toward more and more professionalization, rationalization, and formal regulation in the control of drugs. In these changes, two models we have discussed are at work, corresponding to the ambiguous character of drug use: consumer protection, including public health in the narrower sense associated with physiological medicine; and morality, public tranquility, or public health in the wider social sense. The first model has been more powerful because it covers the area of social life in which individual autonomy is now least valued. When Mill wrote *On Liberty*, absolute freedom of trade still seemed defensible; the disease concept of drug abuse was only an opinion, not an institution; and the medical profession and medical science were relatively feeble. We will never return to the social and intellectual conditions that made possible Mill's opposition to all drug laws. On the other hand, individual freedom of speech and sexual behavior is regarded more highly than in Mill's time. When drug laws are criticized, it is usually on the grounds that drug use has more in common with speech or sexual behavior (or dangerous sports) than with the situations in which medical or consumer regulations apply.

The morality or social health model has served to reinforce the medical–consumer model where necessary; otherwise, the different histories of pleasure drug regulation and ordinary medical drug regulation would be inexplicable. But as we noted in Chapter 1, legal restrictions based on fear of immorality or general social debilitation are notoriously subject to abuse. Common sense in these matters may be nothing more than shared prejudice. Our own common sense, for example, requires us to debate gravely whether possession of marihuana should be decriminalized, even though many obviously more dangerous commodities (alcohol is only one) are sold freely. Attitudes toward minorities, work, worldly success and failure, or sex and family life sometimes turn out to be the real issues in a controversy about drugs. Drugs are symbols charged with cultural tensions. An Asian government's commitment to eliminating opium use or a South American government's determination to stop coca chewing represents symbolically an aspiration to modernize and westernize. Conventional people in our own society may displace repressed anxieties to illicit drugs and their users as a form of scapegoating; rebels may define their difference by using exotic, often illegal drugs and scorning the commonplace ones. Users of disapproved drugs become dope fiends because they are possessed by demons the rest of us have cast out. Drugs become a source of fantasies and fears about excessive control (the chemical robot) and loss of control (the wandering intoxicated mind). Unfamiliar drugs in a given culture come to represent the threat of insidious, unknown evil. In preindustrial societies, fears of spiritual pollution, operating as systematic pressures to hold someone responsible for natural and social maladies, help to keep a group together by setting its members apart from another group (Wildavsky and Douglas 1982). The same fears and pressures affect modern attitudes toward drugs.

The school of social interpretation called "sociology of deviance" pays systematic attention to these issues. In their view, the deviant or abnormal character of an action and the person who performs it constitutes a role created by those who define the rules of society. Certain persons who stray into a "primary deviation" are publicly labeled, and from then on their behavior is reinterpreted to fit a new role. People learn how to behave as mentally ill or alcoholic or addicted; they become secondary deviants. A classic example is Jean-Paul Sartre's account of Jean Genet's career. According to Sartre, the orphan child Genet, caught stealing and labeled a thief, decided to adopt the role and even glory in it. He became a thief by being called one. The deviant label is hard to shake off, especially if it is a "master status" that defines the social identity of its possessors and cuts them off from conventional society. Deviants who are being judged by rules they do not accept may form their own subcultures.

New deviant roles are created by "moral entrepreneurship," which busily extends the area of life subject to rule making and moral judgment, shaping vague values such as social order, liberty, equality, and family solidarity into specific rules of behavior. Ascription of a master status or trait usually expresses an uncertain attitude toward the stigmatized person and behavior; the stereotypes created serve unconscious needs through projection and displacement, while dispelling ambiguity and doubt. In this interpretation, alcohol and drug prohibitions are successful exercises of moral enterprise; they are symbolic victories that impose a cultural hegemony, turning the defeated minority into labeled deviants and enhancing the self-esteem of those who have been able to impose their own definition of the straight path. Drug "abuse" often means involvement in a subordinate or marginal group's cultural ritual; examples can be drawn from the response to American Indian drug use. The purpose of drug laws is seen as symbolic and expressive rather than "instrumental," so that enforcement is not necessarily required (Becker 1963; Gusfield 1963).

The deadpan "value-free" style in which the labeling analysis is usually presented does not disguise its irony. It is implicitly libertarian and un-sympathetic to medical or criminal definitions of drug problems. By redefining "bad" behavior as neutral "deviance" and using the mildly derisive term "moral entrepreneurship," it also works as a critique of legal moralism. In fact, sociology of deviance is partly an oblique attack on the legal enforcement of standards that are "moral" in the senses discussed in Chapter 1; the arguments given there are recast in ostensibly objective terms. The sociology of deviance is a critical description of what Dworkin calls "sociological" as opposed to "discriminatory" morality. The difference is that for his professional purpose, the sociologist has no need of the notion of discriminatory morality; all morality is sociological. This is possible only in a world where moral discriminations are uncertain. The abstract notion of behavioral deviance, detached from all norms and standards, could exist only in a society with no moral majority or moral authority – a modern liberal society.

Labeling theory is hard to refute, since it treats every apparently objective fact of behavior as already contaminated in its definition by social responses and regards most deviance as produced by attempts to record it. The notion of a master status has doubtful empirical content; constant heavy drinking, for example, may dominate a person's life and therefore his or her social status, whether or not the status is master. There is some empirical evidence on alcoholism and addiction opposed to labeling theory. The label of alcoholic or addict is applied very reluctantly, usually at first not by an impersonal social order but by a member of the family. The label is apparently not hard to shake off and does not determine behavior and social status (Clayton and Voss 1981); for example, a history of deviant behavior does not predict experimentation with heroin but does predict addiction (Robins 1975). A study of heroin addicts suggests that secondary deviance through labeling is a minor issue. Addicts often adopt the label themselves before courts of law and treatment agencies apply it to them; they do this partly so that they will be treated as sick rather than delinquent. Family and friends usually respond to the addict as an individual, not to a stereotype. Addicts rarely blame their relapse on the difficulty of reacceptance into straight society. Some keep using the drug but avoid secondary deviance – participation in the addict subculture, stealing, prostitution. Social pressures do not favor but discourage secondary deviance; addicts become known as untrustworthy, manipulative, and offensive, and everyone wants them to change (McAuliffe 1975). Nor does labeling oneself alcoholic, as AA recommends, seem to make the deviance greater. If anything, denial is a problem, and open self-identification may be the beginning of a solution.

Besides, drugs are not just symbols; they are substances with distinct chemical properties and physical and psychological effects. At times it is hard to separate objective from symbolic threats or instrumental from expressive purposes of drug laws, just as it may be hard to distinguish public health in the physiological sense from public health in a broader social sense. If we want to know why cocaine has been classified as a narcotic and the otherwise very similar amphetamines have not, we must look at history. But to explain why, in so many preindustrial cultures, alcohol and opium are considered a social problem but marihuana, stimulants, and hallucinogens are not (Blum and Associates 1969), we must think about the psychopharmacological properties of the drugs themselves.

In any case, labels and cultural symbolism cannot be studied apart from history. Drug use includes magic, religion, medicine, recreation, disease, vice, and crime. In contemporary society we want to keep these categories separate, so classification becomes a problem. In assigning meanings to the experiences produced by drugs, we are confronted by many possibilities and need to make many distinctions. We have separate formal and informal institutions regulating recreation, illness, religion, and so on; much controversy about psychoactive drugs involves conflicting claims by representatives of these institutions, officially sanctioned or outlaw, to be the rightful judges of what drug use means.

The loss of moral authority by many established institutions in industrially advanced countries, together with an efflorescence of drug technology, has made the potential ambiguity greater and the insistence of conflicting claims to transform it into socially acceptable meanings more intense: on one side, authorities proclaiming drug use to be disease and crime; on the other side, rebels declaring it to be fun or even a religious act. Drug use is stigmatized as an irresponsible addiction to kicks and thrills, or praised as delightful and liberating highs, or trips, or consciousness expansion, which lies on the border between religion and fun.

Different drugs have found their way into different cultural categories. Officially, use of morphine, for example, is medicine in certain contexts; otherwise, it is disease or crime, and there is something wrong with anyone who regards it as recreation. Amphetamines prescribed by a doctor for depression might be medicine; amphetamines used by a layman to feel better are disease and crime. Alcohol, self-prescribed, is fun unless you use too much, and then it is disease – alcoholism; it is never medicine, as it was in the nineteenth century. Certain drugs belong in a utilitarian category on the border between medicine and pleasure that is therapeutic in a loose sense: They start users going in the morning, or keep them going during the day, or put them to sleep at night.

Much drug use is vice, the unacceptable kind of fun that offends public morality. Only a few marginal social groups – Mormons, Black Muslims, some fundamentalists – regard all drug use as vice all the time, but a much larger number think that some use of some drugs or any use of other drugs is vice. Once there were two varieties of drug vice: the exotic, fascinating, tempting, and debasing kind associated with illicit drugs, and the homey, domesticated kind connected with a legal drug like alcohol. These differences have become less important as more ordinary people have begun to use illicit drugs. But even within the class of mild or domesticated vice, there are some odd distinctions. Coffee is permissible for children in Latin America but not in the United States, where, however, Coca-Cola, which contains the same drug, is a favorite children's drink. When tobacco was acceptable for men but not for women, spurious health reasons were often given for the discrimination.

Our social categories for psychoactive drug use and our dilemmas about how to distribute drugs among them are not universal features of the human mind or of certain chemicals but products of a specific historical situation. In earlier cultures, the conceptual partitions so carefully erected by our society did not exist. In particular, the distinctions between magic, religion, and medicine have not always been so clear. The words "health" and "holiness" have a common root meaning "whole." Medical diagnosis and prognosis have always partaken of the occult, as a form of divination, and disease has been considered an instrument of gods or evil spirits, sometimes independent and sometimes called forth by the victims' enemies or their own moral delinquency or ritual transgression – as in the plagues of Egypt and Thebes. Shaman, witch doctor, sorcerer, and medicine man are related social roles. The religious–medical or magical–medical ceremony restores the harmony of soul and spirit world, repairing the broken whole and reintegrating the victim into the cultural community.

But today this is an underground theme. Medicine in the West began to separate itself from religion thousands of years ago, and by the early nineteenth century, in Europe and the United States, healers no longer attributed illness to spirits or consciously thought of drugs as magical substances. The scientific revolution and the enormous prestige of Newtonian physics had convinced doctors that most illness had physical and chemical causes. But a medical science created in the image of physics remained only a hope. Even a century after Voltaire's death, his description of doctors as men who poured drugs of which they knew little into patients of whom they knew less remained largely accurate. This uncertain situation, together with the growth of manufacturing, capitalist enterprise, and liberal individualism, made the nineteenth century a great age of self-medication and competing medical authorities. The proprietary drug industry that in some ways expresses the state of medical science and the conditions of medical practice at this stage of history had a great flowering in the late-nineteenth-century United States.

The story of patent medicines is intimately bound up with the history of alcohol, opium, and cocaine. It is more than a comedy-melodrama in which ridiculous or villainous quacks are routed at the end by the forces of honesty, truth, organized medicine, progress, and the criminal law. Even the best histories of the patent medicine era, such as James Harvey Young's *The Toadstool Millionaires* (1961), tend to rely on a framework of amusing or horrifying anecdotes alternating with praise for the triumph of modern medical and legal regulation. But in light of the present conflict over social definition and control of drug use, the moral of the story seems less obvious and less simple.

At the time, doctors tried to discourage the public's interest in entrepreneurial medicine by asking potential customers whether they would trust the repair of a watch to a blacksmith. Unfortunately, this analogy embarrassingly emphasized the inadequacy of physicians as repairmen of the body. The public knew that even the best doctor did not, for practical purposes, understand much more about the human body than a blacksmith understood about watches; no one did. In a time when doctors offered bleeding, emetics, and purges as therapy for many illnesses, it is hardly surprising that people often turned to unlicensed healers and dubious drugs instead. Some of the best physicians, such as Oliver Wendell Holmes, Sr. (who called the patent medicine men "toadstool millionaires") adopted the doctrine of therapeutic nihilism, which declared most current medical practices and materials useless or worse. Holmes may have been right, but a suffering public often preferred the placebo response evoked by the strong personalities or advertising campaigns of the proprietary drug makers.

The relationship between proprietary drug use and orthodox medicine was complicated. Many preparations described in standard pharmacopeias also appeared, often unlabeled or mislabeled, in patent medicines. Both sides searched the same sources in botany and folk medicine, and there was borrowing in both directions. Most doctors in the United States prescribed some proprietary remedies. Pharmacists also concocted proprietary drugs; one of them was Coca-Cola, which originally contained cocaine. In spite of great advances in some fields by the late nineteenth century, neither the state of medical science nor the organization of the profession was yet capable of producing great confidence in the value of reputable as opposed to disreputable or legitimate as opposed to illegitimate medicine.

Psychoactive drugs were in a peculiar position. They were not specific cures for anything but provided relief from suffering of many kinds. Opium, alcohol, or cocaine, like faith in some chemically inactive nostrum, could control the pain while the patient got better. These drugs were important to both orthodox and proprietary medicine. Even Holmes's therapeutic nihilism allowed an exception for opium (and anesthetics).

A list of the drugs most widely used in 1885 shows opiates (for pain) fourth and alcohol (as a sedative and anticonvulsant) sixth (first was iron chloride for anemia; second, quinine for malaria; third, ether for anesthesia; and fifth, sodium bicarbonate for indigestion). By 1910 the list had hardly changed; morphine was fourth and alcohol fifth (Smith and Knapp 1972, p. 161). Hospital pharmacies stocked large amounts of wine as an appetite stimulant, diuretic, sedative, and treatment for psychosomatic illness. Conditions had not changed greatly since the Roman physician Galen recommended laudanum (wine of opium) as a universal remedy.

It had always been known that psychoactive drugs could also be strong poisons. But consciousness of their dangers and demands for restriction began to increase in the late nineteenth century. The new wariness developed because the powers of these drugs began to seem too indeterminate and uncontrollable for medicine – more reliable than the power of quack nostrums, but no less mysterious and potentially monstrous. The first significant federal legislation on drugs, the Pure Food and Drug Act, was a compromise between nineteenth-century liberal attitudes (represented in an extreme form by Mill) and the new reaction against drug misuse. One of the inspirations for this law was a series of articles by Samuel Hopkins Adams entitled "The Great American Fraud," published in *Collier's* magazine in 1905. After considering some of the odder nostrums and the products containing mostly alcohol, Adams devoted an article to the "subtle poisons" that he believed to be "the most dangerous of all quack medicines" because, in a sense, they worked – so well that they would lead astray highly intelligent people. He meant opium and cocaine. The Pure Food and Drug Act forbade interstate shipment of food and soda water containing opium or cocaine, and required that these and certain other drugs in patent medicines be indicated on the label. It was mainly a truth-in-packaging law; the aim was not to eliminate free self-medication but to make it safer by preventing fraud and guaranteeing that the customer would be informed. It was still possible to believe in people's capacity to decide how and when to drug themselves. But soon afterward, far more drastic methods for organized repression of psychoactive drugs came to seem necessary.

The layman's right to make choices about these drugs was repudiated out of a conviction that any use of them outside of a few contexts dominated by medical professionals must be ignorant. These drugs had intrinsic powers of deception, and even the best informed person could be possessed by them, so correct labeling was not enough. Taking opiates to relax or cocaine to feel alert would no longer be legitimated as medical treatment. Soda fountains in drugstores were no longer thought of as medicinal in any way. Coca-Cola, originally sold as a quasimedicinal stimulant, was purged of cocaine and became just a soft drink (with added caffeine). Nineteenth-century ambiguity between health and pleasure began to seem dangerous, just as the conflation of health and holiness in primitive cultures had long seemed absurd. Doctors today may still dispense amphetamines and tranquilizers for the same reasons they once prescribed cocaine, opiates, and alcohol, but laymen cannot prescribe these drugs for themselves, and the medical ritual prevents any confusion between their intended effects and fun.

This control system became established at a particular stage in the development of the medical profession and of (capitalist) industrial society. The process can be observed clearly in the United States, where the first two decades of the twentieth century are generally known as the Progressive era in politics. Some revisionist historians call it a conservative period in which big business consolidated its power against labor and populist threats by means of rationalizing reforms and greater integration with government. In any case, the main political achievement was to bring some order into the chaos of late-nineteenth-century capitalism, and possibly to prevent mass misery that might have led to revolution. The greatest legislative monument of the age was the Federal Reserve Act, which reorganized the banking system; the Pure Food and Drug Act, the Harrison Act, and the Volstead Act were also characteristic Progressive legislation.

The attack on proprietary nostrums and the indiscriminate use of psychoactive drugs not only put a stop to certain dangerous and fraudulent practices but also served to consolidate the strength of organized medicine and pharmacy and the larger drug companies, in cooperation with the federal government. Muckraking journalists, medical professionals, and government officials all agreed that the sale of proprietaries had to be curbed. Narcotics laws aided the institutional growth of the modern health professions by helping to define their areas of competence and exclude unlicensed practitioners. (State licensing for medical practice was first upheld by the Supreme Court in 1888.) The impulse to clean things up and reduce disorder worked against both free self-medication and the small-scale entrepreneurial competition it encouraged.

But advances in the art and science of medicine were just as important as the trend toward consolidation and formal regulation in business and the professions. With the rise of synthetic chemistry, experimental physiology, and above all, bacteriology, the promise of a materialist medicine in the Newtonian image, based on the recognition of specific disease agents for specific diseases, finally seemed about to be fulfilled. The work of Pasteur, Koch, and their colleagues and successors became a model.

It is no accident that this was the era when drug abuse began to be conceived as epidemic disease. A new self-respect and esprit de corps came with the growing social power and professional organization of physicians. In these circumstances, the old psychoactive drugs naturally became more suspect. It required little special training or diagnostic ability to dose patients with alcohol, opium, or cocaine for their complaints and produce satisfied customers who might come back for more indefinitely. This was a challenge to the professional standing of doctors as well as a danger to the patient; intellectual hygiene required clear and enforceable classification of psychoactive drugs.

The law helped to fix the image of drugs that were being used indiscriminately as medicine and for pleasure at a time when changes in social structure and medical knowledge decreed that medicine and pleasure were to be divorced and much of what had been regarded as medicine or pleasure was now to be treated as disease, vice, or crime. Synthetic psychoactive drugs, most of them developed later by a much more highly disciplined, organized, and respected medical profession and drug industry, were at first not treated so harshly, but as their potential for use as pleasure drugs became clear, they were placed under similar controls.

Both doctors and police are part of this arrangement, which serves a protective and conservative function. Disputes about when drug use is illness and when it is crime are often in effect jurisdictional disputes between the medical and police professions; Siegler and Osmond acknowledge this when they emphasize that they favor a medical model rather than a disease concept of drug dependence. Organized medicine has always adjusted its views to those of the government by mutual accommodation (with some open conflict, of course, as in the court decisions forbidding doctors to treat addicts with opiates). Most people regard this as a natural partnership that expresses the nature of public health medicine; even police are happy to turn addicts over to the medical system. Only extreme libertarians such as Szasz, the most faithful intellectual descendants of Mill, think that doctors have sullied their professional purity by turning themselves into police officers and penologists. What matters is that the system of concepts and the institutional structure provide mutual support.

In twentieth-century societies, more and more occupations come to claim the title of profession. A form of work establishes itself as a profession largely through self-consciousness with regard to its technique. Law and medicine are among the oldest professions, with the most highly developed consciousness of technique. The medical and allied professions today, as they expand, divide, and put out new branches, tend to incorporate more and more social functions (Szasz denounces this as "medical imperialism"). In the words of Harold Rosenberg, "A profession becomes really top-rank when it can offer its system of technical redefinition as the key to the human situation, that is, as philosophy" (Rosenberg 1959, pp. 61–3). Medicine may have come closer than any other profession to achieving this status, as more and more kinds of things are defined as illness. For example, the American Psychiatric Association has recently classified habitual cigarette smoking (tobacco dependence) as an illness in certain circumstances.

But medicine has had to make its way by alliance as much as by conquest. Pharmacology and psychiatry, the divisions assigned to psychoactive drugs, operate in relation to the bordering armies of the criminal law by a delicate alternation of skirmishes and treaty conferences. The license of medical professionals to define illness as a social role remains limited, and their right (as well as the law's) to interpret the meaning of psychoactive drug use is persistently contested by people who go on thinking of it as recreation. This challenge has had little effect on formal regulations but a strong effect on informal attitudes, especially since it came into the open in the 1960s. The change came about partly because of a general loss of respect for established institutions and partly as a penalty for professional and government overreaching, especially where marihuana was concerned.

The movement to prohibit alcohol illustrates well how the medical or consumerist side and the moralistic side of drug regulation have been separated and joined at different times and for different purposes. We have always had fewer effective fixed prejudices about alcohol than about other psychoactive drugs and more socially acceptable ways of looking at alcohol problems; alcohol has always been a respectable pleasure as well as a vice and a medical problem, so policy debates have been unusually open and free.

The distinction between drug laws as health and social reform measures and drug laws as symbolic cultural domination is reflected in the way the history of the prohibition movement has been written. Historians during the Prohibition era itself emphasized the progressive and reformist character of the new law. Charles and Mary Beard, writing in 1927, denied that Prohibition was puritan tyranny; Samuel Eliot Morrison and Henry Steele Commager, in a very popular history textbook published in 1930, called it "the most notable of all reforms" of the Progressive generation (Paulson 1973, p. 2). Soon after repeal a reaction set in, and it became standard to regard advocates of prohibition as moralistic fanatics bent on spoiling other people's innocent pleasures. Terms such as "pseudoreform," "status politics," "rural-evangelical virus" (Hofstadter 1955), and "symbolic crusade" (Gusfield 1963) became popular. Prohibitionists were pictured as wanting to impose their provincial, nativistic conception of propriety and self-discipline on the urban, foreign-born, and working-class populations. They were said to be seeking a symbolic victory to compensate for a loss of real power and prestige – a reaffirmation of a way of life that was doomed. The purpose of Prohibition was not instrumental but expressive; that is, its effectiveness was less important than its symbolic and emotional valence. The movement was reactionary and tinged with hysteria and sadism. Alcohol itself was largely a token, an object for displacement of inchoate anxieties. Prohibitionists were projecting what they feared in themselves onto outsiders and repressing it (Sinclair 1962).

This folklore of Prohibition first developed among the more articulate drinking classes during the 1920s. Its most eloquent proponent was H. L. Mencken, politically conservative and derisive about democracy. He summed it up: "A prohibitionist is the sort of man one wouldn't care to drink with – even if he drank." The journalist Franklin P. Adams observed, in a famous verse response to the report of President Hoover's commission on alcohol prohibition:

> It's left a trail of filth and slime;
> It's filled the land with vice and crime;
> It don't prohibit worth a dime.

This opinion of the effects (probably incorrect) made it easier to criticize the prohibitionists' motives as mean, naive, or self-deluded. Later sociological and historical studies elaborated the view more decorously and less polemically – in a more deadpan way.

We all know that alcohol abuse produces disease, accidents, crime, family conflict, and social chaos – effects that would be considered bad under any cultural definition and whatever the symbolic resonances of drinking. And yet for a long time, historians would hardly admit that the prohibitionists' intentions might have borne any rational relationship to these evils. It was as though they were concerned with something quite different from what draws the attention of serious people to alcohol problems today. But a revisionist trend began in the 1960s, and now some historians emphasize the serious concern for health and family life, moral universalism, faith in science and democracy, and utopian social hopes that influenced the Prohibition movement (Paulson 1973; Blocker 1976; Clark 1976).

In fact, provincial moralism and a more universalistic reform impulse were interwoven, often inextricably, in the Prohibition movement, as in all campaigns for the suppression of pleasure drugs. But in other antidrug campaigns, we tend to underestimate the influence of provincial moralism; in antialcohol campaigns, we are more inclined to ignore or explain away the serious effort at social reform. Maybe this is a situation in which too much of the history has been written by the victors; it would do no harm to examine the losing side more sympathetically.

The public campaign against alcohol abuse affected all northern European and Anglo-Saxon countries in the nineteenth and early twentieth centuries. It was a large and complicated movement that started with a crusade for voluntary temperance, then abstinence, and sometimes developed into a drive for government restrictions on alcohol production and sales: passbooks, licensing, nationalization, and finally selective or total prohibition. The Gothenburg system for regulation of spirits (city control of bars, restricted hours, no profits on alcohol) was introduced in Sweden in 1865 and made obligatory in 1905. The Bratt system of individual passbooks for liquor consumption was established in 1919, and liquor stores were nationalized in 1922. Finland imposed national prohibition between 1919 and 1932. Canadians voted for prohibition province by province up to 1919, but then reverted to local option on alcohol sales. England had a serious temperance movement that turned toward prohibition in the 1870s. All of these movements were similar in their social roots, ideologies, and historical development. The U.S. prohibition drive was not unique or uniquely pathological. The campaign against alcohol was a reform movement, often a radical one, associated with other radical causes: social justice, industrial reform, women's suffrage, and, in both Great Britain and the United States, antislavery. It also had much in common with other antidrug movements, especially the crusade against the opium trade, although it faced a much bigger problem and much greater social obstacles.

In medieval England, drunkenness was a matter for the ecclesiastical courts; like other moral issues, it was left to the church. By the fourteenth century there were penalities against the clergy for drunkenness, and laws covering breach of the peace were sometimes used against public intoxication. Taxes, tariffs, licensing laws, and statutes fixing the price and quality of alcoholic drinks were also in effect. There were no secular laws against laymen's drunkenness until an Act of Parliament passed in 1606 allowed local common law courts to punish it. The colonies adopted the English common law system and introduced their own variations. There were the usual licensing, tax, and other regulations, and laws against public and even private drunkenness. Some colonies enacted special laws, usually ineffective, against the sale of alcohol to Indians (to prevent disturbances) or to apprentices and sailors (to preserve property rights in their services). Old records show the same alcohol problems and even more or less the same range of proposed answers that we find today; here not much has changed.

Americans developed a reputation for alcoholic intemperance in the first fifty years after the founding of the Republic; those generations drank more than any before or since. The best estimate is that per capita alcohol consumption in 1830 was two and a half times what it is today, even though drinking is now at a high for this century. Men (and boys) did most of the early-nineteenth-century drinking, and most of it was spirits, especially whiskey. Between 1772 and 1802, consumption of spirits rose from 2.5 to 5 gallons per person per year. The United States before the Civil War was notorious for drinking binges and horrendous drunken degradation of the kind represented by Huck Finn's father in Mark Twain's novel. The alcohol industry was economically important; much of the country's grain production went into the distilleries. Alcohol taxes were intensely resented on the frontier as class legislation. The Whiskey Rebellion of 1794, which forced George Washington to order troops to western Pennsylvania, was an uprising by frontier farmers against a federal excise tax on whiskey. The tax was repealed in 1802, after the Federalist party of Washington and Hamilton fell from power (Rorabaugh 1979).

Licentious drinking habits evoked a public response in the temperance movement that began in the late eighteenth century and became more powerful and more radical after 1830. One of the earliest prominent temperance reformers was the Quaker radical, pacifist, and abolitionist Anthony Benezet, who was especially concerned about the damage liquor did to Negroes and Indians. It was also at this time that the physicians Benjamin Rush and Thomas Trotter began to write seriously about alcoholism; Trotter's study of 1804 is sometimes said to be the first publication treating alcohol abuse as a disease. Although religion in one form or another was the most powerful impulse for temperance reform, it was not an evangelical reaction against Catholics, an Anglo-Saxon reaction against immigrants, or a rural response to urbanism. The nativist Know-Nothing party of the 1850s, for example, gave no consistent support to prohibition.

The movement preceded any significant industrialization and was joined by members of all social classes. It began in the Northeast and was mainly a middle-class and urban or at least small-town phenomenon, rather than a rural one, right up to the twentieth century. It attracted skilled workers, small manufacturers, professionals, and modernizing farmers (Tyrell 1979). For a time, beer and wine were thought to be better than spirits (temperance advocates soon became disillusioned with this notion). Drunkenness was regarded at first mainly as a personal moral problem, to be solved by education, self-discipline, or religious self-purification rather than laws – a position that Mill still held in 1859, when many reformers had abandoned it. The temperance reformers were promoting security, rationality, orderly work habits, and family stability (Rorabaugh 1979).

Disillusionment with voluntary change soon set in. Americans began to drink less whiskey and more beer after 1830, but that seemed to make little difference. Interest turned from temperance to abstinence and then to legal restraints. Prohibition laws of varying severity were passed in several states in the 1840s and 1850s and then repealed: the so-called first wave of prohibition. Mill used them as bad examples in *On Liberty*. Instead of pledge taking and appeals to self-respect, the movement was now calling for state action; the change implied a new view of the citizen's relation to society.

In some of its supporters' dreams, prohibitionism took on a messianic quality: A revolution in human habits would transform society and produce a new birth of liberty and justice. Many abolitionists favored prohibition, including the most famous of them, William Lloyd Garrison. Abolitionists drew an analogy between the two causes; after emancipation one of them, Gerrit Smith, spoke of drinkers as "millions of our voluntary slaves who still cling to their chains" (Sinclair 1962, p. 82). The men who founded the Prohibition party in 1869 regarded it as the true heir to abolitionism.

Temperance reform was even more closely allied with the movement for women's rights and suffrage. Some preliterate societies exercise little control over male drinking because the women, who suffer most from it, have low status and little power (Lemert 1967). Women's rights leaders like Susan B. Anthony and Frances Willard of the Women's Christian Temperance Union (WCTU) pointed out that in Europe and the United States too, women often had to bear the burden of male drunkenness and suffer the hegemony of that quintessentially male supremacist institution, the saloon. The sisterhood of the WCTU was meant to serve partly as a counterweight to the fellowship of the saloon bar. Willard said that she was working to liberate white slaves (women), wage slaves, and whiskey slaves. The alliance between women's rights and the campaign against alcohol was international; the Universal Suffrage Association, founded in Sweden in 1890, united women's rights, socialist, and temperance groups.

Many temperance reformers and prohibitionists thought restraints on the use of alcohol to be necessary for democracy itself. Before the Civil War, elections were sometimes bought with whiskey. After it, brewers and distillers formed alliances with other reactionary groups to work against women's suffrage and other reforms. By the late nineteenth century, most saloons were tied houses, controlled (through mortgages) by monopolistic liquor distributors. The liquor industry strongly influenced the corrupt politics of the Gilded Age, especially by supplying graft to party machines. In 1884 almost two-thirds of the one thousand Republican and Democratic party political conventions were held in saloons.

The campaign against alcohol, like other antidrug campaigns, was also a movement for public health reform. Often parallels were drawn between drunkenness and cholera, the most terrifying epidemic disease of the nineteenth century; like cholera, alcohol abuse was regarded as a symptom of social disorder as well as a disease – something that required indirect solutions. The teaching of physiology and hygiene in public schools was promoted mainly by temperance reformers and prohibitionists; much more space in school textbooks was devoted to the dangers of alcohol in the 1880s than in the 1930s. (Sometimes lurid misinformation was introduced into this educational material – for example, the assertion that alcohol could burn the throat or cause spontaneous combustion in a drunkard. Parallels with more recent antidrug campaigns are evident.)

The temperance movement in Scandinavia, the British Empire, and the United States eventually worked out a critique of free trade and the night-watchman state. In England, early temperance reformers actually thought that a free market – what was known as "free licensing" – would be better than the existing system of government favoritism, which they associated with the corrupt old regime of aristocratic privilege, poor work habits, and lax morality (Harrison 1971). Their belief that this change would reduce alcohol abuse was soon dispelled, and the political philosophy that came to dominate the British temperance movement was best articulated by Mill's great opponent, T. H. Green, who had a strong personal interest in the problem because his brother was an alcoholic. Green's "Lecture on Liberal Legislation and Freedom of Contract," first delivered in 1880, became an important text for the campaign. He recommended prohibition (by local option) on the same grounds as factory acts, health regulations, and laws to protect tenant farmers. Absolute freedom of contract had to be abridged to maintain the conditions for the free exercise of human powers. We must take men as we find them, Green said, rather than treat them as though existing conditions allowed them to live according to an ideal of autonomy. The degradation of drunkenness, like factory abuses and tenancy arrangements detrimental to agriculture, would be perpetuated if the solution were left to casual benevolence, education, and persuasion (Green 1900). It is the familiar argument for enforcing positive liberty.

But with it, all of the old questions about positive liberty arise. It can be asked what interests are really served by laws that deny people the right to make a choice about alcohol, supposedly for their own good or society's. Anthony Benezet's motives for wanting to protect Indians and blacks from liquor may have been irreproachable, but that cannot be said of masters who wanted to get more work out of their slaves or local governments that wanted less trouble from nearby Indians. Like cocaine, whiskey was sometimes regarded as a "Negro" problem by late-nineteenth-century prohibitionists who were also racist. To appeal to manufacturers and landowners, prohibition propaganda mentioned industrial discipline and the danger of pauperism; that was one reason Mill was suspicious of it. The saloon was sometimes vicious and sordid, but it also served the workingman as a union hall, labor exchange, and center of social life.

So the temperance movement sometimes had an undemocratic undertone, with members of the middle class deciding that the poor could not both drink and work. Would prohibition be good for workers and the poor, or would it take away one of their few pleasures? This has always been an issue in drug control. James I put a 4,000 percent customs duty on tobacco in 1604; he hoped to keep the poor from smoking the weed and becoming "riotous." Periodic bans on the sale of gin in eighteenth-century England had the same purpose. The first state prohibition law, forbidding the retail sale of spirits, was passed in Massachusetts in 1838; it was repealed in 1840 after a campaign in which the opposition insisted that it favored the rich, who could afford to buy in bulk. Prohibitionists were naturally sarcastic about the liquor interests' concern for the poor, but it remains true that most forms of drug and alcohol control weigh more heavily on people with less money, and often are designed to do so. This ambiguity in the prohibitionists' notion of liberation allowed a group of brewers and distillers to set up an organization called the Personal Liberty League in 1880.

Especially after 1890, the most powerful prohibition organizations began to adopt (in the words of Joseph R. Gusfield) a "coercive" rather than an "assimilative" attitude toward drinkers (Gusfield 1963). The change was marked by the passage of leadership from the Prohibition party (founded 1869) and the WCTU (founded 1874) to the Anti-Saloon League (founded 1895). The Prohibition party was not leading a one-issue crusade; it was probably the most important reform political organization in the country during the Gilded Age. Although not radical, it favored many changes that were a threat to vested economic interests. Just as abolitionists denounced churches that compromised on slavery, prohibitionists denounced church compromise with the liquor interests. In the 1890s, the Prohibition party lost its more radical constituency to the Populists and its more conservative constituency to the Anti-Saloon

League, which made no broad reform demands but concentrated on alcohol alone. The Anti-Saloon League was led mostly by upper-middle-class people in middle-sized towns and cities. It operated as a centralized, politically manipulative pressure group, appealed to conservative churches, avoided direct attacks on the liquor industry, and sometimes introduced a touch of anti-immigrant prejudice (Blocker 1976, 1979).

It is hard to tell why national prohibition succeeded in Finland and the United States but nowhere else in northern Europe or the British Empire. Finland's parliament passed the prohibition law shortly after the country achieved independence from Russia and became a republic; the law was associated with a new beginning in politics. In the United States, a puritan social messianism, a dream of human perfection, may have been more powerful than it was elsewhere. The drive for national prohibition began in earnest in 1913 after limited success in state referenda. Between 1900 and 1918 there were forty-nine state referendum votes. Before 1912, five of fourteen favored prohibition; after 1912, twenty-five of thirty-five. These were mostly in the less populous states and proposed only a limited form of prohibition. Still, by 1917, half of the states had some form of prohibition, usually a ban on spirits only. Despite the lobbying of the Anti-Saloon League, in the end Prohibition was not imposed merely by a militant minority seeking cultural dominance; it was probably a more popular cause than women's suffrage, which was enacted into law at about the same time.

The limited reach of Prohibition (for example, fruit juice could be legally fermented at home, and the sale of distilling equipment was never outlawed) and its spotty enforcement are sometimes cited as evidence that prohibitionists sought mainly a symbolic victory rather than a real decline in the use of alcohol. But that is probably a misunderstanding of their intentions and the magnitude of their utopian hopes. Prohibitionists did not place their faith in the law alone; they thought that destruction of the saloon system (which Prohibition did achieve), along with other advances in civilization, would lead to a gradual fading of the appetite for alcohol. President Hoover has often been ridiculed for calling Prohibition "an experiment noble in intent," but there was nothing intrinsically foolish about that statement. His mistake was not to admit that the experiment had failed in the simple sense that the public had turned against it. A legend has developed on the assumption that if it failed in this way, it must have been wrong in every possible way. Many histories tell us that drinking and its dangers became worse and that organized crime gained extraordinary wealth and power. Prohibition was "the skeleton at the feast, a grim reminder of the moral frenzy that so many wished to forget, a ludicrous caricature of the Yankee-Protestant notion that it is both possible and desirable to moralize private life through public action" (Hofstadter 1955, pp. 289–90).

But this description itself is a caricature. Although Prohibition was laxly enforced, especially in the areas where it was most unpopular, the law was not ignored; for example, in 1930, 4,000 out of 12,000 inmates of federal prisons were there for liquor trafficking. The law apparently did make it inconvenient to get alcohol and therefore reduced the amount of drinking. Cirrhosis of the liver became much less common. Yearly per capita consumption of alcohol in gallons has been estimated as 2.6 in 1906–10, 1.69 in 1911–14, 0.97 in 1918–19, at the start of Prohibition, 0.73 in 1921–22, 1.14 in 1927–30, and 0.97 in 1934, just as Prohibition ended; by 1940 it was up to 1.56, and today it is 2.6 (Clark 1976).

Admittedly, estimates are uncertain for the Prohibition era; the decline began even before national Prohibition was imposed; and alcohol use also fell off during those years in other countries without Prohibition. It may also be significant that alcohol consumption was lowest in the early years of Prohibition, rather than later on, when the enforcement machinery was putting more people in prison. Still, for whatever reason, the 1920s were apparently the low point rather than the high point of alcohol abuse in U.S. history. Most people never saw a speakeasy, and the publicity given to the conspicuous drinking habits of a few young people of the middle and upper classes created a misleading impression. The poor especially drank much less, apparently because alcohol became relatively expensive. The Wickersham Commission, appointed by President Hoover to investigate the enforcement problem, concluded that Prohibition had probably been good for the health of the poor. There is not even any substantial evidence that Prohibition produced a new wave of lawlessness, apart from the newly created illegality of alcohol trafficking. Organized vice and crime had always been associated with the legal saloon system; the chief business of organized crime was then and still is gambling. Al Capone, the prototypical 1920s gangster, did run a business smuggling beer from Canada, but most of his income and power came from gambling and loan sharking. It is not at all clear whether the history of organized crime would have been much different or its growth much slower if there had been no Volstead Act (Burnham 1968–9).

Prohibition was repealed not because of its scandals, inefficiencies, and nasty side effects (these were never considered good reasons to repeal other drug laws) but because tastes were changing as the middle class became less puritan. People decided that they wanted legal alcohol and found ways to justify the desire. Before the Civil War, William Lloyd

Garrison could make an analogy between the liberation of slaves and the liberation of drunkards. By 1930 Nicholas Murray Butler, the president of Columbia University, was comparing the repeal movement to abolitionism (Sinclair 1962, p. 361). But repeal was not brought about mainly by new ideas of personal liberty. The lobby for repeal was supported by hotel and real estate interests and led by a group called the Association Against the Prohibition Amendment (AAPA), which included a DuPont and John D. Rockefeller, Jr. on its board of directors. The campaign emphasized benefits that seemed attractive in a country suffering from economic depression: taxes, jobs, and the elimination of enforcement costs.

When the AAPA reconstituted itself after repeal as the Liberty League to oppose the Roosevelt government's social programs, it became the president's favorite target of attack and soon collapsed; support for repeal did not mean general opposition to state interference in the economy or a nineteenth-century ideological liberalism. It is no accident that new theories of alcoholism as a disease, developed by AA and the Yale School of Alcohol Studies in the 1930s, emphasized the susceptibility of particular persons rather than the plague germ of alcohol itself. The rhetorical assault on other drugs might continue, but alcohol would no longer be regarded as a menace to society as a whole.

The process that began around 1900 and was completed by the Prohibition experiment eliminated most of the symbolic resonances of the alcohol problem. Today a culturally reactionary movement such as the Moral Majority takes no special interest in alcohol as a moral issue. But prohibitionism also lost its association with other progressive reform movements in Europe and the United States. India offers an interesting contrast; there the Congress party under Gandhi struggled for women's rights and Moslem–Hindu friendship, and opposed British rule, the caste system, alcohol, and opium. The goals of temperance, equality, social cohesion, and democracy were united as they had been in the European and American prohibition movements of the nineteenth century (Paulson 1973, pp. 175–84).

The war against alcohol was produced by the same social changes that provoked the war against opium and other drugs. It involved the same mixture of social and health reform, class interests, and symbolic cultural conflict; the campaign against alcohol was neither more nor less driven by "moral frenzy" than other antidrug movements. Similar medical redefinitions were required; doctors began to think of alcoholism as a disease at about the same time, and in the same at first hesitant way, that they began to define other drug abuse problems as disease. But unlike opium and cocaine, alcohol was not an exotic substance with powers that were frightening because mysterious. It was too familiar to be branded with the narcotic stigma and too closely associated with innocent fun in too many respectable people's minds to be purely a drug menace. Penalties for purchase and possession of alcohol were never imposed, much less enforced. Alcohol use was never reduced to the categories of medicine and vice. The Wickersham Commission concluded that true enforcement of alcohol prohibition was impossible without either religious sanctions or methods intolerable in a liberal democracy, and it admitted that in this respect the only difference between alcohol and other drugs ("narcotics") was public opinion. Here the dream of enforcing positive liberty by law had to be abandoned.

As the Liberty League found out, Prohibition was not rejected because of any theory of state control and liberalism, but because lawmakers finally made a muddled adjustment to persistent public sentiment. Other drugs have always been regarded differently by the public, so government control over them has steadily increased. The temperance movement had difficulty choosing between voluntary self-help and public control as a solution to the alcohol problem – thus its hesitations, backward turnings, and abortive experimentation. By now the Western countries have come down firmly against serious legal restraints. On the control of other drugs, there was little wavering; from the late nineteenth century on, it was not remotely likely that freedom to use them would be included among the rights of classical liberalism.

The international opium trade and most legal opiate use succumbed in the early twentieth century to a long campaign that paralleled the Prohibition movement and was allied with it. The antiopium crusade opposed customary vices, established economic interests and free-market doctrine in the name of public health, morality, and social reform. Like the temperance campaign, it raised questions about liberty and legal moralism. The outcome differed partly because, as a federal judge observed in 1886 while invalidating a Portland, Oregon, city ordinance on opium smoking, "Opium is not our vice" (Bonnie and Whitebread 1974, p. 14); that was one reason we were more likely to go to extremes in our desire to suppress it or to harass those who practiced it.

Well into the nineteenth century, many respectable people considered opium no worse than alcohol. In Europe and the United States, it was freely available and no more expensive than aspirin is today. Moderate habitual use of opium in the form of laudanum was not necessarily considered addiction, and many people regarded addiction itself as less dangerous to individual and social health than alcoholism. In any case, it was rare in the West until the late nineteenth century. Opium smoking, which was common only in China, became a moral and political issue much earlier.

The history of the opium trade conducted by the British government between India and China illustrates the conflicts that arose in an era when the principles of drug control that seem natural today were still struggling for social dominance. Opium had been used in the Far East for thousands of years, but the habit of smoking it apparently began to spread only after tobacco smoking was introduced from Spanish America in the seventeenth century. The import trade was organized first by Arabs and then by Europeans. Imperial China seems to have been the first nation to define opium use as a serious social problem; the emperor issued edicts against it in 1729 and 1799, but enforced them halfheartedly.

In the eighteenth century, England became the dominant power in India, ruling largely through the East India Company, a joint stock trading company that had been operating in Asia since it was chartered by Elizabeth I. The government of Bengal, which was under direct British control, licensed the cultivation of opium, bought it at a monopoly price, refined it, and sold it at auction in Calcutta, taking the profit. Opium transported to Bombay from the western areas of India under indirect British rule was subject to a transit tax. The government of India in the mid-nineteenth century drew a sixth of its revenues from this crop. Private buyers transported the drug to China, where they anchored their ships offshore at Canton and transferred it to Chinese smuggling boats. Chinese officials took bribes from merchants and connived at the contraband traffic.

In the 1820s and 1830s, as opium imports increased, the Chinese government responded more seriously. The demoralizing physical and mental effects of the drug were exacerbated by the debilitating financial effects of the trade. The British wanted China's tea and silk, but had little to offer in exchange. Since the Chinese were not interested in British manufactures, only the sale of opium kept the British treasury from being drained of gold and silver to pay for Chinese products; even so, the balance of trade was unfavorable to Great Britain throughout the first half of the nineteenth century. But the Chinese did not like to lose any precious metals at all in exchange for opium. Some factions in the imperial government therefore recommended legalizing the drug to collect taxes on it, but in 1838 the emperor instead decided to send an honest commissioner to Canton to suppress the commerce. Opium belonging to British merchants was destroyed, and a conflict followed that is now known as the Opium War. The British attacked several Chinese coastal cities, and the Chinese quickly capitulated. By the Treaty of Nanking in 1842, Hong Kong was ceded to Great Britain and five Chinese ports were opened to British trade and residence. Other Western powers soon received similar privileges. Opium smuggling was allowed to continue as before. China did not comply fully with the provisions of the treaty it had been forced to sign, and the seizure of a British merchant ship in 1856 precipitated another war, which ended in 1860 after British and French troops occupied Peking. China now promised to open more ports to European trade, allow foreign legations in Peking, permit Christian missionary activity, and legalize the importation of opium.

These events are sometimes described by saying that the British forced opium on the Chinese. But from the point of view of European governments, the aim of the Opium War and the conflict of 1856–60 was to make China accept the same rules of commerce and diplomacy that Europeans followed among themselves, and treat the representatives of European nations respectfully, as equals rather than barbarian interlopers. The former president of the United States, John Quincy Adams, said that opium figured in the Opium War in the same way that tea figured in the Boston Tea Party; some of the British, oddly, thought of themselves as defending a principle.

Although many people in Europe were slightly ashamed of the traffic and regarded opium smoking as a vice, it had not yet become a powerful moral issue except for a few progressive reformers and missionaries. Defenders of the trade could plausibly say that opium was no worse than gin or whiskey; only a minority of opium smokers were demoralized and degraded addicts, just as only a minority of drinkers were drunkards. Evidence from modern opium-smoking areas suggests that this was true (Kramer 1982). It was also plausible to say that the opium trade would have continued even without the Opium War, given local demand and the weakness and corruption of the imperial government. The Chinese rulers were often told that it was their problem; if the Chinese people did not want the drug, there would be no market for it. The government should either suppress the buying and selling of opium within China or educate the people out of the habit, as temperance reformers were educating Europeans out of the alcohol habit. Imperial China could be seen as an autocratic and corrupt government making sporadic and insincere efforts to enforce a law that its people would not accept. In fact, by the 1850s, China had given up on prohibition; the government willingly accepted legalization and the tax revenues that went with it.

John Stuart Mill was involved in the opium controversy by virtue of his position as a clerk in the London office of the East India Company, where he worked from 1823 to 1858. In 1856 he became chief of the examiner's office, a job his father had also held. It was his duty to write executive orders to the government in India on political subjects; he fulfilled many of the functions of a secretary of state. In 1857 Indian soldiers of the army in Bengal mutinied, and a general uprising followed. After it was put down, the Crown assumed direct rule, despite Mill's eloquent defense of the East India Company's administration (Packe 1954).

The East India Company was removed from power in 1858, the same year that China signed the first treaty legalizing the opium trade. *On Liberty* was completed in 1857 and published in 1859. When Mill defended paternalistic despotism for backward peoples, he was probably thinking of India. When he defended the opium trade in the name of the opium smoker's liberty, he presumably meant either that the Chinese were not backward in this sense, or else that the Chinese government should have taken paternal responsibility for suppressing opium without making demands on the British. It is easy to see how Mill's service in the government of India might have influenced his views on freedom of choice for the Chinese. He was not a hypocrite, and he was never formally inconsistent on this subject, but he was forced by his own and his nation's history into the curious position of defending the freedom of the Chinese to indulge a dubious taste against the opposition of their own autocratic rulers, while himself serving another despotic government that derived profit from supplying that taste.

The campaign to prohibit cultivation of opium in India for export gained strength after the China trade was legalized. The Chinese government still formally expressed disapproval of the imports, but China began to grow its own opium. Cultivation was legalized in the 1860s, and by 1885 two-thirds of the opium consumed in China was produced there (Owen 1934, p. 266). Revenue from the India trade began to lose its importance for Great Britain after 1880. Opium prohibitionists forced the appointment of a Royal Commission that studied the Indian cultivation and manufacturing system from 1893 to 1895. Its report contained 2,500 pages of testimony in which evidence for varying opinions could be found. The commission concluded that the system was a fairly good one that derived maximum revenue from minimum consumption. It said that in any case, the dangers of opium had been exaggerated (this was true; even the most sensible antidrug campaigns always seem to feature lurid exaggeration). Reformers rejected the conclusions as biased by the commission's complicity with the government of India.

Ten years later, heightened public conscience and lowered public revenue made opium prohibition an idea whose time had come. In 1906 the Chinese began to reduce the area of cultivation, close opium dens, and establish a maintenance system for addicts. The British agreed to cut down imports. The republic established in China after the revolution of 1911 extended the antiopium measures taken by its predecessor. The last Indian opium reached China in 1913, and the last imported opium in stock was burned in 1919.

The India trade had ended for good, but despite the government's efforts, cultivation of opium in China went on through the years of internal chaos, civil war, and foreign invasion that followed. Opium smoking was not eliminated until the Communists took control in 1949 and established the first strong central government China had had in many years. Even without imports from India, Chinese addicts (and other opium smokers) found ways to provide themselves with the drug until they were educated or coerced into abandoning the habit by a resolute reforming despotism within China itself. History tends to confirm the opinion of those who said in the nineteenth century that international drug traffic was not the cause of the opium problem in China but a result of it.

Western nations became less tolerant of the opium habit as it began to spread in Europe and especially in the United States. While the opium traffic between India and China declined and the Prohibition movement became stronger in northern Europe and North America, the United States began an attempt to impose strict international controls on narcotics. A series of international conferences at The Hague from 1911 to 1914 drew up a convention that provided for restrictions on the manufacture and distribution of opiates but left the details mostly to domestic legislation; soon afterward the United States passed the Harrison Narcotics Act. The Hague Convention was made part of the Treaty of Versailles in 1919; international control had been fully accepted, at least in theory. Since then, the League of Nations and the United Nations have made a series of arrangements culminating in the United Nations Single Convention on Narcotic Drugs of 1961. This treaty came into force in 1964, setting detailed requirements for the control of opiate manufacture and distribution by the ratifying governments, most of which already had their own highly restrictive laws.

In the United States, concern about narcotics began to mount when vagrants and criminals on the West Coast took up the opium habit from Chinese indentured laborers. San Francisco passed a law against opium dens in 1878; in 1909 the importation of smoking opium was prohibited. The opiate preparations most commonly used in the United States were at first treated more leniently, because most users were middle-class whites (the majority were women). But gradually all opiates came to seem dangerous, and restrictions were introduced, first at the local and state levels and then at the national level. The Harrison Act of 1914 placed all trade in opiates under the jurisdiction of the Bureau of Internal Revenue in the Treasury Department. Every dealer in narcotics and every doctor who prescribed them had to register, record all transactions, and pay a nominal tax (so that the right of Congress to raise revenue could be used as a constitutional justification for the law). A doctor could prescribe opiates only in the pursuit of his professional practice. In form the act was very mild; the police powers granted to the federal government were only implied. But the Treasury Department was able to get the Supreme Court to rule, in the *Doremus* and *Webb* cases (1919) and the *Behrman* case (1923), that addict maintenance was not properly part of professional practice and therefore violated the Harrison Act. After a brief experiment with clinics dispensing opiates in 1920–1 (in Shreveport, Louisiana, until 1923), addicts no longer had a legitimate source of the drug. The problem was defined as a criminal one in 1920 when narcotics enforcement was turned over to Prohibition agents by the establishment of the Narcotic Division of the Treasury Department's Prohibition Unit; this definition faced little opposition until the 1950s. In the 1930s most states made opiate possession a criminal offense by passing the Uniform Narcotic Drugs Act, and many made addiction itself a crime.

A change in medical attitudes followed the change in government policy. When the Harrison Act was passed, many doctors thought that addiction could be cured by supervised withdrawal. The Treasury Department's policy of treating maintenance as an illegitimate professional practice was based on that assumption. When it became clear that there was no easy cure for addiction, the whole medical approach came under suspicion. Even the abstinence syndrome was sometimes said to be psychological in origin. A new kind of criminal addict had become highly visible, and it was now plausible to regard addiction as a vice rather than a disease. This retreat of the medical model and the medical profession had important effects. In the *Linder* case (1925) and the *Boyd* case (1926), the Supreme Court modified its rulings against maintenance, allowing prescription of opiates if the doctor acted in good faith "for relief of a condition incident to addiction" – that is, abstinence symptoms. But by that time doctors were wary of prescribing for addicts anyway, not only because of the law but also because they were such demanding, dishonest, and troublesome patients.

The character of addicts had begun to change in the 1890s as doctors became more conscious of the dangers of opium and introduced new painkillers. The Harrison Act would not have been possible without this decline in medical use and may have had only a minor independent effect.

There were probably fewer opiate addicts in 1920 than in 1895, but the social problems they created, both real and fancied, were greater (Courtwright 1982). Except for the federal narcotics hospitals established at Lexington and Fort Worth, the disease concept of addiction was not reflected again in government policy until the 1950s and 1960s.

The United States has a more serious narcotics problem than other industrial countries, but the principles of control in the twentieth century have been similar everywhere. England, for example, began to pass restrictive narcotics laws before the United States. The British system of addict maintenance by individual doctors, which lasted from 1926 to 1967, has often been cited as an alternative to the U.S. system. But the British preserved this arrangment only as long as addiction was a minor problem, affecting only a few hundred people. Even under the old system, no one had a right to receive opiates; the choice of whether to treat was the doctor's alone. In the 1950s and 1960s addiction began to rise, a black market in narcotics developed, and a new kind of addict appeared – younger, more manipulative, and criminal; in 1967 clinics were established in place of the individual prescription system. Great Britain now has about 1,000 opiate addicts; it has been estimated that a clinic system of the same quality as the one introduced in Great Britain in 1967 would require 1,500 clinics, 2,300 psychiatrists, and 4,000 nurses for New York City alone (Judson 1975, p. 95). Anyway, most of the British clinics have now shifted from intravenous heroin maintenance to oral methadone, the synthetic opiate that prevents a withdrawal reaction without producing a heroinlike intoxication. The present British system resembles American methadone maintenance programs.

Government control over therapeutic drugs regarded as nonnarcotic developed more slowly and in a somewhat different way. Here the symbolic, cultural, and moral concerns were slight compared to the medical and consumer interest. But the trend has taken more or less the same direction as opiate laws; the assumption has been that authoritative knowledge about the efficacy and safety of drugs makes free individual choice illusory and pointless. The story has been described as a passage from "customary" to "command" regulation, with little space for "instrumental" regulation by consumer choice in a more or less free market (Temin 1980). In this interpretation, only the Pure Food and Drug Act, of all the federal drug laws in the United States, was designed to encourage instrumental behavior because it was the only law aimed at simple fraud – false statements about the contents of a drug preparation. The Bureau of Chemistry in the Department of Agriculture, set up to enforce this law, eventually became the Food and Drug Administration (FDA), which interpreted the Food, Drug and Cosmetics Act of 1938 so as to establish a class of drugs available only on prescription (just as the Bureau of Internal Revenue had administratively interpreted the Harrison Act to deny doctors the right to maintain addicts). An amendment passed in 1951 codified the distinction between prescription and nonprescription drugs into law and gave the FDA sole power to decide which drugs could be sold only on prescription.

This step only transferred power from consumers to doctors, who acted according to "customary" norms, the established practices of the profession. With many new prescription drugs coming onto the market, that seemed insufficient protection for consumers, so the government moved to decide which drugs would be made available to doctors. Amendments passed in 1962 gave the FDA considerably greater powers, and specifically allowed it to withdraw approval of a drug if there was no substantial evidence for its effectiveness. The evidence was to be judged by adequate and well-controlled investigations conducted by experts. Effectiveness was no longer a matter of opinion, including the ordinary doctor's opinion; even the medical market was unreliable.

"Well-controlled," "experts," and "effectiveness" were not yet carefully defined, so more restrictions were inevitable. In 1961–9 the FDA arranged for the National Academy of Science to conduct a Drug Efficacy Study. The scientific panel rejected as ineffective a certain fixed combination of antibiotics marketed by the Upjohn Company, and the FDA moved to ban it. Upjohn sued, but a federal court ruled that the company could not even get a hearing without presenting reasonable grounds. Commercial success – the general approval of doctors – did not constitute reasonable grounds because it did not constitute an adequate and well-controlled study. In 1970 the FDA issued regulations defining "adequate and well-controlled"; the most demanding form of experiment, with placebo control and double-blinding, was not required, but mere clinical experience without some quantitative comparisons was excluded (Temin 1980).

Safety was no longer the issue now. Doctors and patients alike were assumed to need protection from the dangers of wasting their money on prescription drugs. Even if fully informed, they would not be allowed to choose harmless drugs of unproven usefulness. Such extraordinarily strict rules are applied only in medicine; in other kinds of commerce, usefulness or efficaciousness is left mostly to individual judgment, and consumer regulations are supposed to protect us mainly against products that are unsafe.

There were many reasons to control "narcotics" strictly, but only one reason for strict controls on drugs defined as purely medicinal. Much depended on what was regarded as a narcotic. This problem gave rise to some anomalies at first, since the social classification of a drug did not depend entirely on its pharmacological effects or even on its attractiveness as a pleasure drug. Certain synthetic psychoactive drugs that had been developed and introduced under medical control in the twentieth century did not have the same disreputable aura as the natural drugs used for centuries by ordinary people. Barbiturates, amphetamines, and tranquilizers could be used for pleasure in a way that might create serious health and social problems, but for a long time they were handled legally in the same way as other prescription drugs. One odd result was that we had severe penalties for possession of marihuana and none for illicit possession of amphetamines and barbiturates, which are much more dangerous. (In the same way, opium smoking had been made illegal before the quasimedical opium use of the middle class.) The situation began to change in the 1960s, and the Comprehensive Drug Abuse Prevention and Control Act of 1970 finally subjected the synthetic psychoactive drugs, old and new, to the same regulations as the older natural drugs. It took a long time, because the law is often a conservative institution that preserves obsolete social distinctions. The major international drug conventions still formally distinguish between "narcotics" (opiates, cocaine, and marihuana) and "psychotropic drugs."

Technical progress is one reason for the new restrictions. In the second half of the nineteenth century, pure chemicals were isolated from many natural drugs, the hypodermic syringe made intravenous injection possible, and the manipulation of molecules to create synthetic drugs began. Since then, thousands of new drugs have been introduced, and mass production has supplied vast quantities of them for medical use. Mill's advocacy of free individual choice was more plausible in a time when few drugs were in use and so little was known about them that the average consumer might have as good a claim as anyone to judge their safety and usefulness. Things are much more complicated now, and social control of biological technology in general is more acceptable.

But the campaign against recreational drugs began (with alcohol and opium) before any important technological change; here a free market or control by custom seemed dangerous for reasons other than consumer ignorance of technical complexities. More important than any purely scientific development is the fact that in twentieth-century society, experience and behavior that are hard to classify make us anxious. Except for alcohol control, the present system of drug control has developed almost entirely in this century. Institutions have been created to impose certain legal and social categories that are different for different drugs. These rules may represent some collective historical wisdom, but we do not have an undivided good conscience about them. Political scientists doubt the validity of enforcing morality; sociologists talk of moral entrepreneurship, symbolic status wars, the creation of deviance by labeling, and the stigmatizing of unpopular groups. Many ordinary people simply refuse to take the laws very seriously.

Our society both needs and mistrusts the kind of rule that prevents people from acting in ways that have undesirable consequences for the quality of their own lives. Whether we think of these regulations as paternalistic or not, there is always some doubt whether education and protection are not just excuses for the domination of a majority's (or even a minority's) psychological needs or material interests. The complexity and diversity of modern societies make the basis of legal authority uncertain. Since there is no common morality or accepted idea of natural human ends, anything presented by one group as necessary for morals or social order can be rejected by others as prejudice and mystification. Cultural ideals may be poorly understood without prescriptions that establish models of conduct, and prescriptions must often be codified into laws. But once they are fixed in this way, it may become harder to reinterpret ideals for changed social circumstances. And where consensus has become weak, enforcement is likely to seem arbitrary.

As we noted in Chapter 1, a kind of solution is provided by the social and political institutions concerned with health, which have grown so much in scope and power in this century. Anyone living before 1800 would probably have found it hard to comprehend the notion of an international body called the World Health Organization assigned to such oddly assorted tasks as eradicating malaria and discouraging marihuana use. As long as anything involving drugs is a health issue, the political institutions dealing with drugs will not have to take much account of variations in habits and values. They will inevitably prefer authority to liberty, even when the authority of doctors over patients has to be transferred to a government that has learned that doctors themselves are unreliable.

Serious government and medical control over alcohol is so thoroughly discredited that we are hardly prepared to acknowledge even in historical retrospect that the temperance and prohibition movements were concerned with the same issues of health and safety as other drug control movements; we remember mainly the moralism and cultural conflict. In the case of ordinary medical drugs, there is no cultural conflict, so that effective controls are easily imposed. In the case of illicit pleasure drugs, controls came earlier and are still stricter, partly because symbolic and moral concerns as well as health and safety interests are involved. But in twentieth-century industrial democracies, it has become hard to impose rules of moral comportment even when they are also health and safety regulations, so these drug laws are hard to enforce and often shamelessly, guiltlessly flouted. In some cases (especially marihuana), the health and safety justifications for prohibition may appear to be largely a pretext, and this typical twentieth-century confusion about drug control takes on the appearance of pure hypocrisy.

4   Varieties of drug control

Assume a modern society not troubled by Mill's libertarian scruples, but also not torn by battles for cultural dominance or paralyzed by historically fixed definitions. What would be the most sensible ways for it to deal with the use of drugs? Obviously, the range of solutions is wide, and any society would have to use a mixture, but they can be assigned generally to two categories: informal prescriptions and sanctions and formal (mostly legal) ones. The distinction between informal and legal sanctions is not equivalent to the distinction between consensus and coercion. Even Mill included among threats to liberty the informal tyranny of majority opinion as well as formal acts of government. The law differs from social pressures not in coerciveness but in its use of explicit rules and penalties. Societies have differed vastly in the extent to which they manage drug use by legal compulsion as opposed to education, persuasion, and social pressure to act in accordance with accepted customs and values. A society like ours, complicated in organization and culturally diverse, with many strangers encountering one another or affecting one another's lives, is more likely to want and need formal rules (Turk 1972).

Where alcohol is concerned, there is still some serious argument about the virtues of legal versus informal controls, expressed in a debate between advocates of the integration or sociocultural model of alcohol control and those who favor the distribution of consumption model. The integration model proposes that the seriousness of a society's alcohol problem is independent of the total amount of alcohol consumed. Instead it depends on the informal arrangements and sanctions surrounding alcohol use: the occasions on which people use it, how children are taught about it, and so on. Alcohol should be properly integrated into daily life, used at family gatherings and at meals. Drinking should not become a center of attention; it should usually be subordinated to another activity that goes on at the same time. Both prescriptions and proscriptions for drinking should be clear. Drinking alone and drunken sprees should be discouraged by custom. Abstinence should be socially acceptable, but drinking should not be

99

material for moral enterprise. Feelings about alcohol should not oscillate between puritanism and license. Drinking lore should be transmitted from generation to generation; teachers and learners should not be the same age. If these intermediate social controls can be established, we will not need either state intervention or desperate appeals for individual restraint. Certain ethnic groups – Jews, Chinese, Greeks – are held up as model integrated drinkers with few alcohol problems.

Integration theorists have recommended such policies as advertising that shows families drinking together and education for responsible drinking. They have also proposed mild legal measures to help shape custom: taxes to make wine and beer relatively less expensive than liquor, licensing laws that discourage the sale of alcohol where no food is sold, suspending bartenders' licenses for serving drunks, and even a lowered drinking age, supposedly to prevent furtive and uncontrolled adolescent drinking (Wilkinson 1970). A few daring writers have also suggested integrated use as an approach to the control of illicit drugs (Harding and Zinberg 1977; Zinberg and Harding 1982).

Some theory and evidence support the integration model. For example, alcohol tends to narrow the range of attention and to impoverish conceptual thinking, so that the drinker notices a smaller variety of cues and may be more likely to respond immoderately or violently. A well-established drinking etiquette means fewer indeterminate cues, a secure cognitive framework for central environmental cues, and enough external cues to prevent chaotic impulses from dominating action (Pernaen 1976). Certain family attitudes toward alcohol seem to be related to later drinking problems among the children – especially situations in which one parent, usually the mother, is an abstainer and hostile to alcohol, and the other parent drinks too much. A smaller proportion of alcoholics than control subjects have parents who do not drink at all, but a larger proportion have parents who disagree about drinking (Wilkinson 1970).

But there are serious objections to the integration model. Certainly the example of France puts the virtues of integrated drinking in doubt. Drinking is highly integrated there; wine is drunk at meals, in most festival and ritual social situations, and as an accompaniment to many daily activities. Children learn to use it from their parents. Yet France has what is possibly the highest rate of chronic alcohol problems in the world and a high rate of acute alcohol abuse. In the case of parents who disagree about drinking and whose children grow up to be alcoholics, it is possible that the parents are in conflict mainly because one of them (usually the father) is an alcohol abuser, who passes on the tendency to his children either by heredity or by example. Even if these empirical difficulties can be evaded, there is likely to be a conceptual one. Unless you are very precise about what integrated drinking means, it is too easy to define it in such a way that it becomes incompatible with alcohol abuse. If integrated drinking means no more than moderate and disciplined drinking, that kind of alcohol use causes few problems by definition.

But the main objection to the integration or sociocultural model is that it suggests no policies that seem likely to be effective. The model has a certain common sense appeal; some ethnic and social groups or cultures manage to discipline their drinking and drug use without total abstinence. But this moderation is almost always the product of a long history, not current injunctions and instructions. It is doubtful how far drinking and drug-taking practices can be manipulated as a conscious policy. There is no simple way to identify how some group does it and to get others to emulate them. The usual suggestions for advertising, drug education in schools, encouraging the use of beer and wine instead of liquor, and so on appear to be very light ammunition against established customs that are deeply embedded in the life of a society. And in fact, they usually prove ineffective. The nineteenth-century temperance movement had to give up believing that beer is better than whiskey. Studies of drug and alcohol education generally fail to show that it changes anyone's behavior very much (Abrams et al. 1973). It is not misleading to say that most people who could profit from a formal drug education course do not need it, because they would learn how to control their drug use anyway.

Current education about illicit drugs is limited in effectiveness because whatever facts are taught, the message ultimately has to be never to use the drug at all. In some cases, the facts and the warning may be hard to reconcile, so that responsible, integrated drug use seems plausible by comparison. But deliberate education for responsible alcohol use has not been a great success, and it is doubtful whether the proposed reform of drug education (even if it were politically conceivable) would help much either. One kind of policy that sometimes works is a religious injunction; Mormons and Moslems have few alcohol problems. Maybe the integration model too would work best in a theocracy, but that is not what its advocates have in mind.

The greatest service of studies on the integration model has been to make it clear how illicit drug users establish "sanctions and rituals" (as Norman Zinberg calls them) that keep ill effects to a minimum. If advocates of the integration model for alcohol were consistent, they would have to recommend it for other drugs too. Except that they are established outside the law, informal social controls on illicit drug use are in principle no different from similar controls on drinking. They vary according to the properties of the drug; they include instructions for using the drug, sumptuary rules, social relations that encourage certain ways of using it, and informal sanctions enforcing the rules (Maloff et al. 1982). In a way, this should be obvious, but the reminder is necessary, since so many people have an image of illicit drug use as an uncontrolled epidemic of disease or criminality. The integration model can teach us to make necessary distinctions and not respond hysterically to all illicit drug use, but it does not tell us much about what to do when drugs and alcohol are abused.

Supporters of the distribution of consumption model believe that alcohol problems vary with the total amount of alcohol consumed in a society, and suggest that the best way to reduce alcohol abuse is to restrict the supply legally through pricing, taxing, and licensing (Popham et al. 1976). In particular, they say that the distribution of alcohol consumption in any population is unimodal (has a single peak) and, with proper mathematical adjustments, can be made to approximate a normal curve. Height, IQ, and many other features of a large population vary in a normal distribution. The shape of a normal curve is symmetrical; it depends only on the mean, which gives its height, and the standard deviation, which defines its spread. In general, whenever values of a variable differ from their mean because of many independently acting influences that sum to produce their effects, the resulting probability distribution is close to a normal curve.

The curve describing the consumption of alcohol by individuals in a population is actually not symmetrical but highly skewed to the right. This means that most people drink only a little alcohol and a few elevate the mean by drinking a great deal. In the United States, for example, 10 percent of the population uses 57 percent of the alcohol, and 20 percent uses 78 percent of the alcohol (Gerstein 1981). This kind of curve often appears when independent random variables combine as a product rather than as a sum to produce an effect. It is then known as a lognormal distribution. This means that the curve, which is highly skewed when plotted using the amount of alcohol consumed by each individual in the population, will be close to a normal curve when plotted using the logarithms of those amounts.

According to this model, the range of individual variation is more or less fixed (zero on one side, the limit of physical toleration on the other), and the shape of the curve depends only on the mean in a given population. If the average person drinks somewhat less, the heaviest users will drink a great deal less. That is true of any normal distribution; if the mean height in two populations is slightly different, the proportions of people more than six feet tall will differ enormously. The conclusion is that policies designed to cut total alcohol consumption will greatly reduce alcohol problems. There is no need to be selective or try to educate the populace. The most effective methods are restricted hours of sale and, above all, increased taxes.

A universal lognormal distribution would refute the integration model, which requires differences in the shape of the consumption curve in different societies. The number of heavy alcohol users or abusers should not necessarily be determined by the same forces that determine how much the average person drinks. Appropriate customs are supposed to ensure that almost everyone drinks moderately and almost no one drinks too much or not at all. It should be possible to find two societies in which the one with the greater average alcohol consumption has less serious drinking problems. The empirical and statistical assumptions of the distribution of consumption model have therefore been strongly challenged, and the challenge has engendered a complicated dispute about consumption measures, sampling, and statistical theory (Room 1978; Pittman 1980; Beauchamp 1980, pp. 102–11; Hunt 1982).

Whatever the precise shape of the consumption curves, there is strong evidence that raising the relative price of a drug or restricting access to it cuts down its use. Heroin addicts apparently adjust the size of their habit to the price of heroin; it is not true that they must have a certain daily dose at all costs (Goldman 1981). And one of the main reasons they stop taking heroin is that the drug becomes too hard to get (Vaillant 1970). England imposed a tax and sales control on gin in 1751 and reduced consumption from eleven million to two million gallons in a few years (Coffey 1966). When Finland liberalized its laws on beer in 1968–9, lowering the drinking age and allowing more outlets, alcohol use increased 46 percent per capita in the first year, and arrests for drunkenness rose substantially (Beauchamp 1980). As we have mentioned, alcohol consumption in 1918–23, at the start of Prohibition, is estimated as one-third of the 1913 average, and in 1927–30 as two-thirds of the 1913 average. Today the level of state taxes on alcohol is correlated with total consumption (Cook 1981). The price of alcohol is relatively low in France, where consumption is very high, and relatively high in Ireland, where (despite myths about Irish drinking) consumption is low. In the United States, the real cost of alcohol dropped substantially from 1960 to 1980 (by 48 percent for liquor, 27 percent for beer, and 18 percent for wine), and consumption rose greatly (Moore and Gerstein 1981, p. 68).

It also seems to be true that where the population as a whole uses less alcohol, there are fewer serious alcohol problems. The rate of cirrhosis of the liver in the United States was 21.5 per million in 1911 and 10.7

per million in 1929 (Aaron and Musto 1981). Between 1969 and 1979, consumption of wine and spirits doubled in Great Britain; so did the rate of alcoholism (Royal College 1979, p. 134). In American states where alcohol taxes are high, there are fewer drunken driving accidents as well as less cirrhosis (Cook 1981). During wartime, when alcohol is rationed, cirrhosis rates drop – for example, in occupied Paris during World War II (Kalant 1981). Countries and peoples held up as models of integrated drinking do not have a low level of alcohol problems unless the drinking level is also relatively low. Italy is often contrasted favorably to France for its sensible drinking customs, and it is true that conspicuous drunkenness and the homeless alcoholic are less common there; but Italy also has a high average consumption of alcohol, close to that of France, and a high level of serious chronic health problems, including cirrhosis. Israel, on the other hand, has few alcohol problems, not just because of integrated drinking but because its average alcohol consumption is the lowest in the industrialized West. Scandinavians, despite their reputation for lone drinking and bingeing, which integration theorists abhor, use little alcohol compared with most other Europeans and have relatively mild acute and chronic alcohol problems. Even if the relationship between per capita consumption and alcohol problems does not follow exactly the pattern suggested by the distribution of consumption model, there is much evidence that the relationship exists.

Does cutting down the supply of a drug simply cause its users to replace it with another drug? If marihuana smokers turn to alcohol or heroin when the price becomes higher, it might be better not to allow that to happen. The evidence is not entirely clear, but very commonly, at any rate, one drug is added to another rather than substituted for it, at least up to the limit of physiological toleration. In one study, patients in a drug treatment program tended to use more alcohol when they were using illicit drugs less often, but the difference was not statistically significant (Simpson and Lloyd 1981). In an experiment in which subjects were supplied with marihuana alone, alcohol alone, or marihuana and alcohol, they used more of both when both were available (Mello and Mendelson 1978). A study of two villages in Pakistan, one in which half of the population used opium and one in which only 5 percent used it, showed that alcohol and marihuana use was about the same in both (McGlothlin 1975).

Another reason for taking legal controls on alcohol seriously is that if raising prices and restricting access do not lower the average consumption of a drug, or if lowering the average consumption does not reduce its ill effects, then the twentieth-century regulatory system for most recreational drugs makes no sense at all. This system does not distinguish between moderate and excessive use or integrated and unintegrated customs; it simply aims to keep everyone from using the drugs, and for that we are willing to pay a substantial price. Serious defenders of current heroin policy admit that it actually makes life worse for addicts, but they contend that heroin must be as expensive and inaccessible as possible to keep down the number of new users and therefore the number of addicts (Moore 1977). Even in the rare cases in which a respectable public body proposes legalization (as opposed to decriminalizing possession) of an illicit drug, it assumes that legalization will lower the price, increase the availability, and therefore increase the total consumption and the problems created by abuse of the drug; the only question is whether the price paid for the current laws is too high (National Research Council 1982).

The evidence for legal restraints has nevertheless been challenged. The gin law passed in England in 1751 reduced alcohol problems, but a harsher law passed in 1736 proved ineffective and led to riots. Was the earlier law too harsh? Was it the spread of coffee, tea, and Methodism that made the English poor more sober? During our Prohibition years, alcohol consumption dropped not only in the United States but throughout the industrial world. As so often happens in social science, the problem is how to distinguish cause from effect when there is no accepted theoretical framework. Legal restraints on alcohol may be just a symptom of a popular trend toward disapproval of alcohol use; liberalization of laws or lowering of prices may be a byproduct of a change in attitudes that makes people tolerate more alcohol use: stateways following folkways. Apparently there are no prospective studies of a geographical region before and after a new alcohol restraint or pricing system is introduced, with a control region for comparison (Smart 1976). And no doubt even if there were, reasons could be given to explain why the control region was not precisely comparable to the experimental region.

There are other related problems. If use of a drug is well enough entrenched in a society, the people will simply not tolerate prices that are too high. High legal prices and restricted legal availability may defeat their purpose by creating a vast black market for that drug or increasing the interest in another one. Some people think that we reached that point with alcohol during Prohibition and are reaching it with marihuana now. Besides, a drug may create such a strong dependency that demand becomes inelastic and raising the price has only a limited effect. This is often said about heroin, but it is more clearly true of tobacco. When James I of England put a confiscatory customs duty of 4,000 percent on tobacco to keep it out of the country, smuggling became so common and lucrative that a few years later he had to reduce the duty and use it for revenue instead of prohibition.

Laws work best in the short term, and especially when the drug problem is concentrated in a small sector of the society. New relaxations or tightenings of alcohol laws often have their greatest effect in the first few months. Japan in the 1950s and Sweden in the 1960s dealt with serious but limited amphetamine problems partly by cutting off the legal sources of supply. India dealt similarly with opium addiction in the 1950s and 1960s. Great Britain kept a small heroin problem from growing by instituting a clinic system in 1968 to replace prescriptions by individual doctors. In all of these cases, the drug users were a small, socially marginal group, often seriously disturbed or criminal; the legal change had no effect on the habits of the majority or even a substantial minority. And because there was no established illicit mass distribution system, the problem could be eliminated fairly quickly, without a long-drawn-out struggle.

A natural suggestion is to combine laws that reduce the total supply with efforts to promote integrated drinking or drug use. Some studies of preliterate societies suggest that the total consumption of alcohol is correlated highly but not perfectly with drinking problems; the rules for alcohol use also make a difference (Frankel and Whitehead 1979). The law can be used to reinforce socially accepted values and make marginal people conform, as in the Swedish and Japanese treatment of the amphetamine problem. It helps put temptation out of the way. Restrictions on a drug's availability may help to promote safer and healthier ways of using it. Illicit drug users on the verge of serious abuse sometimes approve of the law, even when they intend to go on disobeying it. In the same way, a posted speed limit may keep drivers moving more slowly even when they do not obey it.

One interesting combination of sociocultural and legal controls is the local option system. Each small, culturally homogeneous geographical area makes its own laws on alcohol sales, so that legal restrictions are reinforced by social attitudes. In the political terms discussed in Chapter 1, an illicit drug user who wants his or her favorite drug to remain illegal is in the position of Ulysses ordering his men to protect him from his own attraction to the sirens. A small town that bans alcohol sales is close to the position of workers who have collectively agreed to a contract that forbids any one of them to accept longer hours or lower wages than those agreed on by the union (as opposed to workers obeying a minimum wage and maximum hours law for which they have not contracted).

Pricing policies might be regarded as a way of making people buy insurance for the risk to themselves and others in their misuse of alcohol or drugs. With taxes on alcohol, we pay to solve the problems created by alcohol abuse. But this idea has serious difficulties. It goes without saying that existing taxes on alcohol are not nearly high enough to pay for the costs of alcohol abuse. But more important in principle is the fact that the price of this insurance is not paid by the right people. Alcohol abusers pay more in taxes than moderate drinkers, but not nearly enough to cover the extra expense they create. Mill complained that this kind of restraint makes everyone suffer for the intemperance of a few. In particular, the cost, if it is a cost, falls on people who have less income. Any law that makes a commodity relatively more expensive obviously reduces the amount used by the poor more than the amount used by the rich.

If alcohol is an evil, this does the poor a favor; so prohibitionists sometimes argued. But as we saw in our historical survey, the motives of paternalism are always open to question. In the seventeenth-century debate on tobacco or the eighteenth-century English debate on gin, it was quite acceptable to talk about keeping those drugs out of the hands of the dangerous classes – dangerous to themselves and others. Since then we have become more democratic; an open appeal to class fears is out of the question, and even paternalistic attitudes toward the poor are not in favor. But the effect of high prices remains the same.

The idea of reducing alcohol problems by reducing per capita consumption is less plausible if the pathological condition of alcohol abusers makes them immune to legal measures that might change the habits of the average drinker. So, some advocates of the disease theory of alcoholism have been especially hostile to the distribution of consumption model, with its implication that there will be fewer abusive drinkers if the average drinker uses less alcohol. It is significant that the disease theory in its modern form was first successfully promulgated after Prohibition had failed and the effort to regulate drinking by law was in bad repute. This is not to say that the distribution of consumption model is logically incompatible with the disease theory. Whatever the definition of alcoholism, not all alcohol problems are alcoholism problems. In any case, lack of easy availability might prevent some susceptible people from becoming alcoholics, just as heroin law enforcement is supposed to prevent susceptible people from becoming addicts. But obviously, to vary Mill's language, it would be better not to make everyone suffer because of the illness of a few; and that is a more serious danger if diseased and healthy alcohol consumers represent two different populations rather than different points on a single unimodal distribution curve. Those who insist on total abstinence as the only cure for alcoholics are most likely to reject the distribution of consumption model, because it suggests that even abusive drinkers can improve merely by drinking less. Conceiving of alcoholism as a single disease fits the distribution of consumption model less well than conceiving of it as a mixture of alcohol abuse problems that have numerous sources and come in numerous combinations.

Pricing, licensing, and restrictions on hours of sale are accepted as ways to keep alcohol consumption down. But the gulf between alcohol and other abusable drugs is enormous when it comes to a special kind of legal restraint, the criminal law. Only a few drinking practices are criminal – mainly drunk driving and public intoxication. But decriminalizing marihuana or other drugs means only making the laws slightly less lenient than the Volstead Act. Criminalizing sale or possession is no longer taken seriously as a way to control alcohol, but it is the first line of defense against other forms of drug abuse. Social pressure is directed mainly toward getting people to obey the law, that is, not to use the drugs at all. Despite the interesting work on informal social controls over illicit drug use, we are not likely to see a campaign for "responsible" use of marihuana, cocaine, or LSD resembling the publicity for "responsible drinking." The argument for using the criminal law is very simple: If less drastic means of raising prices and restricting availability work, this one should work even better; and even if less drastic means will not work, this one may. As one authority puts it, harassment by the criminal law is worthwhile if it can increase the time needed to obtain an intoxicating dose of heroin from five minutes to two hours (Moore 1977).

Criminal laws differ qualitatively from other legal restraints. To discuss what acts should be criminal raises in a new form the issues of legal moralism and cultural symbolism. Especially when the user is made a criminal, morality has often taken precedence over health and consumer protection. The strange argument that removing criminal penalties on marihuana would amount to public endorsement of the drug reflects the symbolic weight given to the criminal law as a mark of social disapproval. For our purposes the symbolism is important only insofar as it provides a deterrent in itself, apart from the formal penalties. But where drugs are concerned, the value of criminal law symbolism as a deterrent is much smaller than its value as a mark of cultural dominance; that is one reason the public will often refuse to give it up even when the deterrent effect seems close to nil.

Against criminalization there is a long list of objections: the enormous burden on police, courts, and prisons; the preemption of resources that could be devoted to other crimes; the forgoing of tax revenues on a legitimate commodity; the unavoidability of unequal and selective law enforcement; promotion of disrespect for the law when large numbers of people do not accept it and disobey it shamelessly; ruined lives or careers of convicted drug users who have done no harm to others; economic niches created for organized crime; occasions for police corruption and violation of citizens' rights; increased dangers of drug misrepresentation and adulteration; addict crime made necessary by high black market prices.

There is a large critical literature with plenty of evidence on these disadvantages and unpleasant side effects of the criminal law approach to drug control. But most of it does not suggest general rules for judging when criminal penalities for the possession or sale of a particular drug in particular circumstances are unwarranted. The proper limits of the criminal sanction are an old topic of debate. We mentioned the paradox that people who could profit from formal drug education probably do not need it. The legal scholar E. A. Sutherland stated an analogous paradox: Where customary restraints are adequate, laws are unnecessary; where customs are inadequate, laws are useless. If this saying were wholly true, an anarchist utopia of positive liberty would be the only solution. We want to know when it applies in the existing imperfect world.

In the following general situations, criminal sanctions are likely to be wrong:

1. The act under consideration does more good than harm, or only slight harm, or the facts are just not known well enough.
2. There are ways of dealing with the problem that impose less serious restrictions on liberty – education, civil penalties, the whole range of solutions suggested for alcohol problems.
3. The law is not backed by a popular consensus and therefore has little symbolic value as a mark of disapproval.
4. The cost of enforcement, direct and indirect, in money, time, resources, and side effects, is a greater burden on society than the consequences of the crime. In the extreme, the law is unenforceable. As Jeremy Bentham pointed out long ago, sometimes the danger of detection is so small that enforcement would have to be disproportionately harsh to make the law a true deterrent:

   > With what chance of success, for example, would a legislator go about to extirpate drunkenness and fornication by dint of legal punishment? Not all the tortures which ingenuity could invent would encompass it. . . . The great difficulty would be in procuring evidence; an object which could not be attempted . . . without spreading disarray through every family, tearing the bonds of sympathy asunder, and rooting out the influence of all social motives. (Sinclair 1962, p. 178)

5. It is too hard to formulate the law in a way that prevents inequities in punishment. As the Canadian Commission of Inquiry into the Non-Medical Use of Drugs reported (*Final Report* 1973, p. 98), any criminal classification of drugs will be

subject to "incoherences and anomalies," and drug laws "do not distinguish the extent of harm" very well.

If one of these situations exists, others are likely to exist as well. If a law lacks popular support, the cost of enforcement will be burdensome; a law will become unpopular if the means necessary to enforce it outrage many people; inequities in punishment are more likely if the act usually does little harm; and so on. (For more discussion, see Packer 1968; Kittrie 1971; Turk 1972; Irwin 1973; Greenawalt 1974).

If drug enforcement is taken seriously, enormous resources have to be devoted to it. We mentioned that under Prohibition, a third of the inmates in federal prisons were there for alcohol trafficking. Today the Drug Enforcement Administration (DEA) has an annual budget close to $1 billion. About three-quarters of all search warrants are issued for drugs or evidence of drug offenses; electronic surveillance and wiretapping are reserved mostly for drug enforcement under the official designation of "organized crime." Here is what the public money pays for: "DEA's second command post in El Paso, Texas looks like the War Room in *Dr. Strangelove*. Some men sit hunched over video display terminals while others monitor drug flow charts and airspace indicators. The agency also employs surveillance satellites, fixed radar and microwave installations, AWACS, radar planes, and one of the largest computerized intelligence files in the government" (Dubro 1981, p. 13).

Altogether, probably more than $10 billion a year is spent to suppress drugs. Much of it is used to stop smuggling, but at most 10 percent of imported illicit drugs are seized. A relaxation of the marihuana laws in California saved at least $7.4 million in court costs in the first six months (Report 1977, p. 28). According to a study conducted in Los Angeles County in the early 1970s, more than a third of all felony arrests were on drug charges, most for possession; 40 percent of these were rejected in court, mainly because of insufficient evidence (Silberman 1978, p. 357). The attorney general of the United States reported in 1977 that 55 percent of the cases in federal courts in Tucson, Arizona, involved drugs. When the harsh Rockefeller laws were passed in New York and plea bargaining in drug cases became more difficult, court dockets were immediately flooded; there was no evidence of a decline in heroin use (Pekkanen 1980).

The zeal of police against violators can have very unpleasant effects:

In separate actions [on April 23, 1973, in Collinsville, Illinois] these agents [of a Justice Department drug abuse task force] conducted raids at the homes of Mr. and Mrs. Herbert Giglotto and Mr. and Mrs. Donald Askew. The shabbily-clad unshaven raiders barged in on the two houses without . . . search warrants . . . they kicked in the doors without warning while shouting obscenities and threatening the inhabitants with drawn weapons. The Giglottos and Askews . . . were forced to stand idly by while their homes were ransacked and their lives threatened. At no time . . . did the agents satisfactorily identify themselves. . . . When they discovered that they had raided the wrong premises, they simply left – no apologies, no explanations, no offers to fully compensate for the damage they had done.

The agony of the Giglotto and Askew families ended only temporarily when the agents departed . . . both families suffered intermittent harassment . . . late-night threatening telephone calls. . . . But perhaps more demoralizing . . . has been the social ostracism both families have suffered. . . . By July, the intimidation and social pressures had become so intense that the Giglottos were forced to permanently flee Collinsville. (Percy 1974, p. 5)

Another example: "A New Jersey man left his jacket lying in a neighbor's back yard, where it was found and taken in to the police. The man was arrested because there were eight Libriums in the pockets. Even though he had a prescription . . . he was arrested for carrying them in an unmarked bottle. That, according to New Jersey law, is an offense that carries the maximum of three years imprisonment and a $1000 fine" (Dubro 1981). Presumably that man was not jailed, but he may have a criminal record, like the hundreds of thousands arrested each year for possession of marihuana.

In a fascinating pamphlet (Kirkpatrick 1975), prosecuting attorneys charged with enforcing the drug laws speak anonymously. On strict laws and selective enforcement: "Borrowing some pills from a friend – every time someone borrows even penicillin from you . . . they are in technical violation of the drug laws and could get a severe sentence, but *wouldn't*, of course" (p. 9). On community response to the drug menace: "they knew that drugs are supposed to be a big issue. Well, they don't have any drug problem yet, but they feel like they ought to. . . . But you can't say, 'Well, you people are out of your minds,' or you're earmarked as somebody who's anti-law enforcement or soft on drugs or soft on crime" (p. 26). On questionable enforcement methods: "undercover agents were placed in a school for the deaf and they posed as deaf workers for six months . . . in order to catch people enrolled at the college for the deaf who were using marihuana. And when the police came in here with a case like that, that they're so proud of, and you appear maybe a little shocked or reluctant to get involved . . . then it's bad for your relationship" (pp. 29–30).

On drug searches and seizures: "When you ask for a warrant knowing that it's going to be quashed, when you know it's bad to begin with, you can still get one issued in most counties, make the search, and have it thrown out later. You've busted in the guy's house and ransacked the joint, or you've impounded his car and torn the insides out of it. So the warrant is quashed, so what? . . . And some people are quite willing to abuse the law in that way, to make life unpleasant for people they have in their minds identified as criminal anyway" (p. 39). All of these statements bring to mind Bentham's comment about procuring evidence to extirpate drunkenness and fornication by legal punishment; it is "an object which could not be attempted . . . without spreading disarray through every family, tearing the bonds of sympathy asunder, and rooting out the influence of all social motives." (For further examples and discussion, see Manning 1981.)

The police have several strategies for controlling drug traffic, all adjusted to the absence of complainants and the problems of obtaining evidence. (The test for possession of a drug is formally quite demanding – either immediate or exclusive access to the drug or dominion and control.) General street patrol is ineffective as long as search and seizure are not permitted without probable cause. But people who are stopped for some other reason can be searched and then charged if drugs are found. Most drug arrests are made by ordinary patrol officers on possession charges, but they yield relatively few convictions; in one study of six cities, only 14 percent of those arrested served time in jail, and most of them were sellers (Johnson and Bogomolny 1973). Most crimes are solved by retrospective investigation, but that is rather ineffective in drug cases except on rare occasions when an informer has been planted at a high level in a distribution network. Long-term covert operations are difficult and uncommon. A better technique is planting an informant to get a search warrant; often the key to drug law enforcement is the use of informers who cooperate to reduce their own sentences (Moore 1977). This practice obviously creates enormous potential for gross error and injustice. The most important police strategy for arresting the larger dealers is "buy and bust." After buying drugs several times to establish a reputation and a business relationship, the undercover police officer arranges a new sale and makes an arrest when the money and drugs have changed hands. The procedure creates many opportunities for corruption, since the police collect so much untraceable cash.

The institutionalized corruption, betrayal, chaos, and terror promoted by drug law enforcement are not only unfortunate byproducts of a nasty but necessary business, they are essential means of attaining the law's ends. The most serious defenders of the criminal law's regulatory system recognize this explicitly (Moore 1977). Only a small proportion of drug users or even dealers are actually arrested and convicted. But they have nowhere to turn when they are robbed, cheated, or assaulted by other users and dealers. By making the business as nasty and risky as possible, law enforcement is supposed to limit supplies and keep retail prices high. So those who support the system are in an uneasy position when they profess outrage at contemptuous, cruel, and lawless behavior by narcotics agents. It is certainly hypocritical to pretend to indignation and alarm about the murderousness of drug trafficking itself, since we have in effect deliberately tried to shape it in a way that makes it attractive to the most reckless and callous people and as nerve-racking as possible for everyone involved. The main reason marihuana and heroin dealers leave the business is apparently not the threat of prison but "interpersonal strain" – an indirect but no less powerful effect of the criminal control system (Fisher and Bruhnsen 1982). The unpleasantness is sometimes even blamed on the drugs themselves, as though it were a pharmacological effect, but that is largely myth making and only confuses the issue. To be honest, we must admit that guaranteeing the existence of an underworld of treachery and terror is simply one of the methods society has reluctantly chosen to prevent drug abuse, or at least to quarantine the carriers of the drug traffic.

Drug laws notoriously ask more of the criminal justice system than it can deliver. Political principles and social realities that are ignored when the laws are passed must be considered when it comes to enforcement. We make laws that cannot be enforced without paying a price, in money or in liberty, that we are unwilling to pay. The cost of the enforcement machinery is only part of the story. Vested interests of a capitalist economy become involved (we will say more of this later), and so do vested interests of a liberal political system. Mill anticipated some present dilemmas of drug law enforcement when he wrote in *On Liberty*,

> It is only because the institutions of this country are a mass of inconsistencies, that things found admittance into our practice which belong to the system of despotic, or what is called paternal government, while the general freedom of our institutions precludes the exercise of the amount of control necessary to render the restraint of any real efficacy as a moral education. (Mill 1859, chap. 5)

It is useless to ignore questions of liberty in a cost–benefit analysis of the effect of drug laws. The tactical problems cannot even be defined without some acknowledgment of the freedoms we are committed to protecting, whether commercial enterprise or individual rights. The "general freedom of our institutions" is what precludes full exercise of the paternal control written into the drug laws. The Wickersham Commission admitted that alcohol prohibition could never be fully enforced without the use of methods intolerable in a democracy; the same is clearly true of other drug laws, however necessary they may be. A study in New York City in 1969–70 found that 70 percent of the misdemeanor charges and 33 percent of the felony charges involving drugs were dismissed in court, more than half of them because of faulty police procedures, especially insufficient evidence or illegal search and seizure (Cooper 1973).

Of course, costs and individual rights have to be weighed in judging any criminal law, but the drug laws create such a peculiar situation quantitatively that they seem qualitatively unusual. The issues we neglect in making substantive drug legislation return to haunt us in the form of problems that are described as procedural. In a standard textbook on criminal law (Vorenberg 1975), drug and alcohol offenses compose about half of the cases reprinted in four full chapters on admissibility of evidence, stops and arrests, search and seizure, and entrapment. Police and advocates of law and order tend to regard procedural scruples as merely an obstacle and a nuisance, an elaborate game in which the authorities are prevented from doing their work. But just as, according to Sir Henry Maine's famous saying, the substantive common law of England seems to have been secreted in the interstices of procedural decisions, so the substance of our drug laws, which are formally so harsh, is often created in procedural guise.

An interesting symptom is the repeated efforts to impose mandatory minimum sentences for drug offenses. Before 1970, narcotics crimes were the only ones for which the federal criminal code both specified a minimum sentence and denied the possibility of probation or parole. The Drug Abuse Prevention and Control Act eliminated most mandatory sentencing, but state laws since then have repeatedly imposed it. The implication here is that in its day-to-day workings, the criminal justice system cannot be trusted to be harsh enough; the substance of the law will be undermined by the procedures for applying it in drug cases. The most common effect of such laws is to give prosecutors sentencing power by allowing them great discretion in deciding what crimes they will impute to a drug dealer for purposes of plea bargaining. Sometimes the result is that the defendant pleads guilty to a lesser crime that could not have occurred in order to avoid conviction and a mandatory jail term for a more serious crime. These distortions arise because of our unwillingness or inability, for technical and principled reasons, to follow through on the laws we make.

Drunk driving is one kind of behavior related to intoxicant use for which criminal sanctions apparently make sense. Here the harm is obvious, the danger is immediate, and cause and effect seem clear. Even Mill would probably have admitted penalties for drunk driving, just as he was prepared to penalize soldiers for being drunk on duty. But even in this case, many studies suggest that the law has little effect. First, only a small minority of drunk drivers are caught; we could not catch many more of them without devoting more resources to the job than we are willing to make available. When roadblocks and breathalyzer tests are introduced, drunk driving may become less common for a while – until people realize that it is too costly to use roadblocks and breathalyzers long enough on a large enough scale to be effective. Second, when the laws are made harsh, judges, juries, and prosecutors are unwilling to apply them (Waller 1978), and not only because most of them can easily conceive of themselves as getting into the same kind of trouble. After all, only a small proportion of drunk drivers become involved in serious accidents; even fewer such accidents cause deaths, and if anyone dies, it is much more likely to be the drunk driver than an innocent stranger. Any punishment harsh enough to deter might not be defensible as a criminal sanction. License suspension would be a good alternative if only enough drunk drivers could be caught. Scandinavian countries are famous for their strict drinking–driving laws, but there is some evidence that habits and moral education are responsible for their impressive record of highway safety rather than the laws, which are more a symptom than a cause of the regard for prudent driving (Ross 1975, 1982).

Removing penalties for possession of drugs is a widely recommended solution for some of the problems created by the criminal law. Possession of narcotics did not become a federal crime until 1914, but by 1960 it was actually a felony under federal and most state laws. Public opinion then viewed illicit drug use as a vice and the illicit drug user as immoral. Although federal possession penalties were added for amphetamines, barbiturates, and other psychoactive prescription drugs in 1968, attitudes had already begun to change; the illicit drug user had begun to seem more a victim than an evildoer. Federal possession penalties are lower under the 1970 law, and more than thirty states as well as the federal government now allow conditional discharge of first offenders after trial without an adjudication of guilt. The Canadian Commission of Inquiry into the Non-Medical Use of Drugs and a recent National Academy of Sciences report have both suggested decriminalization of marihuana possession, and several states have reduced the penalty to something like a traffic ticket. In the Netherlands, marihuana and hashish can even be sold openly; the police have an announced policy of not interfering with small-scale distribution. In Alaska, cultivation of marihuana at home for personal use is legal. Although arrests for drug possession, especially marihuana possession, are still very common, few of those arrested now go to jail if that is the only charge.

Putting the burden of criminal sanctions entirely on the grower, man-ufacturer, and distributor rather than the user, sometimes called the "vice" model of drug control, has many advantages, both tactical and moral. By cutting off the drug supply where it is concentrated in a few hands, it seems possible to achieve the maximum effect at a minimum cost. The problem of enforcement is reduced to more manageable proportions, since we are no longer making criminals of a large part of the population, with all of the complications and injustices entailed. And whatever the effect of criminal sanctions on suppliers, decriminalization of possession alone does not necessarily increase the use of a drug, if surveys on marihuana in states where the law has changed are correct.

Punishing only the seller also eases some of our moral and political doubts about paternalism. Even Mill was willing to consider punishing people who profit by persuading others to do what is bad for them; brothel keepers and gambling house proprietors were his examples. The evil reputation of the large-scale drug trafficker today is even greater than that of the brothel owner in Victorian times, and he is a suitable object of outrage. The symbolic value of the criminal law is greater if it is directed at the seller rather than at the user. Even people who use the drug may despise the dealer, just as slaveholders in the ancient world and in the American South often felt contempt for slave traders. The consumer or medical model of drug control also dictates that users be left alone, since they are at most victims; we do not fine or jail the patients of someone who practices medicine without a license or the customers of a manufac-turer who disobeys consumer protection laws. Finally, the incoherencies and anomalies in the distribution of punishment that are hard to avoid in any criminal classification of drugs seem less troubling when only the person who profits from other people's drug use goes to prison.

But not too much should be expected from this kind of change in the law. Alcohol use was not criminalized during Prohibition, which still produced most of the same evils as current drug laws. The idea that the conviction of a few big drug traffickers would break up the whole commerce is seductive but false. The problem ultimately lies with the user, not the dealer. As long as there is a market, any so-called kingpin is replaceable. Besides, it has been argued that the possession penalty is useful to get convictions for sale and distribution; for example, persons arrested for possession can serve as informers. One student of heroin policy notes that small-time dealers, especially those who are also addicts, are least cautious and therefore tend to bear the brunt of enforcement; but he regards that as acceptable, since the least cautious dealers are the ones who accommodate new heroin users (Moore 1977). Another reason suggested for preserving the possession penalty is to induce drug abusers to enter treatment. That is a neat solution for anyone who adopts the disease–crime model of drug abuse discussed in Chapter 2. Faced with a crime whose perpetrators need treatment more than punishment, which is also a disease for which the sufferers refuse to take a cure, we might do best with this two-stage procedure: Arrest them as criminals and then impose treatment on them as sick people.

Principle and practice, substantive and procedural problems, abstract rights and concrete actualities confront one another most directly in cases involving constitutional issues. We have already discussed the courts' reluctance to invalidate civil commitment of addicts on constitutional grounds. They have also rejected almost all constitutional challenges to the substance of the drug laws. But drug laws continue to provide the most common occasions for raising many procedural issues.

The main possibility for a constitutional challenge to drug laws lies in the right of privacy, which developed slowly out of interpretations of the First Amendment (freedom of expression, the right to read), the Fourth Amendment (against unreasonable searches and seizures), the Fifth Amendment (against forced self-incrimination and deprivation of life, liberty, or property without due process of law), and the Ninth Amendment (the people may retain rights not specifically enumerated in the Constitution). The Fourteenth Amendment charges states to abide by the due process clause of the Fifth Amendment; in 1973 the Supreme Court ruled that this required states as well as the federal government to respect the right of privacy, which had become incorporated into the Court's interpretation of the Bill of Rights. The idea is that in some areas the control of individuals over their own thoughts and actions should be nearly absolute, and government interference is warranted only if there is an unusually strong reason for it. When an action involves a right "fundamental to ordered liberty," the Fourteenth Amendment prohibits interference with it unless there is a "compelling state interest." The protected areas of intimacy are the mind, the body, and the home.

The right of privacy is an obstacle to legal moralism and therefore provides some of the same protections as Mill's principle of liberty. In a sense, the distinction between the moral and the legal is better stated as a distinction between the private and the public (Shklar 1964). Some people may feel distaste for what goes on in other people's homes or minds, or what they do with their bodies, but the law, in effect following Mill's recommendation, will not treat this distaste as injury to the public. The affront to sensibilities in a breach of public order or decency is distinguished from feelings of disgust or annoyance about what is happening somewhere behind the scenes. Any act may eventually have public consequences, but that is not considered a good enough reason to invoke the law.

Abortion, birth control, and much pornography now come under this rule, but drug use does not. The Supreme Court has upheld the legality of abortion and birth control and the right to have pornography in the home. But drug laws are not considered to be invasions of the private realm. Federal courts have rejected the claim that a right to use any drug, in the home or anywhere else, is fundamental to ordered liberty. By refusing to hear appeals in which people demand the right to use the cancer drug laetrile, the Supreme Court has indicated that it intends to leave this issue to the legislatures. Only the Supreme Court of Alaska has ruled that cultivation of marihuana for personal use is legally protected by an explicit guarantee of the right to privacy in the state (not federal) constitution. And no court will ever rule that the right of privacy protects any commerce in drugs.

Even if a right is not judged fundamental to ordered liberty, it may be guaranteed by the due process clause, or by the clause in the Fourteenth Amendment that requires states to provide equal protection of the law to all people within their jurisdiction. But the courts have interpreted legislative restraints as constitutional under these clauses so long as they have some rational relationship to a permissible state end; no compelling state interest is necessary. In particular, alleged inequities and anomalies in the distribution of penalties are not generally judged to be in violation of equal protection or due process. Only in the case of a fundamental right like freedom of speech will the Constitution be said to forbid serious disparities. In obscenity cases, the courts always look for a consistent rule that justifies banning some books or pictures and not others. But no principle is required to establish the constitutionality of a legislative distinction between two drugs.

The courts will not provide a judicial remedy for every dubious law, and they will rarely invalidate the legislature's classification of crimes. They would not overrule a state law that made picking pockets a more serious crime than shoplifting, or a law that required safety devices on chainsaws but not on power mowers. For similar reasons, they have not been willing to overrule penalties for marihuana possession and sale on the ground that they are too severe in relation to the penalties for other drugs or the dangers of marihuana itself. They have upheld state laws imposing a considerably longer maximum sentence for the sale of cocaine than for the sale of amphetamines, which are pharmacologically similar. And the special treatment of alcohol is not a constitutional problem because the Twenty-First Amendment, which repealed Prohibition, has been interpreted so that it supersedes other applicable constitutional provisions and gives the states full power over alcohol regulation. The problem of distinguishing the extent of harm, as we mentioned earlier, may reduce the effectiveness of criminal laws on drug use and sale, but it has not been made into a constitutional obstacle.

Despite its rejection by the courts as a substantive right in drug cases, privacy has had an important indirect influence on the enforcement of drug laws. The Fourth Amendment's guarantee against unreasonable search and seizure, extended to the states through the due process clause of the Fourteenth Amendment, has served as a constitutional protection for drug offenders. The relationship to privacy is obvious in the Fourth Amendment's reference to protecting "persons, houses, papers, and effects" against searches and seizures. Because the provision was hard to enforce in any other way, the Supreme Court ruled in 1961 that evidence obtained by illegal searches was not admissible in state criminal trials. The ruling has been subjected to much criticism, and the Court is reconsidering it. Important exceptions to the exclusionary rule may eventually be established.

The Fourth Amendment is now interpreted as allowing two kinds of legal search. First, police may obtain a warrant "upon probable cause, supported by vow or affirmation," with a suitably precise description of the place to be searched and the things to be seized. Probable cause is a difficult requirement. Exploratory searches based on mere suspicion do not come up to this standard. The hardest cases involve anonymous informants, and here the courts have not known where to draw the line. Questions arise about when informants have a good enough reputation for reliability and when their names must be disclosed. A warrant is required for telephone tapping unless the police have the consent of one of the parties to the conversation. The courts have also had to decide whether drug courier profiles providing a formal list of suspicious characteristics give probable cause for a search.

Searches incident to arrest are much more common than those conducted with warrants. They are permissible in order to find weapons or to prevent escape or the destruction of evidence; normally, anything in plain view can also be seized. Since the decision excluding illegally obtained evidence from admission in court, the police have taken to lying about this issue. They tend to regard the exclusionary rule as a meaningless obstacle to law enforcement, and they are unwilling to allow it to interfere with the conviction of people who, as they see it, are clearly guilty. Thus they often feel no compunctions about perjuring themselves. There has been an epidemic of what is called "dropsy" testimony; a police officer states that the defendant "dropped" a package of drugs on the floor in plain view while being apprehended. Police also refer to "furtive gestures" that made them think that the defendant was reaching for a gun or trying to get rid of evidence. To justify legally a successful search undertaken after a tip by an informer, the police will sometimes fabricate a history that makes the informant seem reliable (Heller 1973).

The Eighth Amendment's prohibition against cruel and unusual punishments has also been extended to the states through the Fourteenth Amendment, and under this principle both state and federal courts have invalidated a few particularly savage sentences in drug cases. For example, in *People v. Lorenzen*, decided by the Supreme Court of Michigan in 1972, a twenty-year prison term for the sale of a small amount of marihuana was invalidated under a Michigan state constitutional clause prohibiting "excessive" punishment, interpreted by the court as cruel or unusual. Noting that the maximum penalty for assault with intent to maim was ten years, for cruelty to children four years, for selling a machine gun five years, and for adulterating food ninety days, the court ruled that the marihuana sentence shocked the conscience. Criminal penalties for drug transactions are generally severe, but as we have said, the courts have never invalidated any of them under the equal protection or due process clause. Only occasionally, in extreme cases, will courts challenge the legislature's distribution of penalties by invoking the Eighth Amendment and its equivalents.

Another issue that occasionally arises in drug enforcement is the Fifth Amendment's protection against self-incrimination. In 1952 the Supreme Court decided the case of *Rochin v. California*, in which the defendant was convicted of possessing morphine. He had swallowed the morphine capsules as Los Angeles police officers broke into his house and burst into his room. The police took him to a hospital and ordered a doctor to give him an emetic through a tube inserted into his stomach. The morphine was recovered, and the defendant was sentenced to sixty days in jail. The Supreme Court's majority said that the breaking and entering, assault, and torture sufficiently shocked the conscience so that the due process clause was violated. Justice Black considered this statement too vague; he said that the due process clause of the Fourteenth Amendment extended to defendants in state courts the protection of the self-incrimination clause of the Fifth Amendment, which was violated here.

Drug cases raise so many procedural issues so often because of the peculiar nature of the laws. Since drug use and sale are common activities that have been made serious crimes, the number of cases is large. The consensual nature of the crime makes evidence difficult to get. Penalties sometimes seem excessive or irrational, but courts have been unwilling to say that drug laws violate any substantive rights. As a result, the procedural system has to bear the burden of our doubts and second thoughts. In establishing limitations that are formally procedural, judges in a given case are often influenced by substantive questions – what drug is involved, how much, whether there is a sale or an organized criminal enterprise. Procedural adjustments have to accommodate distinctions in degree of harm not effectively made by the statutes, enforcement problems not anticipated by legislatures, and potential rights violations otherwise ignored.

Nevertheless, if the obstacles are overcome and a drug conviction is obtained, it is rarely invalidated for constitutional reasons. Big drug dealers especially fall under what has been called the "bad guy exception" to the Bill of Rights. An appeals court may declare a procedural error committed during the trial to be harmless even when it was in fact substantial. The court may also reject a drug dealer's appeal because his lawyer did not fill out the legal forms in exactly the right way. When it can find no constitutional justification at all for the trial procedure, the higher court may deny the appeal without giving a reason – a recourse that is supposed to be used only for appeals that are entirely frivolous. So, especially in drug cases, "The Constitution is rhetorically overvalued by the courts and then systematically devalued in legal practice" (Hughes 1982, p. 27).

Taxation, restrictions on the time or place of sale, and criminal sanctions on users or sellers are the most common legal methods of reducing the supply of a drug. But the problem can also be approached more specifically by making the drug legally available only to designated users or for designated purposes. The most nearly universal designated user group, of course, is adults. Even Mill made the obvious distinction between adults and children. Other forms of discrimination among classes of users are less acceptable today. We mentioned the early American attempts to prohibit alcohol to sailors, servants, and Indians. Plato, in the *Laws*, proposed that slaves, magistrates, and soldiers should not be allowed to use alcohol. In the Soviet Army, only officers, not enlisted men, are permitted to drink. These forms of discrimination now seem inequitable, to say the least. The passbook system that operated in Sweden for many years was meant to limit the amount of alcohol any person could consume, thus restricting it to moderate drinkers; that system failed. It is true that even the methods now in use often have the indirect effect of designating classes of consumers. High prices exclude the poor; criminal sanctions may exclude people not adventurous or reckless enough to ignore them. But except for children, we now rarely consider using the law explicitly to keep drugs away from a specific class of people who are thought to be especially subject to their ill effects. The reasons are partly empirical – we simply cannot predict well enough who is at risk – and partly a matter of democratic principle.

Legal limitation according to the purpose of drug use is much more common and effective. One form of limitation by purpose is confining a drug to religious use; for example, during Prohibition, sacramental use of alcohol was licensed. The only legitimate religious use for a banned drug today is in the Native American Church ritual, discussed in Chapter 1. In an important case, *People v. Woody* (1964), the California Supreme Court ruled that no compelling state interest justified a ban on peyote use in the Native American Church. The "burden" on religious practice created by a ban on peyote would amount to an infringement on the free exercise of religion. The case was different from that of polygamy in the Mormon Church because here the practice being challenged was "central": It could not be eliminated without destroying the church, and it could not be replaced. In *Leary v. United States* (1967), a federal appeals court refused to extend this right, saying that a compelling state interest in preventing drug abuse outweighed the petitioner's claim to the use of marihuana in his religious practice as a Hindu.

It is hard to find any consistency in the principles used in cases decided under this clause. Courts have not questioned the good faith of claims to a religious exemption; that issue has always been left to juries. And they have not tried to define religion, out of fear that any definition might violate the First Amendment clause prohibiting the establishment of religion. But the court stated in the *Leary* case that conduct otherwise criminal would not be made legal by a religious justification – a comment that, if taken literally, would not only contradict the *Woody* decision but also make the free exercise clause meaningless (On these cases, see Phillips 1968 and Hallucinogens 1968.)

Possibly one of the unstated principles is a rejection of paternalism; for example, people have been allowed to refuse blood transfusions for religious reasons. Quoting a remark in the state attorney general's brief that peyote "obstructs enlightenment and shackles the Indian to primitive conditions," the court in the *Woody* case declared that making this paternalistic judgment was not the attorney general's business. But the judges also had something more in mind, as suggested by their reference to "subcultures that flow into the mainstream of our national life and give it depth and beauty" (Uelman and Haddox 1974, p. 239). It was important that in this case, as opposed to the *Leary* case, the religious practice created a cultural community. The integration model of drug control emphasizes informal social sanctions and rituals as a protection against wrong use of drugs. By making impulsive and careless drug use unlikely, the seriousness of purpose implicit in a religious ritual adds to the protection. Religious sanctions are always among the most effective; as we have suggested, the integration model might work best in a theocracy. This legal limitation on purpose is supposed to ensure a community in which the drug is used in a decorous and disciplined way.

But religious purpose does not guarantee that drug use will be beneficial. It is not only that some religious drug use – think of the Dionysian rites – is not decorous and disciplined. Religion is too equivocal a notion. In two novels published thirty years apart, Aldous Huxley portrayed two contrasting types of religious drug use. The "soma" of *Brave New World* is a euphoriant or hallucinogen used by the people of a dystopian future society to cement their communal solidarity. They take the drug as they sit and chant ritually about melting into the Greater Being, which they identify with the Social River. Soma is a tool for the quiet suffocation of individuality and independence in a world where even human beings are cultured in laboratories according to a formula (Huxley 1932).

The religious drug use in Huxley's last book, *Island*, is very different (Huxley 1962). Here he presents a true utopia in which a decentralized political system is guided by a Western technology and science stripped of their excesses and a religious–philosophical tradition derived largely from Buddhism. A psychedelic or hallucinogenic drug called "moksha medicine," after the Sanskrit word for spiritual liberation, is used on carefully defined social and personal occasions. The emphasis on community, tradition, and discipline prevents the drug use from being merely an experience to be enjoyed or endured, and the guidance of religion and science ensures that it will encourage rather than stifle individuality, variety, and freedom.

But Huxley is pessimistic about the prospects of any such utopia. The island society is stable and successful only because it has been isolated for more than a century from the forces of modernity by the ocean and a benevolent government. In the horrifying last chapter, it is taken over and its culture is destroyed by a nearby tyrant who represents a combination of all the worst features of capitalism, communism, and Third World nationalism. Huxley almost admits that in the modern world his dream is a hopeless one.

The courts have in effect given the Native American Church an exemption from modernity resembling the one that Huxley granted his island. The rules that put drugs and religion in two different categories, protecting religion from contamination, are modified only for a special kind of culture. When official policy toward Indians was assimilation, peyote was regarded as a drug abuse problem. Now that Indians are being allowed to reclaim their cultural identity, peyote has been made legal. But if any other group were involved – say, hippies – the courts would not be so indulgent.

Even apart from the law, it is hard to build modern religious institutions based on drug use. From older forms of religious drug use, we might learn how to shape a drug experience through ritual and how to balance democracy and authority in allowing access to it. But these lessons are hard to learn because we lack the traditions and consensus that would make consciousness changes produced by drugs religious in the old sense. What serves some as moksha medicine may look like soma to others.

The other major limitation by purpose is medicine. Although it emerged from a religious background, medicine is obviously much more important than religion today as a basis for drug control. Religious and medical control both now require government endorsement; aside from that, they are formally similar in certain ways. Both methods have a customary rather than a legal origin, and the medical gatekeeper with Aesculapian authority plays an almost priestly role. Modern medicine has even been sarcastically likened (by Thomas Szasz, for example) to a state religion, with imposing organizational strength, an intellectually powerful ideology, and the support of civil authority. Medicine has its divine powers (medical miracles and wonder drugs), and can also call forth and exorcise demons (drugs of abuse). It even borrows images of purity from religion, and it regards unorthodox healing practices as heresy or superstition to be eliminated by a mixture of official coercion and missionary activity.

The priestly pretensions of doctors may sometimes seem arrogant, and they were challenged by the open invitation to experiment with drugs, issued during the 1960s, which many people continue to accept. But it could be argued that in modern industrial societies the medical profession has to supply the ritual context that makes drug technology relatively safe. Where the ritual of prescription is unavailable, as with alcohol, the results can be disastrous. Some control is needed, and nineteenth-century individualism or openly religious restrictions are impossible in present social conditions.

As we mentioned in discussing the issues of risk and liberty, a medical definition provides a stay against confusion. That is one reason it has become important in public thinking. In a poll taken in the early 1970s, people were asked to choose the best of several definitions of drug abuse; 27 percent chose "excessive use," but 30 percent chose "use for nonintended purpose, nonmedical use" (National Commission 1973, p. 12). Despite occasional scandals confined to a small minority of doctors and patients, people in general tend to be conservative about prescription drugs, including psychoactive ones; they rarely take more than the doctor recommends and often take less (Manheimer et al. 1973; Boffey 1981). Medical control, if it could be imposed without explicit penalties, merely by respect for the authority granted to doctors, would be a kind of integration model; for example, it supplies clear prescriptions and proscriptions, and it provides for transmission of drug lore by knowing elders. The rituals and social sanctions are somewhat more restrictive and formal than those contemplated by the integration model, but the principle is not necessarily different. In preliterate cultures in which medical and religious uses are not always clearly separated, the similarity is obvious; the religious-medical use of hallucinogens in some preliterate cultures (and on Huxley's utopian island) is a model of integrated drug use.

In all drug controls that are legally imposed according to purpose, the main problem is to make sure that the purpose is defined narrowly enough. Because courts have not dared to define religion for fear of establishing a church or churches, they have had to use roundabout methods of narrowing the qualifications for a religious exemption from the drug laws. Legal limits on the definition of medicine are both direct and indirect. The government, through the FDA, now decides what drugs will be made available to doctors. Pharmacists must also keep records of prescriptions for controlled substances, and doctors who seem to be prescribing too freely may be called on by the government to justify themselves. The famous Supreme Court decisions against opiate maintenance imposed a more explicit legal definition of medical purpose in drug use.

Despite these legal sanctions at the margins, the decision on what is a medical purpose has been left largely to the medical profession itself. Any doctor with the proper license may still legally prescribe a psychoactive drug for almost any purpose, subject to the threat of malpractice suits and professional discipline. We discussed the historical development of the idea of a medical purpose in Chapter 3. It has left us with the need to distinguish medicine from pleasure, or more often from the kind of casual therapy used to ease problems of daily life. Medicine must also be distinguished from the enhancement of performance in some task or enterprise. Obviously there are many borderline cases. People attending funerals have long used wine and whiskey as medicine for grief, and today a doctor or friend may supply diazepam (Valium) to a mourner. Many people also use Valium for everyday stress. A writer describing her use of the drug says that it gives her a feeling of detachment and makes it easier for her to feel both joy and anger by dispelling anxiety

(Carpenter 1980). Whether this use of the drug is nonmedical (and therefore wrong?) is a hard question. When amphetamines are given to children with attention deficit disorder (hyperactive children), some regard it as a highly questionable pedagogical technique, others as simply a treatment for a disease.

One purpose for which most drug use has become unacceptable is sports. It seems almost self-evident to most people today that using drugs in athletic competition is wrong, and many consider it potentially disastrous for sports. But it is curiously difficult and complicated to justify this position. What seems self-evident is not so at all. In 1900, for example, a patent medicine whose active ingredient was cocaine won a prize at an English exhibition with a citation calling it "wine for athletes." This drink, Vin Mariani, was openly and unapologetically used at the time by athletes in many sports. If by now it seems almost unnecessary to give justifications for not allowing drugs in sports, that is largely because since the time of Vin Mariani medicine has annexed more territory. Medical use has become the only acceptable use of most drugs, and medicine is defined more strictly now than it was in 1900. Without this medical background, the arguments against drug use in sports might seem feeble.

Four standard reasons given for banning drugs from sports are that they are dangerous, they are unfair, they produce abnormal states of the body and mind, and they are artificial or unnatural. Taken at face value, these reasons would hardly be good enough. For example, it is just not plausible that drugs are banned because they are so risky. Athletes in many sports are not only permitted but constantly required to take much more serious risks, both short-term and long-term, than those usually involved in drug use. To cite only the most obvious example, everyone knows that professional boxers often die in the ring or suffer severe brain damage, because the threat of damaging blows to the head is essential to the excitement of the sport. It would be implausible to say that any effect of drugs could be worse. But drugs are under medical control, and boxing is not.

Maybe we are implicitly assuming that the risk is not voluntarily assumed in the case of drugs because drug takers simply do not understand what they are doing. A boxer *is* supposed to know what he is letting himself in for when he climbs into the ring, but not when he takes a pill to fight better. But this is easy to believe mainly because our system of drug regulation is based on the assumption that most people are not fit to make their own choices about the more powerful drugs. And that is because most drug use is now acceptable only under the control and supervision of physicians.

The charge that drug use is unfair makes little sense when examined closely. The implication is that a player who gets his strength and spirit from a pill is not winning by his own efforts, but the same case could be made against any sports equipment. No one says that fielders using gloves or auto racers using mechanics and pit crews are not winning by their own efforts. It is hard to see why drug use is any different in principle. Drug use happens to be unfair right now because it involves breaking the rules to gain special advantage, but we could eliminate that unfairness simply by changing the rules.

There is also a suspicion that athletes who take drugs to perform better are using them in abnormal amounts and in an abnormal way. That sounds sinister until we try to define exactly what it means. Probably the best interpretation is that drugs are acceptable only for normalizing, not for optimizing. They can be legitimately used to cure disease or bring physical condition up to par, but not to improve performance at the high level of athletic competition, where they would violate some standard of human normality. We can even argue that this is what makes drug use unfair: Taking a drug to become well enough to play is all right, but taking it just to play better is a form of cheating.

Whether this position makes any sense depends on what normality means. If it is only a statistical average, there is no reason not to try to raise it. Giving drugs to pole vaulters to improve their jumping is no different from giving them fiberglass vaulting poles. If normal use of drugs or other equipment means use that is conducive to health, there may be a case for the objection. We sometimes think of sports as a way to cultivate a superior or ideal naturalness and balance – the classical Olympic ideal. But this standard, or even the distinction between normalizing and optimizing, is not applied very carefully when whole classes of drugs are permitted or banned by name. The issue is often settled by a kind of medical definition – a decision that the only normal way to use drugs is the way that doctors use them (or should use them): to relieve pain, treat illness, or compensate for disability. Athletes who feel pain because their bodies are demanding rest may take local anesthetics or antiinflammatory drugs to compete, although this is hardly a healthful practice; but a gold medal winner in the Olympics was disqualified when his blood showed traces of ephedrine, an asthma medicine that is banned because it has stimulant side effects. According to some accounts, amphetamines are used in football mainly by older players who feel a loss of their youthful energy and competitive enthusiasm. The drug brings them up to what could be regarded as a normal level – the level of their past play (Mandell 1978). The question is why is this wrong if antiinflammatory drugs are acceptable, or if wearing eyeglasses to compensate for deteriorating vision is acceptable. The answer seems to be that prescribing antiinflammatory drugs or local anesthetics to relieve pain is something that doctors do, and giving stimulant drugs is something they are not supposed to do. Talk of normalizing, optimizing, and abnormality misses the operative distinction here.

The final complaint against drug use in sports is artificiality or unnaturalness. But this assumes a totally unworkable distinction between natural (good) and artificial (bad) ways to improve performance. It is natural for human beings to use artifices; artifacts and artificiality are pervasive in sports. Bare feet are natural, so shoes must be artificial. To say that using drugs to cure illness or relieve pain is natural, but using them to run faster or throw farther is artificial, would be equivalent to calling the use of shoes to protect the feet natural and their use in track competition artificial. The charge of artificiality is really a variant on the charges of unfairness and abnormality; we have already seen how much our idea of what is unfair or abnormal where drugs are concerned depends on medical definitions, usually implicit rather than explicit.

Limitation by purpose in the legal regulation of controlled substances is so important that we tend to be suspicious of any proposal for using them that leaves the purpose ambiguous or vague. The modern doubt about what qualifies as religion makes it hard to justify drug use for religious purposes. The federal court in the *Leary* case must have wondered, apart from all questions about good faith, whether the petitioner's purpose in using marihuana was religious in any sense that differentiated it clearly from other purposes. The same difficulty arises with most social arrangements suggested for the use of psychedelic or hallucinogenic drugs. Any mixture of medical with religious and other claims now makes us uneasy. There have been proposals for psychedelic centers where people could take LSD and related drugs in a safe environment surrounded by helpful people. But the proponents do not know whether to conceive of these centers as analogous to resorts, religious retreats, psychiatric clinics, or scientific research institutions, and the ambiguity is enough to create suspicion. Our laws exclude such institutions not just incidentally but by the very categories in which they are framed.

The historical troubles of opiate maintenance illustrate this mistrust of ambiguity. The Supreme Court itself could not decide conclusively whether the addict's problem was a medical one and maintenance a medical solution. To some people, it has always seemed outrageous that we should give free opiates to addicts. Do we provide free whiskey to alcoholics or, if that example is too absurd, do we supply free ski lift tickets to skiing fanatics? These doubts about opiate maintenance are, of course, just one of the social complications created by the disease concept of drug abuse. It has occasionally been suggested that we establish recreational drugstores, analogous to liquor stores, but with the safeguard of requiring a doctor's permission for each customer – a procedure that resembles licensing for airplane pilots. The prospects of this idea are very poor, and not only because of the obvious administrative problems. What troubles so many people about opiate maintenance is precisely that it appears to be a kind of licensed recreational drug use that casts medical professionals in an inappropriate role. The practical problems of opiate maintenance schemes make this anxiety plausible.

Andrew Weil (Weil 1972) recommends that we use drugs for positive reasons, to enhance life rather than just to relieve boredom, pain, and misery; he is rejecting the standard medical notion of appropriate drug use, which is almost exactly the opposite. And for most drugs, medical use is the only kind considered appropriate. Yet by the World Health Organization's definition of health as "total well-being, physical, mental, and social," Weil is promoting health just as much as another doctor who thinks that no one who is already feeling fairly well should ever take drugs. What happens here is that the social definition of health varies according to the context. When we talk about the dangers to health caused by drugs, we tend to use the broadest possible definition of health in order to justify the strongest restrictions. When we establish legitimate purposes for using drugs, of which health is obviously one, we try to define health narrowly so that again we can justify severe restrictions. Health as positive liberty – total well-being – is a legitimate reason for banning drugs but not for using them.

If any generalization can be drawn from this survey of the types of direct drug control, it is that they are all of limited effectiveness. The integration model of prudent, moderate drug use for everyone may be an excellent goal, but it is hard to see how to turn it into a policy. Legal controls, including criminal sanctions, have some effect, but we pay a substantial social price for them. Legally limiting drug use to certain classes of people is generally no longer acceptable. Drug use can be limited to narrowly defined religious or medical purposes, but this policy creates difficulties of its own and often proves irrelevant in solving the larger drug problem. Maybe we are not looking at things the right way when we devote too much attention to controls on drug use. Perhaps we can get a better view by moving back a little.

5   Solution or dissolution of the drug problem?

The worst, most corrupting lies are problems badly stated. *Georges Bernanos*

Everything is a dangerous drug except reality, which is unendurable. *Cyril Connolly*

In a recent report commissioned by the National Academy of Sciences (Institute of Medicine 1980), the authors complain that research on alcohol abuse is seriously underfunded in comparison with research on cancer and heart disease, whether the standard is prevalence, mortality, or economic cost. For example, when mortality rates are adjusted, heart disease gets 10 to 20 times as much research money as alcoholism; adjusting for comparative prevalence, cancer gets 200 times as much; in relation to economic loss, cancer gets 75 times as much and heart disease 15 times as much. The report goes on: "Among many scientists, the field of alcohol studies has a reputation of extreme variability and questionable solidity . . . all of which gives the field a soiled cloak of respectability" (p. 23). The same could be said of other drug abuse research. This allegation of neglect is reminiscent of the complaint (see Chapter 2) that medical professionals are reluctant to confer the role of patient on drug and alcohol abusers. But there may be deep reasons why addicts and alcoholics are bad patients and drug and alcohol abuse are bad research topics. Medical researchers constantly warn us that advances in cancer treatment will come not from a "war on cancer" but from basic research in genetics and cell biology. But at least cancer is a relatively well-defined problem. Even less can be expected from a war on drugs or from a crash program of drug abuse research because we have so little idea of what enemy we are fighting or what needs to be studied.

When an adult beats a child, we do not talk about a "physical strength abuse problem," and we do not refer to the danger of drowning as the "deep water problem." The idea of a drug problem is not necessarily much more coherent. John Dewey said that an end in view is not an absolute ideal but only a guide to action. It is judged by the company it keeps among means. When the means seem distasteful or confused, it may be necessary to redefine the end. Suppose the drug problem is largely a misconception, a misleading way of dividing up reality for explanatory purposes. Sometimes we give signs that we suspect it is. An extraterrestrial creature who listened to our declarations about the terrible problems created by drugs, and then compared our approach to marihuana with our approach to alcohol and tobacco, would have conclude that we do not quite mean what we are saying.

It does seem perverse to deny that there is an alcohol problem, and in many senses there obviously is one. A report published in 1979 by the Royal College of Psychiatrists in England gives some idea of it (Royal College 1979, pp. 57–88). Half of all wife abusers in Great Britain are heavy drinkers; more than half of the prisoners have serious drinking problems; half of the homicides are committed by people who have been drinking; half of the people who die in car accidents have a blood alcohol level above the statutory limit. In one hospital studied, half of the head injuries were in some way connected with drinking. These figures could be matched in many other industrial countries. In the United States, alcoholic cirrhosis of the liver is as common a cause of death as diabetes and arteriosclerosis. Alcohol also causes stomach ulcers, cancer of the esophagus, birth defects (fetal alcohol syndrome), and severe brain damage (Korsakoff's syndrome). The cost of alcohol abuse in lost productivity and medical and psychiatric services is reckoned in the tens of billions of dollars. The indirect and incalculable price of the havoc created in the lives of the alcoholics' families may be even more important. This is no phantom problem.

But it is not that simple. The great majority of drinkers do no serious harm to themselves or anyone else, or do more good than harm. As we noted in Chapter 1, being explicit about the benefits of alcohol or drug use (except strictly medical ones) is not popular. There is a kind of taboo on the subject, and in any case the benefits are hard to state. Heightened creativity and productivity are claimed for stimulant use and religious value for psychedelic drugs. Alcohol is praised for facilitating friendship and commerce, marihuana for enhancing sensitivity and sensuality. But the effects are so variable, so dependent on set and setting, so hard to distinguish from the activity to which the drug use is a background that when the benefits of drug and alcohol use are considered at all in serious discussions of the problem, it is usually in the misleading guise of an inquisition on motives and causes, as though drug use could be explained only by the users' unfortunate past or personal defects, and never by what it does for them in an ordinary way.

Even when the harm is obvious, the alcohol or drugs may not be obviously to blame. When the studies are looked at closely, it is hard to say just how much of the physical and social pathology and economic losses associated with alcohol use are actually caused by it (Gerstein 1981, pp. 205–7). Most studies on alcohol and crime, for example, do not distinguish alcoholism among criminals from criminality among alcoholics, or crimes caused by alcohol from crimes in which drinking is present. It might be that drunken offenders are more likely to be caught, for example. There is also the danger that alcoholism will be defined partly by the social and legal problems it seems to create, which may make hypotheses about the relationship of alcohol abuse to crime circular (Greenberg 1981).

Alcoholism, as opposed to acute alcohol intoxication, may or may not be important as a cause of crime; definitions of alcoholism vary so much that it is hard to make use of the data. Sometimes other factors obviously matter much more than alcohol; for example, France, with its high rate of alcohol abuse, has a low rate of homicide. Scandinavian studies find that higher alcohol use is associated with more violent crime, but intervening variables have to be considered. Both alcohol consumption and violent crime increased in Finland from 1956 to 1974, but the proportion of violent crime associated with alcohol use did not increase, as would be expected if this parallel were regarded as proof that the rise in alcohol consumption alone produced more violence. Possibly something else causes both alcohol abuse and violence – low frustration tolerance, aggressive personality, stress, childhood neglect, organic brain damage. The real cause of violence might also be something usually associated with alcohol use, such as a high frequency of personal interactions or being in an all-male group. Different explanations might apply in different circumstances (Pernaen 1981). The problems are analogous to those that arise in trying to define the disease of alcoholism.

On an epidemiological scale, the connection between illicit drug use and the social ills attributed to it is even harder to prove. One of the best analyses of prospective studies of drug use concludes that "few unfavorable outcomes of drug use, especially marihuana use, have been identified" (Kandel 1978, p. 30). Most differences between drug users and nonusers apparently precede the drug use. For example, the causal connection between illicit drug use and juvenile delinquency seems to be spurious; that is, the statistical association is canceled out when conditions preceding both drug use and delinquency are factored in (Clayton 1981). Delinquents charged with violent offenses use the same amounts and kinds of drugs as nonviolent juvenile offenders (Tinklenberg et al. 1981). A study of crime and drug use among 9,945 Philadelphia men in their late twenties conducted in 1972 for the National Commission on Marihuana and Drug Abuse found that "available data did not permit a conclusion that drug use caused more crime or more serious crime" (Jacoby et al. 1973, p. 300). Other studies have found that moderate drug use had no effect on academic performance at a selective college (Mellinger et al. 1978) and that there were few differences between college undergraduates who used drugs and those who did not – even fewer differences in 1978 than in 1969 (Pope et al. 1981).

If there is one social consequence of drug use that almost everyone admits, it is the relationship between heroin addiction and crime. But even this turns out to be less solidly established than most of us think. Again, the complication is that addiction and criminal behavior have common roots. A study of 590 addicts in the federal hospital at Lexington, Kentucky, found the relationship between addiction and crime to be unclear (Voss and Stephens 1973). Addicts are usually criminals before they become addicts, and addicted criminals are much like nonaddicted criminals, who themselves often use heroin as well as other illicit drugs (Vaillant 1966). The addict's "need" for heroin is not necessarily more compulsive or irresistible than a nonaddicted criminal's "need" for gambling money, fancy cars, or expensive women, which "drives him to crime" as heroin drives the addict. Addicts are quite capable of adjusting the size of their habits to the price of heroin. A study in Washington, D.C., found that over a four-year period in the 1970s, higher heroin prices coincided with a lower rather than a higher rate of property crime (Goldman 1981). Another study of men who were both heroin and alcohol abusers revealed that their most common crimes were selling drugs (73.4 percent) and commercial vice (17.5 percent). About 17 percent had committed burglaries, 13 percent shoplifting, and 6 percent armed robbery. The criminal behavior almost always started before they were addicted (Chambers 1981). Addicts do commit fewer crimes during periods of voluntary abstention (Waldorf 1970; Ball et al., 1979). That might be simply because the reason they are abstaining is that they feel less capable of any active street hustling; or, in contrast, they may be disciplining themselves better in general. It may be wrong, but it is certainly not implausible, to say that a policy aimed mainly at getting the addict to stop using the drug "confounds a relatively minor symptom with the disease" (Chein et al. 1964, p. 14).

Studies show that everyday judgment in certain situations tends to be systematically distorted in several ways (Tversky and Kahneman 1974; Kahneman et al. 1982). It is easy to see how these biases affect views on drug abuse. One finding is that certain kinds of dangers are particularly vivid and memorable, and therefore appear to be much more common than they really are. People tend to overestimate the number of deaths from accidents and violence and underestimate the number caused by chronic illness. Damage from drug abuse, especially acute intoxication, is highly visible to the public even when relatively rare, and it is made even more interesting by lurid publicity involving celebrities. Many people hardly ever hear about illicit drugs except when there has been a disaster or an arrest. Ordinary drug use is usually inconspicuous, a background to other activities. Most people have no clear image of social drug use, except for alcohol, but vivid scenarios of drug abuse are common and easily called to mind.

Another finding is that some things are regarded as explaining others, even when there is no good reason to suppose that they do. For example, people judge that a person described as tall is likely to be heavy rather than light, but they do not judge that a person described as heavy is more likely to be tall than short, even though logically the inference should go both ways. Height seems somehow to account for weight, but not the reverse; the representative or stereotypical heavy person is visualized as fat rather than tall. More generally, people tend to ignore diagnostic inferences and favor causal ones. Given the hypothetical assumption that more solar energy is being used in the 1980s, most people judge that fuel prices will be lower in the 1990s (use of solar energy as the cause), even though increased use of solar energy might more plausibly indicate (diagnostically) a growing fuel shortage and therefore higher future prices.

Revising any accepted explanatory model is a form of diagnostic inference; it involves figuring out what features of the model might be giving rise to error, which implies ceasing to regard them as causes. Experimental subjects were told that a certain person took a projective test in high school that showed him to be cold and self-centered; now he was teaching handicapped children. The subjects developed ingenious ways to explain how this person had changed or why he was compensating for his personal deficiencies, but they rarely suggested that the test might have been wrong. In the same way, some people might try to understand why a student does well in school despite marihuana smoking, without ever challenging the idea that marihuana smoking makes for poor schoolwork. Drug use is to crime, social disaster, and personal troubles as height is to weight; it is easier to make inferences in which drugs explain things than inferences in which drug use is what needs to be explained. The diagnostic view is more difficult. There are too many causes, and they are too uncertain; no vivid picture emerges. We are not inclined to see the relationship between, say, heroin addiction and crime as incidental or indicational (both having a common cause, like height and body weight) rather than causal. The stereotypical addict is a criminal, but the stereotypical criminal is not an addict, so we are likely to make the inference in only one direction.

People also tend to judge conjunctive probabilities badly. In one experiment, the subjects were given a fictional description of a woman who had had artistic and radical political interests in college; then they were presented with a list of occupations and activities, and asked which of them she was most likely to be pursuing ten years later. "Feminist," understandably, was chosen often and "bank teller" seldom. "Feminist bank teller" was chosen less often than "feminist" but more often than "bank teller"; subjects noticed the logical contradiction only when it was pointed out to them. The added detail in "feminist bank teller" made it more vivid and plausible than the description "bank teller," more representative in a psychological sense, even though it was by definition less probable. The imaginary stereotypical college radical is less likely to become a bank teller than to become a bank teller who is also a feminist.

We have a vivid image of the pale, ragged addict injecting heroin into his vein with a dirty needle in an abandoned house or going through withdrawal agonies in a jail cell. In a sense, this figure is more real to us than the generic heroin addict and much more real than the average heroin user, who is not addicted – just as the college radical who becomes a feminist bank teller is more vivid and plausible as an image, though less likely as a reality, than one who becomes a bank teller.

Everyday judgment also fails in assessing covariation. When people consider evidence for the statement that redheads are hot-tempered, they may try to remember the proportion of redheads they have known who are hot-tempered. But this means very little unless compared with the proportion of nonredheads who are hot-tempered – a fact people tend not to consider. Even worse, someone who is biased toward the opinion that redheads are hot-tempered may unconsciously stretch the definitions of the vague terms "redhead" and "hot-tempered" so as to validate the correlation. This is an enormous problem in making judgments about drug abuse. Persons inclined to think that, say, habitual marihuana use causes poor performance at work or in school – a very common belief not established by evidence – will remember the habitual marihuana users they have known who work badly or do poorly in school. But they will forget the marihuana users who work or study well, and they will never try to compare the proportions of marihuana users and nonusers who do poorly. Even more important, they are likely to adjust their definition of habitual marihuana use and their understanding of poor work or school-work, so that anyone they do not regard as a poor student or worker will not seem to be a habitual marihuana user.

Uncertainty about cause and effect was one of the main reasons for mistrusting legal moralism in general. Many of the sexual practices that have been regulated by law are actually at most symptoms, and rarely causes, of the social problems the regulation is supposed to solve. That objection seems less applicable to drug laws because the ill effects of drug use are sometimes immediate and obvious. But on closer study of the social conditions in which drug abuse occurs, it often becomes much less clear what is cause and what is symptom. The imagery of simple poisoning seems less apt, and laws or other control techniques directed at the drugs themselves seem less useful. Even among serious drug abusers, the problems related to drug abuse are not necessarily worst for those with the biggest habits, and abstinence often does not even help much (McLellan et al. 1981). Thomas Szasz has gone so far as to say that the chapter on drug abuse in standard reference works on pharmacology is no more appropriately placed than a chapter on prostitution would be in a textbook on gynecology (Szasz 1974, p. 10). That is, drugs cause drug abuse only in the sense that female sexual organs cause prostitution. By vivid exaggeration, this statement indicates what the issue is. To the extent that drug abuse is a social problem rather than a physiological one, we may be missing the point by concentrating our attention on the drugs themselves.

Even the idea of a social problem is not as obvious as it seems. Sociologists studying the alcoholism movement that began in the 1930s have emphasized what they call the "construction" of social problems (Gusfield 1981; Wiener 1981; Beauchamp 1980). Even seemingly raw facts do not exist until they are shaped for public presentation; a social fact is a symbolic thing, a human creation. It takes on reality when it is collectively defined and legitimated by groups that appropriate it and make it their own. The way a problem is defined depends on what society is willing to recognize and take seriously. Before Prohibition, alcohol itself was a legitimate social problem, "owned" largely by the temperance crusaders and the churches. During Prohibition it was also the government's business. After 1933, reconstruction and a transfer of property were necessary; now the problem was the alcoholic and alcoholism, including "hidden alcoholism," and it was owned by the health professions and groups like AA. Since the establishment of the National Institute on Alcoholism and Alcohol Abuse, the problem has become government property again in a different way.

This view of how social problems are defined is an aspect of the sociology of deviance. The moral entrepreneurs who create deviant labels are like the groups that appropriate social problems; often they are the same people. And like the neutral notion of deviance labeling, the idea that social problems are constructed rather than given is implicitly a critique. It implies that what seems obvious and straightforward is not so. The choice of what to regard as a problem often depends on interests and feelings hidden even from those who make the choice.

Recent studies have illustrated fluctuations in the definition of social problems by using the example of drunk driving (Gusfield 1981). For many years, this problem was largely disregarded. People knew that there were drunk drivers, but no one concentrated on them as a social cause. There were alcoholics, there were auto accidents, and there were sad stories about people who had one too many and died or killed on the road. It was no more regarded as a distinct social problem than falling off a ladder in the home; it belonged to the residual category of miscellaneous accidents. The laws against drunk driving were rarely enforced in a serious way for the reasons discussed in Chapter 4: Few drunk drivers were caught; prosecutors, judges, and juries felt more sympathy than contempt for those who were. (France had no laws against drunk driving until 1962, and even afterward police at the scene of accidents did not routinely record whether there had been drinking.)

In the last five or ten years, at least in the United States, attitudes have changed. Drunk driving has become a center of attention, and the killer drunk has become a mass media villain. Legislatures are passing harsher laws against driving under the influence, and politicians are promising that they will be enforced more strictly. Whether this will make much difference in the long run is doubtful, given the problems of detection and the persistent reluctance to follow through. What is certain is that the problem is being dramatized in a particular way – blame is placed primarily on the driver and secondarily on alcohol abuse. Liquor companies are allowed to disown it (unlike heroin dealers, who are held socially responsible for addict crime). Automobile manufacturers also disown it. There is not much talk about reducing alcohol consumption, nor is the subject changed to improving automobile safety, highway design, the siting of bars, or emergency medical services (Gusfield 1981). In the midst of a public campaign against criminally negligent drivers, we tend to forget that the present proprietorship of the problem and the present way of construing it are not the only possible ones, or even necessarily the best.

The National Commission on Marihuana and Drug Abuse suggested that drug use be divided into five classes. Experimental use means trying a drug once or twice to find out what it is like. Recreational-social use is the pattern of the ordinary social drinker or marihuana user, and even that of many heroin users who are not addicted. Situational use is use for special (nonmedical) purposes – stimulants for work or study, tranquilizers for public speaking, psychedelic drugs for religious or personal insight. Most people are quite capable of using most drugs only in these ways, which produce relatively little harm. The last two categories, intensive use and compulsive use, cause most of the trouble. But here, unusual personalities and social circumstances often matter more than the drug. The same compulsive drug user will shift from LSD to amphetamines, from amphetamines or cocaine to alcohol or heroin, from alcohol to heroin, from heroin to barbiturates or back to alcohol. The ways of redefining drug problems parallel the ways of accounting for addiction and dependence, which are alternative descriptions of intensive and compulsive use. Instead of concentrating on the drug, we can think about the person, the situation, the society, or even the human condition. A direct assault on drug problems, in this view, is aimed at the wrong target. Even if it succeeded, other symptoms would replace drug abuse. That is why modern societies look for indirect solutions (even as they police drug use itself more closely).

We have already discussed many of these solutions, but others are worth mentioning. In nineteenth-century England, the temperance movement tried to encourage "counterattractions" that would keep people away from taverns. Supply the poor with clean water, milk, decent housing, parks, sports, and adult education, and they will want less alcohol (Harrison 1971). The problem is redefined as a question of what liquids to drink or how to spend leisure time. An analogous idea that has been popular recently in the United States is "natural highs." This term itself shows that the drug culture has made some inroads on our vocabulary, but the principle is the same: Take the emphasis off the dangers of drugs and put it on better ways to get what drugs provide. Students of alcohol abuse have also called the technique "diversion." As a variant of the sociocultural or integration model, it is subject to the same criticism: It is a good idea that is almost impossible to turn into an effective policy. Diversion may work best in special situations in which men are isolated in a group and drink simply because there is nowhere to go and nothing else to do – a logging camp or a battleship (Lemert 1962).

Another indirect approach to drug problems is through social psychology. Preliterate societies have been studied to determine what cultural characteristics encourage moderate drinking habits. Attitudes toward dependency, aggression, and impulse control are considered important. It has been suggested that serious drinking problems are more likely in a culture that curbs impulses heavily but imperfectly, or one in which dependency needs are frustrated and there is anxiety about achievement and power (Bacon 1976; Boyatzis 1976). In a study of 247 hunter-gatherer cultures, it was found that a low level of alcohol and tobacco use was associated with a harsh environment and difficulty for the men in finding wives. Males drank a great deal in societies in which games of chance were popular, feats of war were admired, and self-reliance was demanded (Blum and Associates 1969). Another study found aggressive drunkenness to be associated with low social complexity, fear of ghosts, and weak families (Schaefer 1976). Still another study found that a low level of drunkenness in communal drinking festivals was unrelated to the level of anxiety in a culture but was associated with collective property, patrilocal residence after marriage, bride price, village life as opposed to nomadism, and severe restraints on aggression in children (Field 1962).

If we knew what childrearing practices or what modal personality in a culture produced moderation in drug use, and if we knew how to influence childrearing or personality development, we would have a way to prevent drug and alcohol problems. But we understand too little about what cultural features cause drug abuse and have little idea what to do about it in any case. This approach too is subject to the same objections as the integration model of drug control.

One limitation of these studies is that they are still, however indirectly, aimed at resolving something that is conceived primarily as a drug problem. The analogy of epidemic disease is inadequate for many purposes but interesting in this context. Classically, epidemiologists divide their field of study into disease agent, host, and environment. It is often better to work on the host or the environment rather than try to eliminate the agent. Smallpox has been wiped out by vaccination, a direct assault on the virus that produces the disease. But the decline in tuberculosis over the past century in advanced industrial countries has more complicated and obscure causes. It began long before antibiotics were available, and many people today carry tuberculosis bacilli in their bodies all their lives with no symptoms of illness. Better nutrition, greater public cleanliness – the main deliberate changes have been in the host and the environment, and most of them were not aimed directly at the tuberculosis problem. Apart from any conscious efforts, we may also have seen a biological reconciliation between the bacillus and its human host, a process of mutual adaptation with its own rhythm (Dubos 1965).

There are parallels in the case of drugs. The integration or sociocultural model of drug control is an attempt to regulate the environment rather than the agent or host. It is unsuccessful as a policy directed from above by public institutions and aimed directly at the drug problem. But mutual adaptation does arise, often quite rapidly. When psychedelic or hallucinogenic drugs first appeared on the illicit market, there were many casualties. But after a few years people learned how to use them, and adverse reactions became much less common. This knowledge was transmitted informally and not by official institutions. In many cultures, controlled, integrated drug use has evolved historically with little conscious attention devoted to a drug problem, just as the tuberculosis bacillus and the human body have become mutually tolerant. A society in which everyone drinks a little but no one becomes an alcoholic is analogous to one in which many people carry the tuberculosis bacillus but few are made ill by it. Another analogy is our symbiotic relationship with the intestinal bacteria that help us digest food: "What grape, to keep its place in the sun, taught our ancestors to make wine?" (Connolly 1983, p. 39).

It is interesting to press this comparison between drugs and microorganisms. Both derive their power from a microscopic structure that is intimately attuned to the structure of our bodies and therefore allows them to infiltrate our defenses. Migrations and conquests always lead to general exchange of both drugs and microorganisms. In the last great exchange, which took place in the sixteenth and seventeenth centuries, the Western Hemisphere was introduced to cannabis, opium, and distilled alcohol, as well as smallpox and measles; the Eastern Hemisphere received tobacco and possibly syphilis; coffee and tea spread from Asia to Europe and America. Adaptation to either drugs or microorganisms takes time and often remains imperfect; some of the cultures to which Europeans introduced alcohol five hundred years ago have not become adapted to it yet.

One kind of redefinition that avoids taking the drug problem seriously on its own terms is the socialist revolutionary analysis. When Karl Marx called religion the opium of the people, he meant that it was a consolation for the oppressed in a class society that would become unnecessary and lose its hold after the revolution. A direct attack on this spiritual drug problem was pointless; it would solve itself when social conditions changed. The same was true of the material drug problem. Engels wrote of the English working class in the 1840s that the only pleasures left to it were drink and sex. A revolutionary could say that when there are no more poor and no more rich, no pauper will need to drink to feel like a millionaire, and there will be no more millionaires to become alcoholics out of idleness and dissipation. Being an alcoholic or addict is, so to speak, one of the roles provided by a class society, like being a household servant or a stockbroker. As the socialist economist J. H. Hobson put it, "There is no separate Drink Problem" (Harrison 1971, p. 405).

But the attitudes of radicals and revolutionaries on this issue have varied. In general, they have been suspicious of psychological explanations, and they have regarded antidrug crusades as a distraction from the real task at hand. Karl Marx scorned the people he called "temperance fanatics," as he scorned feminists and other bourgeois reformers. When the British Parliament was debating a liquor licensing law in 1909, a socialist member said, "There are thousands of people dying in the streets while you are trifling with this Bill" (Harrison 1971, p. 425). On the other hand, the Bolsheviks made an abortive attempt to ban vodka after they took power, and the socialist and communist movements in Scandinavia often supported prohibition in the early twentieth century.

When Marx said that the people were drugged by religion, he did not mean to imply that the ruling class did this deliberately to pacify them; it was only the inevitable outcome of their oppression, "the heart of a heartless world." But the matter can also be viewed more simply: The ruling class uses religion (or drugs) to keep the masses quiet. Some blacks think that about heroin. The accusation is hard to prove or disapprove, but if it implies that the people who are now addicts might otherwise have become political radicals, there is reason to doubt it. It is equally hard to believe that even reactionary racists would not be delighted to see heroin disappear from the ghettos.

A more interesting kind of radical analysis concentrates on the recreational drug market and its functions in the political economy of drug use and abuse. We have already mentioned the direct and indirect economic interests in the commercial drug trade that are threatened by serious drug law enforcement. The world market created by European imperial expansion in the seventeenth century has made the exchange of drugs and drug technologies much more effective. The rum trade was a mainstay of the New England economy, and tobacco cultivation was almost the sole support of Virginia and North Carolina in colonial times. Coca was an important source of income for king and church in Bolivia and Peru under Spanish rule. Just before Prohibition, almost half of the revenue of the U.S. government came from taxes on alcohol. Today a good part of Great Britain's balance of trade depends on the export of Scotch whiskey, just as Britain's Indian empire depended on the export of opium 150 years ago. Major portions of the economies of whole countries are now given over to growing coffee and tea for export. As for the illicit drug market, farmers in Turkey, Iran, Afghanistan, and Burma depend on American heroin addicts for their income; the marihuana and cocaine traffic is transforming the economies and societies of Bolivia, Colombia, and Jamaica. Marihuana has become one of the most important cash crops in the United States itself, just as grain for whiskey was one of our most important crops in 1830. It is harder to eliminate drug use once it has become an integral part of the world economic system.

The legal control system also has some unexpected economic functions. Heroin addicts, for example, steal things and sell them to fences or to local people at far less than their retail price. People who despise heroin addicts and other fences will nevertheless buy from them, as slaveholders might feel contempt for slave traders or rich cocaine users for the people who sell them cocaine. Stores lodge inflated claims for the thefts, insurance companies raise their premiums, and manufacturers have a market for replacements (O'Connor et al. 1971). The overall effect is a redistribution of wealth toward the inner-city poor.

The moral of these interesting historical and sociological stories remains unclear. The cocaine traffic may be bad for Colombia and Bolivia, even if it does bring in a great deal of money, but that has nothing to do with the intrinsic properties of cocaine. Knowing how bananas affect the Honduran economy or how sugar affects the Cuban economy does not tell us whether bananas and sugar are good or bad. If many of the problems of Colombia, for example, are caused by a system of cash crop cultivation for export in an economy dominated by the United States, it makes just as much sense to denounce the legal traffic in coffee as the illicit traffic in cocaine. The cocaine traffic is more corrupt, violent, and obviously destructive in its social effects, but that is mainly because of its illegality.

The radical analysis takes into account both supply (the concern of the distribution of consumption theory) and demand (the concern of the alcoholism movement and the integration theory). On the supply side, it is an extension of the idea of hunting down the big traffickers, the drug profiteers. Only instead of going after individual traffickers, radicals want to eliminate the economic context in which they (and all businessmen) operate. But the Soviet Union's attempt to ban vodka showed that this will not succeed if enough customers still want the drug. So the demand side must also be dealt with by eliminating the conditions that create drug abusers and alcoholics. It is something like diversion, greatly elaborated. Supply elimination and demand elimination correspond to the two faces of positive liberty – authoritarian and anarchist. At the start, suppliers are put out of business, but once the demand no longer exists, coercion will no longer be needed to cut off the supply. Demand will be eliminated not by a direct attack on the drug problem but by liberating the masses from exploitation and making life much better for everyone. The desire to abuse drugs fades as civilization advances and the new socialist humanity replaces the Old Adam – the Prohibitionist dream was similar. Lenin wrote that in the future socialist world, state coercion would be needed until everyone learned socially responsible habits. By then, humanity would have graduated from its tutelage, and social excesses would wither away along with the state. In this stateless utopia there would be no place for prescribed liberties of the kind advocated by Mill, and no need for them.

As the difficulty of turning diversion or the integration model into a conscious policy suggests, socialist revolutions have been more effective on the supply side than on the demand side. China apparently did away with its opium problem by long prison terms and executions and by disrupting the commerce – not by liberating addicts from their desire for opium through the thoughts of Mao. When the Old Adam has persisted after the revolution, socialists have not developed original solutions. The state that Lenin founded has tried to eliminate the capitalist milieu in which the alcohol trade used to be conducted (there is still a large black market in illicit spirits), but the alcohol problem remains about average for an industrial country (Trent 1975), and the people who study it find themselves falling back on most of the old explanations (only economic and social conditions can no longer be blamed). The official Soviet position is that prerevolutionary Russian cultural traditions are at fault. That is beginning to sound implausible now that sixty-five years have passed since the revolution and there is no sign of a decline in alcohol abuse. Otherwise, Soviet theories about the causes and treatment of alcoholism are not very different from those prevalent in capitalist societies. Alcoholism is associated with an underclass more than it is in the United States. Although the Soviet Union is still more moralistic than we are about alcoholism – drunks may be publicly humiliated by having their heads shaved – it is beginning to medicalize the problem. The explanation of cultural tradition is beginning to give way to biological theories. Group therapy techniques resembling those of AA are used; factories have compulsory alcoholism programs; liquor is heavily taxed. In short, the Soviet Union is facing the same problems and is trying more or less the same solutions as capitalist countries (Roman and Gerbert 1973). The Communist utopia without alcohol problems is not approaching, and the Soviet state, notoriously, shows no signs of withering away.

We will all have to learn to live with more compromise and ambiguity on drug issues. There is something absurd and irrelevant about the martial imagery often evoked: drugs versus society, a war on drugs. A drug-free society remains a mirage. We must learn to live with drugs in a way that, as Mill would say, promotes individuality, self-development, variety of human situations, the highest and most harmonious development of human powers. The complexity of modern society and the powers of modern technology make this harder to do. So does the growth of leisure time and disposable resources. And attempts to control drugs are subject to the conflicting influences of a decline in enforceable moral authority and a heightened consciousness of the need for public protection against common risks. If, as E. O. Wilson suggests, "Most and perhaps all of the prevailing characteristics of modern societies can be identified as hypertophic modifications of the biologically meaningful institutions of hunter-gatherer bands" (Wilson 1978, p. 95), it is not surprising that we have hypertrophied drug problems too.

But even societies that consider themselves plagued by drug and alcohol abuse do not handle the problem nearly so badly as is sometimes thought. In the United States today, despite easy availability of cheap alcohol, a third of the adult population does not drink at all, and another third drinks three times a week or less. Most people do not find it hard to exercise self-restraint in using drugs. Attitudes toward tranquilizers, for example, are very conservative in all racial, social, and economic groups, but especially among the poorest and least educated. People regard them as temporary palliatives that cure nothing; they believe that using them is a sign of weakness and may prevent real solutions to personal problems. Most people disapprove of using drugs to enhance normal functioning; by association, they tend to be suspicious of antidepressants and drugs for energy or alertness (Manheimer et al. 1973). Volunteers allowed to regulate their own intake of amphetamines for weight loss used less than the amounts usually prescribed (Bigelow et al. 1978). The picture of drug abuse as a potentially uncontrollable epidemic is vastly overdrawn.

Drug problems are partly self-limiting. For example, in France, one of the hardest-drinking countries in the world, per capita alcohol consumption dropped from 6.8 gallons per year to 5.9 gallons between 1955 and 1972 (Moore and Gerstein 1981, p. 36). Drug problems also limit themselves biologically, since many of them belong to a certain stage of life. Like street crime, drug abuse is a symptom of the turmoil of late adolescence and early adulthood. Most people use less alcohol and almost no illicit drugs after the age of twenty-five or thirty. Even heroin addicts often "mature out" in their thirties (Winick 1962; Waldorf and Biernacki 1982).

Besides, overemphasizing safety may put unnecessary limitations on human possibilities and powers. Consider this comment by a man who was known for asceticism:

One may decide, with full knowledge, that what one is doing is worth the damage it inflicts on one's liver. For health is not the only thing that matters. . . . I doubt whether, on balance, even outright drunkenness does harm, provided it is infrequent – twice a year, say. The whole experience, including the repentance afterwards, makes a sort of break in one's mental routine, comparable to a weekend in a foreign country, which is probably beneficial. (Orwell 1968, p. 257)

Similar claims are made for occasional LSD use, including the bad trips. The point is that people sometimes have to be allowed to make these judgments for themselves. Some writers have promoted the ideal of a completely safe pleasure drug, as though it were something like the desirable ideal of a completely safe medicine. But it is more like the insipid ideal of a completely safe sport or adventure. Some risk, if only a risk of unpredictable change, is essential to the meaning of the activity. The completely safe pleasure drug resembles its utopian opposite, the completely drug-free society. Knowing that drug use can never be made perfectly safe, we can still afford to place more confidence in the judgment of the average person and the recuperative powers of society than we have been willing to show where drugs are concerned.

A natural human desire to alter consciousness is one of the reasons sometimes given for the use of drugs. But altering consciousness does not have to be conceived as something abrupt, unusual, and mysterious. Our primate curiosity makes us seek new things to see, feel, and think, and adventurousness implies some risk. Drug or alcohol use, within limits, can sometimes promote the development of human powers by heightening individuality and variety of experience, in accord with Mill's prescriptions as well as the more communitarian theories of positive liberty. Just as it would be a mistake to impose an impoverished conception of sexual naturalness and normality for the sake of what is alleged to be pubic morality, it can be a mistake to use what is thought to be public health or social cohesion as an excuse to impose an impoverished conception of naturalness and normality on the search for new experience by changing consciousness.

The special danger of drug use is that it may drastically reduce real variety and novelty in human experience. Even when there is no drug abuse in the ordinary sense, no danger to health or individual pathology, drug technology can be destructive to humanity – as in Huxley's *Brave New World*. Soma at first seems to be the harmless pleasure drug that some have wished for, but as used in Huxley's dystopia, it is not harmless. It narrows rather than broadens the range of effective human choice. This example suggests why fears about drugs go deeper than any mere struggle for cultural dominance or classification into strange-sinister-theirs and familiar-benign-ours. Drugs are an intimate technology with the apparent power to distort our humanity, so the dangers that are called objective and those that are called symbolic, or the instrumental and expressive purposes of drug laws and antidrug movements, cannot always be distinguished at the deepest level.

The difficulty, even impossibility, of distinguishing so-called objective from so-called symbolic dangers is illustrated by the example of drug use in sports. As we noted in the last chapter, the common reasons given for banning drug use in sports would also justify banning many other practices and items of equipment that are considered quite acceptable. It would be hard to show that allowing athletes to use drugs is any more unfair than allowing them to use fiberglass vaulting poles, or any more dangerous than allowing them to drive automobiles at 180 miles per hour, or any more artificial than using Nautilus machines or, for that matter, running shoes. Nor is it easy to see why eyeglasses to correct defective vision have a normalizing effect but stimulants to correct defective enthusiasm and energy have an optimizing effect, or why painkillers are acceptable as a substitute for needed rest when stimulants are not.

We mentioned the medicalization of drugs as one reason for this distinction. The use of drugs can be banned for medical reasons, although blows to the head with a boxing glove or blows to the neck during a football tackle cannot. But medicalization is only a symptom of a deeper uneasiness. The runner Sebastian Coe has said that drug use has the capacity "to destroy sports, to chip away at the foundations" (Wallace 1982). No one has ever said that about the effect of blows from gloved fists on boxers' brains, because the threat of head injury *is* one of the foundations of boxing, one of the things that makes it exciting and defines the boxer's skills.

The charges of danger, unfairness, abnormality, and artificiality against drug use in sports are mainly ways of expressing our feeling that drug use is somehow inappropriate in an aesthetic or conventional sense that is hard to formulate clearly. The point is that some techniques and instruments seem to change the nature of a sport and others do not. Fiberglass vaulting poles are admitted, but a motorized pole or one containing a spring would presumably not be allowed – not because it would be dangerous, unfair, or artificial, and certainly not because the jumper's talent and training would no longer be important, but simply because the sport itself would no longer be pole vaulting as we now know it. We might even introduce motorized pole vaulting in addition to ordinary pole vaulting, just as we have both motorcycle and bicycle races, with the understanding that these are entirely different sports. Where the line should be drawn is a matter of form and propriety, the aesthetic shape of the game. Fiberglass does not change pole vaulting beyond recognition, but a motor or spring would.

It does not seem that drugs, at least the existing ones, change the shape of a game more than the fiberglass pole or the lively ball in baseball. And even if they did or could change things that much, we might allow an equivalent of the bicycle–motorcycle distinction – separate competitions for athletes who do not use drugs and for those who do. But obviously this proposition is hopeless, scandalous. Drugs today are regarded as a peculiar kind of equipment that destroys the aesthetic shape or form of any game by changing the nature of the athletes themselves. It is sometimes complained that training methods used in one country or another make its athletes into robots or mechanical men; not coincidentally, improper drug use is usually part of this charge. The implication is that sports become meaningless if the competitors are something both more and less than athletes – self-made robots whose freedom and humanity have been deliberately impaired for the sake of victory in a game. Fear of the athlete's transformation or degradation lies behind the suggestion of robotism in the word "artificial," as well as the charge that drug users are not winning by their own efforts. Talk of artificiality is just another way to express a feeling of inauthenticity or inappropriateness.

The standard of genuineness and appropriateness that we are implicitly applying is a mixed one. It cannot be reduced to a simple moralistic formula, and it has not always been the same. The athletic establishment in 1900 did not feel the sense of impropriety in using stimulant drugs that we feel today. But more than convention and fashion have changed; our idea of what it means to be an athlete is different now. At this level convention touches on something deeper, something on the border between the aesthetic and the moral, or, in other terms, between the symbolic and the instrumental.

Whether the violated convention seems to be deep and important depends on what kind of game we think is being played. For example, the problem of stimulant use in football might be posed by asking whether it would be better to open up some positions for younger players by preventing drug use, or to allow more experienced older players to keep going a while longer. If we did that, the issue would become almost a technical one and would lose its flavor of scandal. We would no longer be looking for ways to cope with a "drug abuse problem" that enters football from outside and corrupts it; we would simply be asking what form we wanted the game to take.

But everyone knows that the question will never be seriously put in that form. By contrast, consider the ban on spitballs. It was introduced to make hitting easier and to clean up the image of baseball. No one claimed that the spitball was especially dangerous, unfair, or abnormal. The new rule was aimed at molding the shape of the game to make it more interesting and attractive, and, incidentally, more profitable. The rule is often violated but not strictly enforced, partly because throwing spitballs does not, after all, change the shape of baseball very much. Drug violations are taken more seriously. It somehow seems more terrible for an athlete to be hurt by a toxic reaction to a drug than hit by a spitball, even if the injury is no worse. Amphetamine dependence in a football player is more scandalous than brain damage in a boxer, because more or less severe brain damage is regarded as an unfortunate but natural effect of the way professional boxing is conducted, but we do not accept the possibility that more or less severe drug dependence might become one unfortunate but natural effect of the way professional football competition is conducted. Drug use somehow changes the nature of the game.

An analogy with language may be helpful. The grammar of a sport permits a risky and exciting display of human powers by disallowing many actions as inappropriate. We ask what the shape of the game requires, just as we ask what human communication in a given language requires. A spitball in baseball is like a solecism or a mild obscenity in the wrong place. Many people regard drug use in sports as analogous to talking gibberish; it takes the meaning out of what you are doing.

The distinctions made in sports are also made in broader contexts. Most drugs that are believed to optimize moods or mental states (pleasure drugs and performance enhancers) are prohibited; drugs thought to normalize moods or mental states (medical or psychiatric drugs) are acceptable. Drugs are banned both in sports and in other settings because they are supposed to be dangerous and people are not supposed to know enough to avoid the dangers. They are also described as "artificial" paradises, which ought to be abandoned for "natural" highs. Only the charge of unfairness is not heard outside of sports, because there the standard form of the game is less rigidly defined by convention.

In his novel *The Futurological Congress*, Stanislav Lem imagines a society in which drug use has deprived life itself of its proper form (Lem 1974). In the "psychem society," as he calls it, the nearly intolerable living conditions produced by overcrowding and changes in climate are masked for the great majority of people by a variety of marvelously precise and efficient hallucinogenic drugs that make them think they are living in a paradise. They are not obviously suffering, and they are not benumbed or narcotized. In a sense, they are using drugs to normalize their condition by making it humanly bearable. A character in the novel, defending the system, even dares to use the analogy of eyeglasses. Instead of correcting defective vision, the psychem society corrects the vision of a defective world. One reason for our uneasiness about the use of stimulants in sports is that it might be justified using the same analogy.

The psychem society has institutionalized illusion and inauthenticity so comprehensively that human life becomes meaningless. The problem is not that this way of using drugs is dangerous (it may be, but so is life without it in the world of the novel) or abnormal (by what definition?). The trouble is that this is a deeply inappropriate way for human beings to live. It is not just that perceptions, feelings, and thoughts are being manipulated chemically; we do that every time we drink alcohol, and in any case, all of our mental activity is mediated by chemical neurotransmitters. The horror, as a character in the novel explains, comes from eliminating the very distinction between natural and manipulated feelings. In sports the parallel would be an elimination of the difference between victory by one's own efforts and victory by chemical manipulation. Considering the actual nature of athletic drug use, the imagery of mad sports engineers and their manipulated creatures may seem rather farfetched and melodramatic. But it expresses a genuine concern that drug use is somehow dehumanizing and aesthetically false, transgressing the formal limitations that make excellence possible – like writing a sonnet with the wrong rhymes and rhythms or, still worse, programming it on a computer.

Existing drugs do not really have the power to make athletes into robots or guinea pigs or supermen any more than they have the power to create precisely defined illusions that can be imposed by governments. The structure of the brain is too complicated for that. Even the most effective drugs are a clumsy and undirected form of interference in a complex interaction of organism and environment. But the psychem society is a powerful nightmare vision, because the primitive character of drug technology as an instrument for specific purposes is much less obvious than its capacity to produce enormous changes in consciousness very fast. As the poet A. E. Housman says, "Malt does more than Milton can/to justify God's ways to man." If the subjective effects of drugs could be directed toward specific forms of perception and belief as easily as the explosive force of a rocket engine is directed toward its target in space, we might be able to create a society in which our present conception of humanity would be seriously violated.

Imagine a species of extraterrestrial beings whose natural sensory world resembles Lem's psychem society. We can reliably change everything in our field of vision by turning our heads 180 degrees. These creatures could produce similar reliable changes by putting various substances into their mouths and swallowing them. The bizarre drugs described in Lem's novel would seem as ordinary to them as alcohol seems to us. If these creatures discovered alcohol, they might consider its relatively unpredictable and undirected effects to be as weird and terrifying as Lem's drugs appear to us. And that is the way we ourselves tend to regard new drugs. Unless a drug is as integral a part of traditional human life as alcohol is, we fear that it will create a strange and somehow distorted human environment. Lem's society seems a wrong way for people to live. Human life might take on a meaningless, inhuman shape if drug technology were allowed free rein.

In this borderland between the aesthetic and the moral, pornography supplies an analogy. Some of it is deeply offensive, even though there are no universally accepted standards of naturalness and normality in sexual display. It is even harder to achieve agreement on general matters such as the authentically and meaningfully human or the forms appropriate to human life. Most of us no longer believe in natural law. The standards are vague and subject to historical change, yet some uses of drugs seem deeply offensive or wrong. In the last hundred years, the rules against pornography have been relaxed, and we find less and less violation of propriety in more and more forms of public sexual display. But the rules against drugs have been tightened, mainly because they now seem to be a form of technology that, as Lem implies in his novel, has the power drastically to distort the shape of human life.

Unfortunately, the standards are so vague that it is often hard to say when they are being violated. We do not want to prevent desirable change by insisting on a historically, geographically, or culturally provincial notion of appropriateness. A drug that tripled the human life span or, worse yet, made us immortal could be regarded as either a wonderful new medical treatment or a sinister transformation of the conditions of life. We know very well that using a motor or a spring in vaulting poles, for example, would require a redefinition of the sport of pole vaulting. But it is hard to say what redefinition of humanity would be required if people became immortal.

By this standard most existing drugs are very feeble. The complexity of the human body and brain puts such engineering miracles as the immortalizing drug far beyond our present technical capacities. The threat to our notion of what it means to be a human being is symbolic, or at most potential rather than actual. The sense of inauthenticity or impropriety takes many forms. And however much it may be derided by sociologists of deviance as a response to symbols rather than reality, we cannot rid ourselves of it.

Denunciation of drug use by athletes covers an underlying confusion about the proper conduct of sports – about the kinds of risks that are permissible, the demands made on athletes, the purpose of sports medicine, and the suitability of training practices. Similar questions lie behind the argument about drug use in general. Which dangerous practices should be permitted and which ones forbidden? Are some demands or desires created by modern social conditions intolerable? What is the proper role of medicine? When does a new practice or innovation threaten our sense of what humanity should be? The focus on drugs may not be right, despite some historical fantasies and current propaganda (and many individual disasters). It is doubtful whether any society has ever been ruined by a drug; certainly no sport has been. But as technology becomes more effective and somehow more menacing, we become more suspicious of this peculiarly initimate and insidious kind of technology. Even if no drug has ruined a sport or a society so far, the symbolic threat remains, and we are not likely to relax our efforts to contain it.

In a technological society, we have to live with the visions of *Brave New World* and the psychem society, as well as with the more commonplace dangers of drugs. But that should not frighten us back into rigidity – into "standing stiffly in the position of flinging a gauntlet or uttering a battle cry," the image G. K. Chesterton used to describe prohibitionism. If a degraded uniformity in human life is one of the main dangers, trying to impose a single simple solution is another variant of the disease for which it pretends to be the cure. The utopian vision of religious drug use in Huxley's *Island* is not necessarily more implausible than the vision of *Brave New World*.

Since neither a drug-using utopia nor a drug-free society is now in prospect, circumstances have been forcing us into greater flexibility. When an illicit drug has been used by tens of millions of people, it can no longer be relegated to a small criminal or pathological category, and we have to start making distinctions among kinds of use and users. That implies a greater variety of controls, and more compromises between social reality and the demands of law enforcement. If the law and public language simplify and stereotype experience too much, they will defeat their own purposes. That is why public and private discourse about drugs has begun to converge.

On the other hand, public rules and public discourse are necessarily less ambiguous and contradictory – more rigid – than private sentiment, because they are less able to survive unresolved conflict (Williams 1979). Modern societies inevitably incorporate conflicting values, and we would lose something by reducing the conflict too much. We cannot expect perfect harmony, and a touch of something like hypocrisy may be unavoidable; the line between confusion or conflict of values and straightforward hypocrisy may be hard to draw. There is even a moral argument in favor of certain kinds of hypocrisy. The nineteenth-century utilitarian ethical philosopher Henry Sidgwick wrote:

. . . it may be right to do and privately recommend under certain circumstances, what it would not be right to advocate openly; it may be right to teach openly to one set of persons what it would be wrong to teach to others; it may be conceivably right to do, if it can be done with comparative secrecy, what it would be wrong to do in the face of the world, and even, if perfect secrecy can be reasonably expected, what it would be wrong to recommend by private advice or example. (Sidgwick 1907, pp. 488–90)

An example would be giving a depressed student an unjustifiably high grade to lift his spirits and help him do better work. Recognizing the paradox of stating publicly that it is sometimes right to do secretly what a public ethical code condemns, Sidgwick added that the above opinion should itself be kept comparatively secret (Singer 1981, p. 166).

Ultimately, the problems surrounding drug use can be neither solved nor dissolved. Freud said that the palliatives needed to make human life bearable include intoxicants that render us insensitive to our miseries; for this purpose, he even put them on a par with art (a "substitute gratification") and science (a "powerful diversion"). Mencken said of the alcohol problem that between the distillers and saloonkeepers on one side and the prohibitionists on the other, "no intelligent man believes the thing is soluble at all." The alcohol problem might be more like the metaphysical problem of evil than like a treatable disease or an adjustable social conflict.

The confusion of attitudes about intoxicants is not just a modern one, even if it is heightened by contemporary conditions; it is in the nature of humanity and the drugs themselves. Baudelaire writes in his essay "On Wine and Hashish":

Wine is like man; we will never know to what extent it should be esteemed and scorned, hated and loved, nor how many sublime actions or monstrous misdeeds it is capable of. So let us not be more cruel to it than to ourselves, and let us treat it as our equal. (Baudelaire 1974, p. 72)

And he adds: "If wine disappeared . . . I believe that it would produce in the health and intellect of the world a void, an absence much more frightful than all the excesses and aberrations for which wine is held responsible" (p. 75). But hashish, he says, "makes neither warriors nor citizens," annihilates the will, isolates the user, and in the end proves useless and dangerous (pp. 92–3). In *Les paradis artificiels*, he adds that it "allows man to violate the laws of his constitution" in his taste for the infinite (p. 101). This distinction does not make sense. It cannot be right to embrace the contradictions in one case and reject them in the other. Chesterton said that the dipsomaniac and the abstainer both make the mistake of treating wine as a drug rather than a drink. But the truth is that alcohol is, among other things, a drug. All drugs produce their dipsomaniacs, their abstainers, and everything in between. If wine is like man, capable of sublime and monstrous deeds, so are other drugs. If we must be cruel to them, that does not mean we have to be so much more cruel than we are to ourselves.

Bibliography

Aaron, Paul, and Musto, David. 1981. Temperance and prohibition in America: An overview. In Mark H. Moore and Dean Gerstein, eds.: *Alcohol and Public Policy: Beyond the Shadow of Prohibition*. Washington, D.C.: National Academy Press.

Abrams, L. A., Barfield, E. F., and Swisher, J. D., eds. 1973. *Accountability in Drug Education*. Washington, D.C.: Drug Abuse Council.

Alexander, B. K., Coambs, R. B., and Hadaway, P. F. 1978. The effects of housing and gender on morphine self-administration in rats. *Psychopharmacology* 58:175–9.

American Psychiatric Association, Committee on Nomenclature and Statistics. 1953. *Diagnostic and Statistical Manual of Mental Disorders*. Washington, D.C.

American Psychiatric Association, Task Force on Nomenclature and Statistics. 1980. *Diagnostic and Statistical Manual of Mental Disorders*, 3rd ed. Washington, D.C.

Armor, D. J., Polich, J. M., and Stambal, H. B. 1976. *Alcoholism and Treatment*. Santa Monica, Calif.: Rand Corporation.

Bacon, Margaret K. 1976. Alcohol use in tribal societies. In Benjamin Kissin and Henri Begleiter, eds.: *Social Aspects of Alcoholism*. New York: Plenum Press.

1976. Cross-cultural studies of drinking: Integrated drinking and sex differences in the use of alcoholic beverages. In Michael W. Everett, Jack D. Wadell, and Dwight B. Heath, eds.: *Cross-Cultural Approaches to the Study of Alcohol*. The Hague: Mouton.

Barry, Herbert, III. 1976. Cross-cultural evidence that dependency conflict motivates drunkenness. In Michael W. Everett, Jack O. Wadell, and Dwight B. Heath, eds.: *Cross-Cultural Approaches to the Study of Alcohol*. The Hague: Mouton.

Baudelaire, Charles. 1974 (orig. 1851, 1860). *Les paradis artificiels*. Paris: Livres de Poche.

Beauchamp, Dan E. 1980. *Beyond Alcoholism: Alcohol and Public Health Policy*. Philadelphia: Temple University Press.

Becker, Howard S. 1963. *Outsiders: Studies in the Sociology of Deviance*. London: Collier-Macmillan.

Bejerot, Nils. 1970. *Addiction and Society*. Springfield, Ill.: Charles C. Thomas.

1972. *Addiction: An Artificially Induced Drive*. Springfield, Ill.: Charles C. Thomas.

Berlin, Isaiah. 1969. Two concepts of liberty. In *Four Essays on Liberty*. London: Oxford University Press.

Bess, Barbara, Jones, Samuel, and Rifkin, Alfred. 1972. Factors in successful narcotic renunciation. *American Journal of Psychiatry* 7:861–8.

Bigelow, George E., Liebson, Ira, Kaliszak, Julia, and Griffiths, Roland R. 1978. Therapeutic self-medication as a context for drug abuse research. In Norman A. Krasnegor, ed.: *Self-Administration of Abused Substances: Methods for Study*. NIDA Research Monograph 20. Washington, D.C.: U.S. Government Printing Office.

Blocker, Jack S., Jr. 1976. *Retreat from Reform: The Prohibition Movement in the United States 1890–1913*. Westport, Conn.: Greenwood Press.

———. 1979. The modernity of prohibitionists: An analysis of leadership structure and background. In Jack S. Blocker, Jr., ed.: *Alcohol, Reform, and Society*. Westport, Conn.: Greenwood Press.

Blum, Richard H., and Associates. 1969. *Drugs I: Society and Drugs*. San Francisco: Jossey-Bass.

Boffey, Philip M. 1981. Worldwide use of Valium draws new study. *New York Times*, Oct. 13, 1981.

Bonnie, Richard J., and Whitebread, Charles H., II. 1974. *The Marihuana Conviction*. Charlottesville: University Press of Virginia.

Boyatzis, Richard E. 1976. Drinking as a manifestation of power concerns. In Michael W. Everett, Jack D. Wadell, and Dwight B. Heath, eds.: *Cross-Cultural Approaches to the Study of Alcohol*. The Hague: Mouton.

Boyd, J. Edwin. 1970. A multidimensional explication of popular notions on alcoholism. *Quarterly Journal of Studies on Alcohol* 31:876–88.

Brock, Dan W. 1980. Involuntary civil commitment: The moral issues. In Baruch Brody and Tristram Engelhardt, eds.: *Mental Illness: Law and Public Policy*. Boston: D. Reidel.

Burnham, J. C. 1968–9. New perspectives on the prohibition "experiment" of the 1920s. *Journal of Social History* 2:51–68.

Carpenter, Teresa. 1980. I'm writing as fast as I can: Two cheers for Valium. *Village Voice* 25 (Jan. 7): 1, 17–19.

Chafetz, Morris E. 1979. Alcohol and alcoholism. *American Scientist* 67:293–9.

Chambers, Carl D. 1981. Characteristics of combined opiate and alcohol abusers. In Stephen E. Gardner, ed.: *Drug and Alcohol Abuse: Implications for Treatment*. NIDA Treatment Research Monographs. Washington, D.C.: U.S. Government Printing Office.

Chappel, John N., Smith, David E., and Buxton, Millicent E. 1979. Training techniques for physicians in the diagnosis and treatment of amphetamine abuse. In David E. Smith, ed.: *Amphetamine Use, Misuse, and Abuse*. Boston: G. K. Hall.

Chein, Isidore, Gerard, Donald L., Lee, Robert S., and Rosenfeld, Eva. 1964. *The Road to H: Narcotics, Delinquency, and Social Policy*. New York: Basic Books.

Chomsky, Noam. 1973. Notes on anarchism. In Noam Chomsky, ed: *For Reasons of State*. New York: Vintage.

Clark, Norman H. 1976. *Deliver Us from Evil: An Interpretation of American Prohibition*. New York: Norton.

Clayton, Richard R. 1981. The delinquency and drug use relationship among adolescents: A critical review. In Dan J. Lettieri and Jacqueline P. Lundford, eds.: *Drug Abuse and the American Adolescent*. NIDA Research Monograph 38. Washington, D.C.: U.S. Government Printing Office.

Clayton, Richard R., and Voss, Harwin L. 1981. *Young Men and Drugs in Manhatton: A Causal Analysis*. NIDA Research Monograph 39. Washington, D.C.: U.S. Government Printing Office.

Coffey, T. S. 1966. Beer street: Gin lane: Some views of eighteenth century drinking. *Quarterly Journal of Studies on Alcohol* 27:665–92.

Commission of Inquiry into the Non-Medical Use of Drugs. 1973. *Final Report*. Ottawa: Information Canada.

Connolly, Cyril. 1983 (orig. 1945). *The Unquiet Grave*. New York: Harper & Row.

Cook, Philip J. 1981. The effect of liquor taxes on drinking, cirrhosis, and auto accidents. In Mark H. Moore and Dean Gerstein, eds.: *Alcohol and Public Policy: Beyond the Shadow of Prohibition*. Washington, D.C.: National Academy Press.

Cooper, S.C. 1973. *Dismissal of Narcotics Arrest Cases in the New York City Criminal Court*. Santa Monica: Rand Corporation.

Courtwright, David T. 1982. *Dark Paradise: Opium Addiction in America before 1940*. Cambridge, Mass.: Harvard University Press.

DeLint, Jan. 1976. The epidemiology of alcoholism with specific reference to sociocultural factors. In Michael W. Everett, Jack D. Wadell, and Dwight B. Heath, eds.: *Cross-Cultural Approaches to the Study of Alcohol*. The Hague: Mouton.

Dershowitz, Alan. 1973. Constitutional dimensions of civil commitment. In National Commission on Marihuana and Drug Abuse: *Drug Use In America: Problem in Perspective*, vol. 4, appendix. Washington, D.C.: U.S. Government Printing Office.

Devlin, Patrick, 1965. *The Enforcement of Morals*. London: Oxford University Press.
   1971. *Morals and the Criminal Law*. In Robert A. Wasserstrom, ed.: *Morality and the Law*. Belmont, Calif.: Wadsworth.

Dubos, Rene. 1965. *Man Adapting*. New Haven, Conn.: Yale University Press.

Dubro, Alec. 1981. Reefer madness. *Inquiry*, March 8:12–16.

Duster, Troy. 1970. *The Legislation of Morality: Law, Drugs and Moral Judgment*. New York: Free Press.

Dworkin, Gerald. 1971. Paternalism. In Robert A. Wasserstrom, ed.: *Morality and the Law*. Belmont, Calif.: Wadsworth.

Dworkin, Ronald. 1970. *Taking Rights Seriously*. Cambridge, Mass.: Harvard University Press.
   1971. Lord Devlin and the enforcement of morals. In Robert A. Wasserstrom, ed.: *Morality and the Law*. Belmont, Calif.: Wadsworth.

Edwards, Carl N. 1974. *Drug Dependence: Social Regulation and Treatment Alternatives*. New York: Jason Aronson.

Falk, John L. 1981. The place of adjunctive behavior in drug abuse research. In Travis Thompson and Chris E. Johansen, eds.: *Behavioral Pharmacology of Drug Dependence*. NIDA Research Monograph 37. Washington, D.C.: U.S. Government Printing Office.

Field, Peter B. 1962. A new cross-cultural study of drunkenness. In D. J. Pittman and C. R. Snyder, eds.: *Society, Culture, and Drinking Patterns*. New York: Wiley.

Fingarette, Herbert. 1970. The Perils of *Powell*: In search of a factual foundation for the disease concept of alcoholism. *Harvard Law Review* 83:793–812.

Fingarette, Herbert, and Hasse, Anne Fingarette. 1972. *The Meaning of Criminal Insanity*. Berkeley, Calif.: University of California Press.

Fink, M. 1972. Electrophysiology of drugs of dependence. In S. J. Mulé and Henry Brill, eds.: *Chemical and Biological Aspects of Drug Dependence*. Cleveland: CRC Press.

Fisher, B., and Bruhnsen, K. 1982. The impact of legal sanctions on illicit drug selling. In Thomas J. Glynn and Jack E. Nelson, eds.: *Public Health Issues and Drug Abuse Research*. NIDA Research Issues 30. Washington, D.C.: U.S. Government Printing Office.

Frankel, B. Gail, and Whitehead, Paul C. 1979. Sociological perspectives on drinking and damage. In Jack S. Blocker, Jr., ed.: *Alcohol, Reform, and Society*. Westport, Conn.: Greenwood Press.

Gerstein, Dean R. 1981. Alcohol use and consequences. In Mark H. Moore and Dean

Gerstein, eds.: *Alcohol and Public Policy: Beyond the Shadow of Prohibition*. Washington, D.C.: National Academy Press.

Glaser, Daniel, and Snow, Mary. 1969. *Public Knowledge and Attitudes on Drug Abuse*. New York: New York State Addiction Control Commission.

Goldman, Fred. 1981. Heroin and federal strategy: A policy in search of evidence. *Journal of Psychoactive Drugs* 13:217–26.

Gottheil, Edward J. 1982. Letter. *American Journal of Psychiatry* 139:1644–5.

Green, Thomas Hill. 1895 (orig. 1882). *Lectures on the Principles of Political Obligation*. London: Longmans, Green.

1900 (orig. 1880). Lecture on liberal legislation and freedom of contract. In R. L. Nettleship, ed.: *Works*, vol. III. London: Longmans, Green.

Greenawalt, Kent. 1974. Some related limits of law. In J. Roland Pennock and John W. Chapman, eds.: *The Limits of Law*. New York: Lieber-Atherton.

Greenberg, Stephanie W. 1981. Alcohol and crime: A methodological critique of the literature. In James J. Collins, Jr., ed.: *Drinking and Crime*. New York: Guilford Press.

Griffiths, R. R., Bigelow, G. E., and Henningfield, J. E. 1980. Similarities in animal and human drug-taking behavior. In Nancy K. Mello, ed.: *Advances in Substance Abuse*. Greenwich, Conn.: Jai Press.

Grinspoon, Lester, and Bakalar, James B. 1978. Drug abuse, crime, and the antisocial personality: Some conceptual issues. In William H. Reid, ed.: *The Psychopath*. New York: Brunner-Mazel.

Gusfield, Joseph R. 1963. *Symbolic Crusade: Status Politics and the American Temperance Movement*. Chicago: University of Illinois Press.

1981. *The Culture of Public Problems: Drinking-Driving and the Symbolic Order*. Chicago: University of Chicago Press.

Hallucinogens. 1968. *Columbia Law Review* 68:521–60.

Harding, Wayne M., and Zinberg, Norman E. 1977. The effectiveness of the subculture in developing rituals and social sanctions for controlled drug use. In Brian M. du Toit, ed.: *Drugs, Rituals, and Altered States of Consciousness*. Rotterdam: A. A. Balkema.

Harrison, Brian. 1971. *Drink and the Victorians*. Pittsburgh: University of Pittsburgh Press.

Hart, H. L. A. 1963. *Law, Liberty, and Morality*. Palo Alto, Calif.: Stanford University Press.

Heller, Dean. 1973. A conflict of laws: The drug possession offense and the Fourth Amendment. In National Commission on Marihuana and Drug Abuse. *Drug Use in America: Problem in Perspective*, vol. 3, appendix. Washington, D.C.: U.S. Government Printing Office.

Himmelfarb, Gertrude. 1974. *On Liberty and Liberalism: The Case of John Stuart Mill*. New York: Alfred A. Knopf.

Hofstadter, Richard. 1955. *The Age of Reform*. New York: Alfred A. Knopf.

Howland, Richard W., and Howland, Joe W. 1978. Two hundred years of drinking in the United States: Evolution of the disease concept. In John A. Ewing and Beatrice A. Rouse, eds.: *Drinking*. Chicago: Nelson-Hall.

Hughes, Graham. 1982. Busting the people's case. *New York Review of Books* 29 (June 24):27–9.

Hunt, Leon Gibson. 1982. Growth of substance abuse and misuse: Some speculations and data. In Norman E. Zinberg and Wayne M. Harding, eds.: *Control Over Intoxicant Use*. New York: Plenum Press.

Huxley, Aldous. 1932. *Brave New World*. Garden City, N.Y.: Doubleday, Doran. 1962. *Island*. London: Chatto and Winslow.

Institute of Medicine. 1980. *Alcoholism, Alcohol Abuse, and Related Problems: Opportunities for Research*. Washington, D.C.: National Academy of Sciences.

Irwin, Samuel. 1973. A rational approach to drug abuse prevention. Madison, Wis.: STASH Press. Reprinted from *Contemporary Drug Problems*, Spring 1973.

Jacoby, Joseph E., Wiener, Neil A., Thornberry, Terence P., and Wolfgang, Marvin E. 1973. Drug use and criminality in a birth cohort. In National Commission on Marihuana and Drug Abuse: *Drug Use in America: Problem in Perspective*, vol. 1, appendix. Washington, D.C.: U.S. Government Printing Office.

Jellinek, E. M. 1960. *The Disease Concept of Alcoholism*. New Haven, Conn.: Hillhouse Press.

Johnson, Samuel. 1950 (orig. 1748). The vision of Theodore, hermit of Teneriffe, found in his cave. In Mona Wilson, ed.: *Samuel Johnson: Poetry and Prose*. London: Rupert Hart-Davis.

Johnson, Weldon T., and Bogomolny, Robert. 1973. Selective justice: Drug law enforcement in six American cities. In National Commission on Marihuana and Drug Abuse. *Drug Use in America: Problem in Perspective*, vol. 3, appendix. Washington, D.C.: U.S. Government Printing Office.

Judson, Horace Freeland. 1975. *Heroin Addiction: What Americans Can Learn from the English Experience*. New York: Random House.

Kahneman, Daniel, Slovic, Paul, and Tversky, Amos, eds. 1982. *Judgment Under Uncertainty: Heuristics and Biases*. Cambridge: Cambridge University Press.

Kalant, Harold. 1981. Governmental control of individual behavior – philosophical and practical considerations. In Louis S. Harris, ed.: *Problems of Drug Dependence, 1980*. NIDA Research Monograph 34. Washington, D.C.: U.S. Government Printing Office.

Kandel, Denise B. 1978. Convergences in prospective longitudinal surveys on drug use. In Denise B. Kandel, ed.: *Longitudinal Research on Drug Use*. New York: Wiley.

Keller, Mark. 1960. Definition of alcoholism. *Quarterly Journal of Studies on Alcohol* 21:125–34.
    1972. On the loss-of-control phenomenon in alcoholism. *British Journal of Addiction* 67:153–66.

Kirkpatrick, Thomas B., Jr. 1975. *Prosecution Perspectives on Drugs*. Washington, D.C.: Drug Abuse Council.

Kittrie, Nicholas N. 1971. *The Right to Be Different: Deviance and Enforced Therapy*. Baltimore: Johns Hopkins University Press.

Kramer, John C. 1982. Speculations on the nature and pattern of opium smoking. In Norman E. Zinberg and Wayne M. Harding, eds.: *Control Over Intoxicant Use*. New York: Human Sciences Press.

Larkin, Edward J. 1979. Controlled drinking – disease concept controversy: Suggestions for synthesis. *Psychological Reports* 44:511–16.

Lem, Stanislav. 1974. *The Futurological Congress* (trans. Michael Kandel). New York: Seabury Press.

Lemert, Edwin M. 1962. Alcohol, values, and social control. In D. J. Pittman and C. R. Snyder, eds.: *Society, Culture, and Drinking Patterns*. New York: Wiley.

1967. *Human Deviance, Social Problems, and Social Control*. Englewood Cliffs, N.J.: Prentice-Hall.

Lettieri, Dan J., Sayers, Mollie, and Pearson, Helen Wallenstein, eds. 1980. *Theories on Drug Abuse*. NIDA Research Monograph 30. Washington, D.C.: U.S. Government Printing Office.

Levine, Harry Gene. 1978. The discovery of addiction. *Journal of Studies on Alcohol* 39:143–74.

Lindesmith, Alfred R. 1947. *Opiate Addiction*. Bloomington, Ind.: Principia Press.

Lindsey, Robert. 1980. Accident rate of light planes upsets experts. *New York Times*, June 20, 1980.

Linsky, A. S. 1972. Theories of behavior and the social control of alcoholism. *Social Psychiatry* 7:47–52.

Maisto, Stephen A., and Schefft, Bruce K. 1977. The constructs of craving and loss of control drinking: Help or hindrance to research? *Addictive Behaviors* 2:207–17.

Maloff, Deborah, Becker, Howard S., Fonnroff, Arlene, and Radin, Judith. 1982. Informal social controls and their influence on substance use. In Norman E. Zinberg and Wayne M. Harding, eds.: *Control Over Intoxicant Use*. New York: Human Sciences Press.

Mandell, Arnold J. 1978. The Sunday syndrome. *Journal of Psychedelic Drugs* 10:379–84.

Manheimer, Dean I., Davidson, Susan T., Balter, Mitchell B., Mellinger, Glen D., Cison, Ira H., and Parry, Hugh J. 1973. Popular attitudes and beliefs about tranquillizers. *American Journal of Psychiatry* 130:1246–53.

Manning, Peter K. 1981. The criminal justice system and the user. In Joyce P. Lowinson and Pedro Ruiz, eds.: *Substance Abuse: Clinical Problems and Perspectives*. Baltimore: Williams and Wilkins.

McAuliffe, William E. 1975. Beyond secondary deviance: Negative labelling and its effects on the heroin addict. In Walter R. Gove, ed.: *The Labelling of Deviance*. New York: Wiley.

McDonald, William F. 1973. Enforcement of narcotic and dangerous drug laws in the District of Columbia. In National Commission on Marihuana and Drug Abuse: *Drug Use in America: Problem in Perspective*, vol. 3, appendix. Washington, D.C.: U.S. Government Printing Office.

McGlothlin, William H. 1975. Drug use and abuse. *Annual Review of Psychology* 26:45–63.

McLellan, A. T., Lubovsky, L., Woody, G. E., O'Brien, C. P., and Kron, R. 1981. Are the "addiction-related" problems of substance abusers really related? *Journal of Nervous and Mental Diseases* 169:232–9.

Mellinger, Glen D., Somers, Robert H., Bazell, Susan, and Manheimer, Dean I. 1978. Drug use, academic performance, and career indecision: Longitudinal data in search of a model. In Denise B. Kandel, ed.: *Longitudinal Research on Drug Use*. New York: Wiley.

Mello, Nancy K., and Mendelson, Jack H. 1978. Marihuana, alcohol, and polydrug use: Human self-administration studies. In Norman A. Krasnegor, ed.: *Self-Administration of Abused Substances: Methods for Study*. NIDA Research Monograph 20. Washington, D.C.: U.S. Government Printing Office.

Meyer, Roger E., and Mirin, Steven. 1981. A psychology of craving: Implications of behavioral research. In Joyce R. Lowinson and Pedro Ruiz, eds.: *Substance Abuse: Clinical Problems and Perspectives*. Baltimore: Williams and Wilkins.

Mill, John Stuart. 1859. *On Liberty*. London: J. W. Parker.

Miller, William R. 1979. Problem drinking and substance abuse: Behavioral perspectives. In Norman A. Krasnegor, ed.: *Behavioral Analysis and Treatment of Substance Abuse*. NIDA Research Monograph 25. Washington, D.C.: U.S. Government Printing Office.

Moore, Mark H. 1977. *Buy and Bust: The Effective Regulation of an Illicit Market in Heroin*. Lexington, Mass.: D.C. Heath.

Moore, Mark H., and Gerstein, Dean, eds. 1981. *Alcohol and Public Policy: Beyond the Shadow of Prohibition*. Washington, D.C.: National Academy Press.

National Commission on Marihuana and Drug Abuse. 1973. *Drug Use in America: Problem in Perspective*. Washington, D.C.: U.S. Government Printing Office.

National Research Council, Commission on Behavioral and Social Science and Education, Committe on Substance Abuse and Human Behavior. 1982. *An Analysis of Marijuana Policy*. Washington, D.C.: National Academy Press.

O'Connor, Garrett, Wurmser, Leon, Brown, Torrey C., and Smith, Judith. 1971. The economics of narcotics addiction: A new interpretation of the facts. In National Academy of Sciences: *Problems of Drug Dependence, 1971*. Washington, D.C.: National Academy Press.

Ogburn, Alan C. 1978. Patient characteristics and treatment reforms in alcohol and drug abuse treatment. In Yedy Israel, ed.: *Research Advances in Alcohol and Drug Problems*, vol. 4. New York: Plenum Press.

O'Neill, Eugene. 1956. *Long Day's Journey into Night*. New Haven, Conn.: Yale University Press.

Orwell, George. 1968. As I please. *Tribune*, December 20, 1946. In Sonia Orwell and Ian Angus, eds.: *The Collected Essays, Journalism, and Letters of George Orwell*, vol 4. London: Secker and Warburg.

Owen, David Edward. 1934. *British Opium Policy in India and China*. New Haven, Conn.: Yale University Press.

Packe, Michael St. John. 1954. *The Life of John Stuart Mill*. London: Secker and Warburg.

Packer, Herbert L. 1968. *The Limits of the Criminal Sanction*. Palo Alto, Calif.: Stanford University Press.

Palola, Ernest J., Dorpat, Theodore L., and Larson, William R. 1962. Alcoholism and suicidal behaviour. In D. J. Pittman and C. R. Snyder, eds.: *Society, Culture, and Drinking Patterns*. New York: Wiley.

Paredes, Alfonso, Hood, William R., Seymour, Harry, and Gollob, Maury. 1973. Loss of control in alcoholism: An investigation of the hypothesis, with experimental findings. *Quarterly Journal of Studies on Alcohol* 34:1146–61.

Pattison, E. Mansell. 1976. Nonabstinent drinking goals in the treatment of alcoholism. *Archives of General Psychiatry* 33:923–30.

Paulson, Ross Evans. 1973. *Women's Suffrage and Prohibition: A Comparative Study of Equality and Social Control*. Glenview, Ill.: Scott, Foresman.

Pekkanen, John R. 1980. Drug-law enforcement effects. In Drug Abuse Council: *The Facts About "Drug Abuse."* New York: Free Press.

Pernaen, Kai. 1976. Alcohol and crimes of violence. In Benjamin Kissin and Henri Begleiter, eds.: *Social Problems of Alcoholism*. New York: Plenum Press.

1981. Theoretical aspects of the relationship between alcohol use and crime. In James J. Collins, Jr., ed.: *Drinking and Crime*. New York: Guilford Press.

Phallow, Hugh Cann (A. S. Carlin). 1978. Alpinism: Social, scientific and treatment aspects of getting high and its prohibition. *Journal of Psychedelic Drugs* 10:77–8.

Phillips, John R. 1968. Free exercise: Religion goes to "pot." *California Law Review* 56:100–15.

Pittman, David Joshua. 1980. *Primary Prevention of Alcohol Abuse and Alcoholism*. St. Louis: Social Science Institute of Washington University.

Pope, Harrison G., Jr., Ionescu-Pioggia, Martin, and Cole, Jonathan D. 1981. Drug use and life-style among college undergraduates: Nine years later. *Archives of General Psychiatry* 38:588–91.

Popham, Robert E., Schmidt, Wolfgang, and de Lint, Jan. 1976. The effects of legal restraint on drinking. In Benjamin Kissin and Henri Begleiter, eds.: *Social Aspects of Alcoholism*. New York: Plenum Press.

Prentice, Alfred C. 1921. The problem of the narcotic drug addict. *Journal of the American Medical Association* 76:1551–6.

Rawls, John. 1971. *A Theory of Justice*. Cambridge, Mass.: Harvard University Press.

Report of the Select Committee on Narcotics Abuse and Control, Ninety-Fifth Congress, First Session. 1977. *Considerations for and Against the Reduction of Federal Penalties for Small Amounts of Marihuana for Personal Use*. Washington, D.C.: U.S. Government Printing Office.

Robins, Lee N. 1975. Alcoholism and labelling theory. In Walter R. Gove, ed.: *The Labelling of Deviance*. New York: Wiley.

Robins, Lee N., Bates, William M., and O'Neal, Patricia. 1962. Adult drinking patterns of former problem children. In D. J. Pittman and C. R. Snyder, eds.: *Society, Culture, and Drinking Patterns*. New York: Wiley.

Robinson, David. 1972. The alcohologist's addiction. *Quarterly Journal of Studies on Alcohol* 33:1028–42.

Roman, P. M., and Gebert, P. J. 1973. Alcohol abuse in the U.S. and the U.S.S.R.: Divergence and convergence in policy and ideology. *Social Psychiatry* 14:207–16.

Room, Robin. 1978. Evaluating the effect of drinking laws on drinking. In John A. Ewing and Beatrice A. Rouse, eds.: *Drinking*. Chicago: Nelson-Hall.

Rorabaugh, W. J. 1979. *The Alcoholic Republic*. New York: Oxford University Press.

Rosenberg, Harold. 1959. Everyman a professional. In Harold Rosenberg, ed.: *The Tradition of the New*. New York: Horizon Press.

Ross, H. Laurence. 1975. The Scandinavian myth: The effectiveness of drinking-and-driving legislation in Sweden and Norway. *Journal of Legal Studies* 4:285–310.

   1982. *Deterring the Drinking Driver*. Toronto: D.C. Heath.

Royal College of Psychiatrists, Special Committee on Alcoholism. 1979. *Alcohol and Alcoholism*. London: Tavistock.

Sargent, Margaret. 1976. Theory in alcohol studies. In Michael W. Everett, Jack D. Wadell, and Dwight B. Heath, eds.: *Cross-Cultural Approaches to the Study of Alcohol*. The Hague: Mouton.

Schaefer, James M. 1976. Drunkenness and culture stress: A holocultural test. In Michael W. Everett, Jack D. Wadell, and Dwight B. Heath, eds.: *Cross-Cultural Approaches to the Study of Alcohol*. The Hague: Mouton.

Schwartz, Louis B. 1971. Morals offenses and the model penal code. In Robert A. Wasserstrom, ed.: *Morality and the Law*. Belmont, Calif.: Wadsworth.

Seevers, M. H. 1972. Characteristics of dependence on and abuse of psychoactive substances. In S. J. Mulé and Henry Brill, eds.: *Chemical and Biological Aspects of Drug Dependence*. Cleveland: CRC Press.

Shklar, Judith. 1964. *Legalism*. Cambridge, Mass.: Harvard University Press.

Sidgwick, Henry. 1907. *The Methods of Ethics*. London: Macmillan.

Siegler, Miriam, and Osmond, Humphry. 1974. *Models of Madness, Models of Medicine*. New York: Macmillan.

Silberman, Charles E. 1978. *Criminal Violence, Criminal Justice*. New York: Random House.

Simpson, D. Dwayne, and Lloyd, Michael R. 1981. Alcohol and illicit drug use. In Stephen E. Gardner, ed.: *Drug and Alcohol Abuse: Implications for Treatment*. NIDA Treatment Research Monograph Series. Washington, D.C.: U.S. Government Printing Office.

Sinclair, Andrew. 1962. *Prohibition: The Era of Excess*. Boston: Little, Brown.

Singer, Peter. 1981. *The Expanding Circle*. New York: Farrar Straus and Giroux.

Skinner, Harvey A., Glaser, Frederick B., and Annis, Helen M. 1980. *Factors in Self-Identification as an Alcoholic*. Toronto: Addiction Research Foundation.

Smart, Reginald S. 1976. Effects of legal restraints on the use of drugs: A review of empirical studies. *Bulletin on Narcotics* 28:55–65.

Smith, Mickey C., and Knapp, David A. 1972. *Pharmacy, Drugs, and Medical Care*. Baltimore: Williams and Wilkins.

Straus, Robert, and McCarthy, R. G. 1951. Nonaddictive pathological drinking patterns of homeless men. *Quarterly Journal of Studies on Alcohol* 12:601–11.

Swisher, James D. 1971. Drug education: Pushing or preventing? *Peabody Journal of Education* 68–75.

Szasz, Thomas. 1974. *Ceremonial Chemistry: The Ritual Persecution of Drugs, Addicts, and Pushers*. Garden City, N.Y.: Anchor Press.

Temin, Peter. 1980. *Taking Your Medicine: Drug Regulation in the United States*. Cambridge, Mass.: Harvard University Press.

Thompson, Travis, and Pickens, Roy. 1970. Stimulant self-adminstration by animals: Some comparisons with opiate self-administration. *Federation Proceedings* 29:6–12.

Tinklenberg, Jared R., Murphy, Peggy, Murphy, Patricia L., and Pfefferbaum, Adolph. 1981. Drugs and criminal assault by adolescents: A replication study. *Journal of Psychoactive Drugs* 13:277–87.

Torg, J. R., Truex, R., Quendenfeld, T. C., Burstein, A., Spealman, A., and Nichols, C. 1979. The national football head and neck injury registry. *Journal of the American Medical Association* 241:1477–79.

Trice, Harrison M., and Wahl, J. Richard. 1962. A rank order analysis of the symptoms of alcoholism. In D. J. Pittman and C. R. Snyder, eds.: *Society, Culture, and Drinking Patterns*. New York: Wiley.

Turk, Austin T. 1972. *Legal Sanctioning and Social Control*. Washington, D.C.: U.S. Government Printing Office.

Tversky, Amos, and Kahneman, Daniel. 1974. Judgment under uncertainty: Heuristics and biases. *Science* 185:1124–31.

Tyrell, Ian R. 1979. Temperance and economic change in the antebellum north. In Jack S. Blocker, ed.: *Alcohol, Reform, and Society*. Westport, Conn.: Greenwood Press.

Uelman, Gerald F., and Haddox, Victor S., eds. 1974. *Drug Abuse and the Law: Cases, Text, and Materials*. St. Paul, Minn.: West.

Vaillant, George E. 1966. A twelve-year follow-up of New York narcotic addicts: III. Some social and psychiatric characteristics. *Archives of General Psychiatry* 15:599–609.

　　1970. The natural history of narcotic drug addiction. *Seminars in Psychiatry* 2:486–98.

Vorenberg, James. 1975. *Criminal Law and Procedure: Cases and Materials*. St. Paul, Minn.: West.

Voss, Harwin L., and Stephens, Richard P. 1973. Criminal history of narcotic addicts. *Drug Forum* 2:191–202.

Waldorf, Dan. 1970. Life without heroin: Some social adjustments during long-term periods of voluntary abstention. *Social Problems* 18:228–42.

Waldorf, Dan, and Biernacki, Patrick. 1982. Natural recovery from heroin addiction: A review of the incidence literature. In Norman E. Zinberg and Wayne M. Harding, eds.: *Control Over Intoxicant Use*. New York: Human Sciences Press.

Wallace, William N. 1982. Coe cites drug use problem. *New York Times*, February 12.

Waller, Patricia F. 1978. Drinking and highway safety. In John A. Ewing and Beatrice A. Rouse, eds.: *Drinking*. Chicago: Nelson-Hall.

Weil, Andrew. 1972. *The Natural Mind*. Boston: Houghton Mifflin.

Wiener, Carolyn L. 1981. *The Politics of Alcoholism*. New Brunswick, N.J.: Transaction Books.

Wildavsky, Aaron, and Douglas, Mary. 1982. *Risk and Culture*. Berkeley, Calif.: University of California Press.

Wilkinson, Rupert. 1970. *The Prevention of Alcohol Problems*. New York: Oxford University Press.

Williams, Allan F. 1976. The alcoholic personality. In Benjamin Kissin and Henri Begleiter, eds.: *Social Aspects of Alcoholism*. New York: Plenum Press.

Williams, Bernard. 1979. Conflicts of values. In Alan Ryan, ed.: *The Idea of Freedom*. New York: Oxford University Press.

Williams, Bernard, ed. 1981. *Obscenity and Film Censorship*. London: Cambridge University Press.

Wilson, Edward O. 1978. *On Human Nature*. Cambridge, Mass.: Harvard University Press.

Winick. Charles. 1962. Maturing out of narcotic addiction. *Bulletin on Narcotics* 114:1–7.

Wolff, Robert Paul. 1965. Beyond tolerance. In Barrington Moore, Jr., Robert Paul Wolff, and Herbert Marcuse, eds.: *A Critique of Pure Tolerance*. Boston: Beacon Press.

World Health Organization. 1969. *Technical Report Service 407*. Geneva.

Wuorinen, John H. 1931. *The Prohibition Experiment in Finland*. New York: Columbia University Press.

Young, James Harvey. 1961. *The Toadstool Millionaires*. Princeton, N.J.: Princeton University Press.

Zinberg, Norman E., and Harding, Wayne M., eds. 1982. *Control Over Intoxicant Use*. New York: Human Sciences Press.

Index